# DATA MINING
# THE WEB

## THE WILEY BICENTENNIAL–KNOWLEDGE FOR GENERATIONS

*E*ach generation has its unique needs and aspirations. When Charles Wiley first opened his small printing shop in lower Manhattan in 1807, it was a generation of boundless potential searching for an identity. And we were there, helping to define a new American literary tradition. Over half a century later, in the midst of the Second Industrial Revolution, it was a generation focused on building the future. Once again, we were there, supplying the critical scientific, technical, and engineering knowledge that helped frame the world. Throughout the 20th Century, and into the new millennium, nations began to reach out beyond their own borders and a new international community was born. Wiley was there, expanding its operations around the world to enable a global exchange of ideas, opinions, and know-how.

For 200 years, Wiley has been an integral part of each generation's journey, enabling the flow of information and understanding necessary to meet their needs and fulfill their aspirations. Today, bold new technologies are changing the way we live and learn. Wiley will be there, providing you the must-have knowledge you need to imagine new worlds, new possibilities, and new opportunities.

Generations come and go, but you can always count on Wiley to provide you the knowledge you need, when and where you need it!

**WILLIAM J. PESCE**
PRESIDENT AND CHIEF EXECUTIVE OFFICER

**PETER BOOTH WILEY**
CHAIRMAN OF THE BOARD

# DATA MINING
# THE WEB

Uncovering Patterns in
Web Content, Structure,
and Usage

**ZDRAVKO MARKOV AND DANIEL T. LAROSE**

*Central Connecticut State University*
*New Britain, CT*

**WILEY-INTERSCIENCE**
A JOHN WILEY & SONS, INC., PUBLICATION

*Library of Congress Cataloging-in-Publication Data:*

Markov, Zdravko, 1956–
  Data-mining the Web : uncovering patterns in Web content, structure, and usage /
by Zdravko, Markov & Daniel T. Larose.
    p.   cm.
  Includes index.
  978-0-471-66655-4 (cloth)
  1. Data mining.   2. Web databases.   I. Larose, Daniel T.   II. Title.
QA76.9.D343M38 2007
005.74 – dc22

                                                          2006025099

Printed in the United States of America

10 9 8 7 6 5 4 3 2 1

*For my children*
*Teodora, Kalin, and Svetoslav*
— Z.M.

*For my children*
*Chantal, Ellyriane, Tristan, and Ravel*
— D.T.L.

# CONTENTS

# *PREFACE*

## DEFINING DATA MINING THE WEB

By *data mining the Web*, we refer to the application of data mining methodologies, techniques, and models to the variety of data forms, structures, and usage patterns that comprise the World Wide Web. As the subtitle indicates, we are interested in uncovering patterns and trends in the content, structure, and use of the Web. A good definition of data mining is that in *Principles of Data Mining* by David Hand, Heikki Mannila, and Padhraic Smyth (MIT Press, Cambridge, MA, 2001): "Data mining is the analysis of (often large) observational data sets to find unsuspected relationships and to summarize the data in novel ways that are both understandable and useful to the data owner." *Data Mining the Web: Uncovering Patterns in Web Content, Structure, and Usage* demonstrates how to apply data mining methods and models to Web-based data forms.

## THE DATA MINING BOOK SERIES

This book represents the third volume in a data mining book series. The first volume in this series, *Discovering Knowledge in Data: An Introduction to Data Mining*, by Daniel Larose, appeared in 2005, and introduced the reader to this rapidly growing field of data mining. The second volume in the series, *Data Mining Methods and Models*, by Daniel Larose, appeared in 2006, and explores the process of data mining from the point of view of model building—the development of complex and powerful predictive models that can deliver actionable results for a wide range of business and research problems. Although *Data Mining the Web: Uncovering Patterns in Web Content, Structure, and Usage* serves well as a stand-alone resource for learning how to apply data mining techniques to Web-based data, reference is sometimes made to more complete coverage of certain topics in the earlier volumes.

## HOW THE BOOK IS STRUCTURED

The book is presented in three parts.

### Part I: Web Structure Mining

In Part I we discuss basic ideas and techniques for extracting text information from the Web, including collecting and indexing web documents and searching and ranking web pages by their textual content and hyperlink structure. Part I contains two chapters, Chapter 1, *Information Retrieval and Web Search*; and Chapter 2, *Hyperlink-Based Ranking*.

## Part II: Web Content Mining

Machine learning and data mining approaches organize the Web by content and thus respond directly to the major challenge of *turning web data into web knowledge*. In Part II we focus on two approaches to organizing the Web, clustering and classification. Part II consists of three chapters: Chapter 3, *Clustering*; Chapter 4, *Evaluating Clustering*; and Chapter 5, *Classification*.

## Part III: Web Usage Mining

*Web usage mining* refers to the application of data mining methods for uncovering usage patterns from Web data. Web usage mining differs from web structure mining and web content mining in that web usage mining reflects the behavior of humans as they interact with the Internet. Part III consists of four chapters: Chapters 6, *Introduction to Web Usage Mining*; Chapter 7, *Preprocessing for Web Usage Mining*; Chapter 8, *Exploratory Data Analysis for Web Usage Mining*; and Chapter 9, *Modeling for Web Usage Mining: Clustering, Association, and Classification*.

## WHY THE BOOK IS NEEDED

The book provides the reader with:

- The models and techniques to uncover hidden nuggets of information in Web-based data
- Insight into how web mining algorithms really work
- The experience of actually performing web mining on real-world data sets

## "WHITE-BOX" APPROACH: UNDERSTANDING THE UNDERLYING ALGORITHMIC AND MODEL STRUCTURES

The best way to avoid costly errors stemming from a blind black-box approach to data mining, is to apply, instead, a white-box methodology, which emphasizes an understanding of the algorithmic and statistical model structures underlying the software. The book, applies this white-box approach by:

- Walking the reader through various algorithms
- Providing examples of the operation of web mining algorithms on actual large data sets

- Testing the reader's level of understanding of the concepts and algorithms
- Providing an opportunity for the reader to do some real web mining on large Web-based data sets

## Algorithm Walk-Throughs

The book walks the reader through the operations and nuances of various algorithms, using small sample data sets, so that the reader gets a true appreciation of what is really going on inside an algorithm. For example, in Chapter 1, we demonstrate the nuts and bolts of relevance ranking, similarity searching, and other topics, using a particular small web data set. The reader can perform the same analysis in parallel, and therefore understanding is enhanced.

## Applications of Algorithms and Models to Large Data Sets

The book provides examples of the application of the various algorithms and models on actual large data sets. For example, in Chapter 7 data cleaning, de-spidering, session identification, and other tasks are carried out on two real-world large web log databases, from the Web sites for NASA and Central Connecticut State University. All data sets used throughout the book are available for free download from the book series Web site, `www.dataminingconsultant.com`.

## Chapter Exercises: Checking to Make Sure That You Understand It

The book includes over 100 chapter exercises, which allow readers to assess their depth of understanding of the material, as well as to have a little fun playing with numbers and data. These include exercises designed to (1) clarify some of the more challenging concepts in data mining, and (2) challenge the reader to apply the particular data mining algorithm to a small data set and, step by step, to arrive at a computationally sound solution. For example, in Chapter 4 readers are asked to run a series of experiments comparing the efficacy of a variety of clustering algorithms applied to the "Top 100 Websites" data set.

## Hands-on Analysis: Learn Data Mining by Doing Data Mining

Nearly every chapter provides the reader with *hands-on analysis problems*, representing an opportunity for the reader to apply his or her newly acquired data mining expertise to solving real problems using large data sets. Many people learn by doing. The book provides a framework by which the reader can learn data mining by doing data mining. For example, in Chapter 8 readers are challenged to provide detailed reports and summaries for real-world web log data. The 34 tasks include finding the average time per page view, constructing a table of the most popular directories, and so on.

# DATA MINING AS A PROCESS

The book continues the coverage of data mining as a process. The particular standard process used is the CRISP-DM framework: the cross-industry standard process for data mining. CRISP-DM demands that data mining be seen as an entire process, from communication of the business problem through data collection and management, data preprocessing, model building, model evaluation, and finally, model deployment. Therefore, this book is not only for analysts and managers, but also for data management professionals, database analysts, decision makers, and others who would like to leverage their repositories of Web-based data.

# THE SOFTWARE

The software used in this book includes the following:

- WEKA open-source data mining software
- Clementine data mining software suite.

The Weka (Waikato Environment for Knowledge Analysis) machine learning workbench is open-source software issued under the GNU General Public License, which includes a collection of tools for completing many data mining tasks. The book uses Weka throughout Parts I and II. For more information regarding Weka, see `http://www.cs.waikato.ac.nz/~ml/`. Clementine (`http://www.spss.com/clementine/`) is one of the most widely used data mining software suites and is distributed by SPSS. Clementine is used throughout Part III.

# THE COMPANION WEB SITE:
`www.dataminingconsultant.com`

The reader will find supporting materials for both this book and the other data mining books in this series at the companion Web site, `www.dataminingconsultant.com`. There one may download the many data sets used in the book, so that the reader may develop a hands-on feeling for the analytic methods and models encountered throughout the book. Errata are also available, as is a comprehensive set of data mining resources, including links to data sets, data mining groups, and research papers.

The real power of the companion Web site is available to faculty adopters of the textbook, who will have access to the following resources:

- Solutions to all the exercises, including hands-on analyses
- Powerpoint presentations of each chapter, ready for deployment in the classroom

- Sample data mining course projects, written by the authors for use in their own courses, and ready to be adapted for your course
- Real-world data sets, to be used with the course projects.
- Multiple-choice chapter quizzes
- Chapter-by-chapter web resources

## DATA MINING THE WEB AS A TEXTBOOK

The book naturally fits the role of a textbook for an introductory course in web mining. Instructors may appreciate:

- The "white-box" approach, emphasizing an understanding of the underlying algorithmic structures
  - Algorithm walk-throughs
  - Application of the algorithms to large data sets
  - Chapter exercises
  - Hands-on analysis
- The logical presentation, flowing naturally from the CRISP-DM standard process and the set of web mining tasks
- The companion Web site, providing the array of resources for adopters detailed above

The book is appropriate for advanced undergraduate or graduate-level courses. An introductory statistics course would be nice, but is not required. No prior computer programming or database expertise is required.

## ACKNOWLEDGMENTS

The material for web content and structure mining is based on the web mining course that I developed and taught for the graduate CIT program at Central Connecticut State University. The student projects and some exercises from this course were then used in the artificial intelligence course that I taught for the CS program at the same school. Some material from my data mining and machine learning courses taught for the data mining program at CCSU is also included. I am grateful to my students from all these courses for their inspirational enthusiasm and valuable feedback. The book was written while I was on sabbatical leave, spent in my home country, Bulgaria, sharing my time between family and writing. I wish to thank my children, Teodora and Kalin, and my wife, Irena, for their patience and understanding during that time.

*Zdravko Markov, Ph.D.*
Department of Computer Science
Central Connecticut State University
www.cs.ccsu.edu/~markov/

I would like to thank all the folks at Wiley, especially editor Paul Petralia, for their guidance and support. Je suis également reconnaissant à ma rédactrice et amie Val Moliere, qui a insisté pour que cette série de livres devienne réalité. I also wish to thank Dr. Chun Jin, Dr. Daniel S. Miller, Dr. Roger Bilisoly, Dr. Darius Dziuda, and Dr. Krishna Saha, my colleagues in the Master of Science in data mining program at Central Connecticut State University, Dr. Timothy Craine, Chair of the Department of Mathematical Sciences at CCSU, Dr. Dipak K. Dey, Chair of the Department of Statistics at the University of Connecticut, and Dr. John Judge, Chair of the Department of Mathematics at Westfield State College. Thanks to my daughter, Chantal, for her precious love and gentle insanity. Thanks to my twin children, Tristan and Ravel, for sharing the computer and for sharing their true perspective. Above all, I extend my deepest gratitude to my darling wife, Debra J. Larose, for her support, understanding, and love. "Say you'll share with me one love, one lifetime...."

*Daniel T. Larose, Ph.D.*
Professor of Statistics
Director, Data Mining @CCSU
Department of Mathematical Sciences
Central Connecticut State University
www.math.ccsu.edu/larose

# WEB STRUCTURE MINING

**In the** first part of the book we discuss basic ideas and techniques for extracting text information from the Web, including collecting and indexing web documents and searching and ranking web pages by their textual content and hyperlink structure. We first discuss the motivation to organize the web content and find better ways for web search to make the vast knowledge on the Web easily accessible. Then we describe briefly the basics of the Web and explore the approaches taken by web search engines to retrieve web pages by keyword search. To do this we look into the technology for text analysis and search developed earlier in the area of information retrieval and extended recently with ranking methods based on web hyperlink structure.

All that may be seen as a preprocessing step in the overall process of data mining the web content, which provides the input to machine learning methods for extracting knowledge from hypertext data, discussed in the second part of the book.

*Data Mining the Web: Uncovering Patterns in Web Content, Structure, and Usage*
By Zdravko Markov and Daniel T. Larose   Copyright © 2007 John Wiley & Sons, Inc.

# CHAPTER 1

# INFORMATION RETRIEVAL AND WEB SEARCH

WEB CHALLENGES

CRAWLING THE WEB

INDEXING AND KEYWORD SEARCH

EVALUATING SEARCH QUALITY

SIMILARITY SEARCH

## WEB CHALLENGES

As originally proposed by Tim Berners-Lee [1], the Web was intended to improve the management of general information about accelerators and experiments at CERN. His suggestion was to organize the information used at that institution in a graphlike structure where the nodes are documents describing objects, such as notes, articles, departments, or persons, and the links are relations among them, such as "depends on," "is part of," "refers to," or "uses." This seemed suitable for a large organization like CERN, and soon after it appeared that the framework proposed by Berners-Lee was very general and would work very well for any set of documents, providing flexibility and convenience in accessing large amounts of text. A very important development of this idea was that the documents need not be stored at the same computer or database but rather, could be distributed over a network of computers. Luckily, the infrastructure for this type of distribution, the Internet, had already been developed. In short, this is how the Web was born.

Looking at the Web many years later and comparing it to the original proposal of 1989, we see two basic differences:

1. The recent Web is huge and grows incredibly fast. About 10 years after the Berners-Lee proposal, the Web was estimated to have 150 million nodes (pages) and 1.7 billion edges (links). Now it includes more than 4 billion pages, with about 1 million added every day.

**2.** The formal semantics of the Web is very restricted—nodes are simply web pages and links are of a single type (e.g., "refer to"). The meaning of the nodes and links is not a part of the web system; rather, it is left to web page developers to describe in the page content what their web documents mean and what types of relations they have with the documents to which they are linked. As there is neither a central authority nor editors, the relevance, popularity, and authority of web pages are hard to evaluate. Links are also very diverse, and many have nothing to do with content or authority (e.g., navigation links).

The Web is now the largest, most open, most democratic publishing system in the world. From a publishers' (web page developers') standpoint, this is a great feature of the Web—any type of information can be distributed worldwide with no restriction on its content, and most important, using the developer's own interpretation of the web page and link meaning. From a web user's point of view, however, this is the worst thing about the Web. To determine a document's type the user has to read it all. The links simply refer to other documents, which means again that reading the entire set of linked documents is the only sure way to determine the document types or areas. This type of document access is directly opposite to what we know from databases and libraries, where all data items or documents are organized in various ways: by type, topic, area, author, year, and so on. Using a library in a "weblike" manner would mean that one has first to read the entire collection of books (or at least their titles and abstracts) to find the one in the area or topic that he or she needs. Even worse, some web page publishers cheat regarding the content of their pages, using titles or links with attractive names to make the user visit pages that he or she would never look at otherwise.

At the same time, the Web is the largest repository of knowledge in the world, so everyone is tempted to use it, and every time that one starts exploring the Web, he or she knows that the piece of information sought is "out there." But the big question is how to find it. Answering this question has been the basic driving force in developing web search technologies, now widely available through web search engines such as Google, Yahoo!, and many others. Other approaches have also been taken: Web pages have been manually edited and organized into topic directories, or data mining techniques have been used to extract knowledge from the Web automatically.

To summarize, the challenge is to bring back the semantics of hypertext documents (something that was a part of the original web proposal of Berners-Lee) so that we can easily use the vast amount of information available. In other words, we need to *turn web data into web knowledge*. In general, there are several ways to achieve this: Some use the existing Web and apply sophisticated search techniques; others suggest that we change the way in which we create web pages. We discuss briefly below the three main approaches.

## Web Search Engines

Web search engines explore the existing (semantics-free) structure of the Web and try to find documents that match user search criteria: that is, to bring semantics into the process of web search. The basic idea is to use a set of words (or terms) that the user specifies and retrieve documents that include (or do not include) those words. This is the *keyword search* approach, well known from the area of information retrieval (IR). In web search, further IR techniques are used to avoid terms that are too general and too specific and to take into account term distribution throughout the entire body of documents as well as to explore document similarity. Natural language processing approaches are also used to analyze term context or lexical information, or to combine several terms into phrases. After retrieving a set of documents ranked by their degree of matching the keyword query, they are further ranked by importance (popularity, authority), usually based on the web link structure. All these approaches are discussed further later in the book.

## Topic Directories

Web pages are organized into hierarchical structures that reflect their meaning. These are known as *topic directories*, or simply *directories*, and are available from almost all web search portals. The largest is being developed under the Open Directory Project (`dmoz.org`) and is used by Google in their Web Directory: "the Web organized by topic into categories," as they put it. The directory structure is often used in the process of web search to better match user criteria or to specialize a search within a specific set of pages from a given category. The directories are usually created manually with the help of thousands of web page creators and editors. There are also approaches to do this automatically by applying machine learning methods for classification and clustering. We look into these approaches in Part II.

## Semantic Web

*Semantic web* is a recent initiative led by the web consortium (`w3c.org`). Its main objective is to bring formal knowledge representation techniques into the Web. Currently, web pages are designed basically for human readers. It is widely acknowledged that the Web is like a "fancy fax machine" used to send good-looking documents worldwide. The problem here is that the nice format of web pages is very difficult for computers to understand—something that we expect search engines to do. The main idea behind the semantic web is to add formal descriptive material to each web page that although invisible to people would make its content easily understandable by computers. Thus, the Web would be organized and turned into the largest knowledge base in the world, which with the help of advanced reasoning techniques developed in the area of artificial intelligence would be able not just to provide ranked documents that match a keyword search query, but would also be able to answer questions and give explanations. The web consortium site (`http://www.w3.org/2001/sw/`) provides detailed information about the latest developments in the area of the semantic web.

Although the semantic web is probably the future of the Web, our focus is on the former two approaches to bring semantics to the Web. The reason for this is that web search is the data mining approach to web semantics: extracting knowledge from web data. In contrast, the semantic web approach is about turning web pages into formal knowledge structures and extending the functionality of web browsers with knowledge manipulation and reasoning tools.

# CRAWLING THE WEB

In this and later sections we use basic web terminology such as *HTML, URL, web browsers*, and *servers*. We assume that the reader is familiar with these terms, but for the sake of completeness we provide a brief introduction to web basics.

## Web Basics

The Web is a huge collection of documents linked together by references. The mechanism for referring from one document to another is based on hypertext and embedded in the HTML (HyperText Markup Language) used to encode web documents. HTML is primarily a typesetting language (similar to Tex and LaTex) that describes how a document should be displayed in a browser window. Browsers are computer programs that read HTML documents and display them accordingly, such as the popular browsers Microsoft Internet Explorer and Netscape Communicator. These programs are clients that connect to web servers that hold actual web documents and send those documents to the browsers by request. Each web document has a web address called the URL (universal resource locator) that identifies it uniquely. The URL is used by browsers to request documents from servers and in hyperlinks as a reference to other web documents. Web documents associated with their web addresses (URLs) are usually called *web pages*.

A URL consists of three segments and has the format

```
<protocol name>://<machine name>/<file name>,
```

where `<protocol name>` is the protocol (a language for exchanging information) that the browser and the server use to communicate (HTTP, FTP, etc.), `<machine name>` is the name (the web address) of the server, and `<file name>` is the directory path showing where the document is stored on the server. For example, the URL

```
http://dmoz.org/Computers/index.html
```

points to an HTML document stored on a file named "index.html" in the folder "Computers" located on the server "dmoz.org." It can also be written as

```
http://dmoz.org/Computers/
```

because the browser automatically looks for a file named index. html if only a folder name is specified.

Entering the URL in the address window makes the browser connect to the web server with the corresponding name using the HyperText Transport Protocol (HTTP). After a successful connection, the HTML document is fetched and its content is shown in the browser window. Some intermediate steps are taking place meanwhile, such as obtaining the server Internet address (called the IP address) from a domain name server (DNS), establishing a connection with the server, and exchanging commands. However, we are not going into these details, as they are not important for our discussion here.

Along with its informational content (formatted text and images), a web page usually contains URLs pointing to other web pages. These URLs are encoded in the tag structure of the HTML language. For example, the document index.html at `http://dmoz.org/Computers/` includes the following fragment:

```
<table border=0>
<tr><td valign=top><ul>
<li><a href="/Computers/Algorithms/"><b>Algorithms</b></a>
<i>(367)</i>
```

The URL in this HTML fragment, `/Computers/Algorithms/`, is the text that appears quoted in the `<a>` tag preceded by `href`. This is a local URL, a part of the complete URL (`http://dmoz.org/Computers/Algorithms/`), which the browser creates automatically by adding the current protocol name (`http`) and server address (`dmoz.org`). Here is another fragment from the same page that includes absolute URLs.

```
<b>Visit our sister sites</b>
<a href="http://www.mozilla.org/">mozilla.org</a>|
<a href="http://chefmoz.org/">ChefMoz</a>
```

Another important part of the web page linking mechanism is the *anchor*, the text or image in the web page that when clicked makes the browser fetch the web page that is pointed to by the corresponding link. Anchor text is usually displayed emphasized (underlined or in color) so that it can be spotted easily by the user. For example, in the HTML fragment above, the anchor text for the URL `http://mozilla.org/` is "mozilla.org" and that for `http://chefmoz.org/` is "ChefMoz."

The idea of the anchor text is to suggest the meaning or content of the web page to which the corresponding URL is pointing so that the user can decide whether or not to visit it. This may appear similar to Berners-Lee's idea in the original web proposal to attach different semantics to the web links, but there is an important difference here. The anchor is simply a part of the web page content and does not affect the way the page is processed by the browser. For example, spammers may take advantage of this by using anchor text with an attractive name (e.g., summer vacation) to make user visit their pages, which may not be as attractive (e.g., online pharmacy). We discuss approaches to avoid this later.

Formally, the Web can be seen as a *directed graph*, where the nodes are web pages and the links are represented by URLs. Given a web page *P*, the URLs in it are called *outlinks*. Those in other pages pointing to *P* are called *inlinks* (or *backlinks*).

## Web Crawlers

Browsing the Web is a very useful way to explore a collection of linked web documents as long as we know good starting points: URLs of pages from the topic or area in which we are interested. However, general search for information about a specific topic or area through browsing alone is impractical. A better approach is to have web pages organized by topic or to search a collection of pages indexed by keywords. The former is done by topic directories and the latter, by search engines. Hereafter we shall see how search engines collect web documents and index them by the words (terms) they contain. First we discuss the process of collecting web pages and storing them in a local repository. Indexing and document retrieval are discussed in the next section.

To index a set of web documents with the words they contain, we need to have all documents available for processing in a local repository. Creating the index by accessing the documents directly on the Web is impractical for a number of reasons. Collecting "all" web documents can be done by browsing the Web systematically and exhaustively and storing all visited pages. This is done by *crawlers* (also called *spiders* or *robots*).

Ideally, all web pages are linked (there are no unconnected parts of the web graph) and there are no multiple links and nodes. Then the job of a crawler is simple: to run a complete *graph search algorithm*, such as *depth-first* or *breadth-first* search, and store all visited pages. Small-scale crawlers can easily be implemented and are a good programming exercise that illustrates both the structure of the Web and graph search algorithms. There are a number of freely available crawlers from this class that can be used for educational and research purposes. A good example of such a crawler is WebSPHINX (`http://www.cs.cmu.edu/~rcm/websphinx/`).

A straightforward use of a crawler is to visualize and analyze the structure of the web graph. We illustrate this with two examples of running the WebSPHINX crawler. For both runs we start with the Data Mining home page at CCSU at `http://www.ccsu.edu/datamining/`. As we want to study the structure of the web locally in the neighborhood of the starting page, we have to impose some limits on crawling. With respect to the web structure, we may limit the depth of crawling [i.e., the number of hops (links) to follow and the size of the pages to be fetched]. The region of the web to be crawled can also be specified by using the URL structure. Thus, all URLs with the same server name limit crawling within the specific server pages only, while all URLs with the same folder prefixes limit crawling pages that are stored in subfolders only (subtree).

Other limits are dynamic and reflect the time needed to fetch a page or the running time of the crawler. These parameters are needed not only to restrict the web area to be crawled but also to avoid some traps the crawler may fall into (see the discussion following the examples). Some parameters used to control the crawling algorithm must also be passed. These are the graph search method (depth-first or breadth-first) as well as the number of threads (crawling processes running in parallel) to be used. Various other limits and restrictions with respect to web page content can also be imposed (some are discussed in Chapter 2 in the context of page ranking). Thus, for the first example we set the following limits: depth = 3 hops, page size = 30 kB (kilobytes), page timeout = 3 seconds, crawler timeout = 30 seconds, depth-first search, threads = 4. The portion of the web graph crawled with this setting is shown in Figure 1.1. The starting page is marked with its name and URL. Note that due to the dynamic limits and varying network latency, every crawl, even those with the same parameters, is different. In the one shown in Figure 1.1, the crawler reached an interesting structure called a *hub*. This is the page in the middle of a circle of multiple pages. A *hub page* includes a large number of links and is usually some type of directory or reference site that points to many web pages. In our example

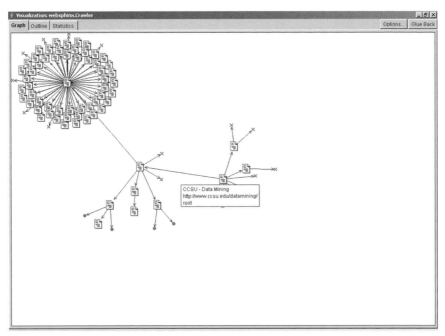

**Figure 1.1**   Depth-first web crawling limited to depth 3.

the hub page is KDnuggets.com, one of the most comprehensive and well-organized repositories of information about data mining.

Another crawl with the same parameters and limits, but using a breadth-first search, is shown in Figure 1.2. The web graph here is more uniformly covered because of the nature of the search algorithm—all immediate neighbors of a given page are explored before going to further pages. Therefore, the breadth-first crawl discovered another hub page that is closer to the starting point. It is the resources page at CCSU—Data Mining. In both graphs, the ×'s mean that some limits have been reached or network exceptions have occurred, and the dots are pages that have not yet been explored, due to the crawler timeout.

The web graph shown by the WebSPHINX crawler is actually a tree, because only the links followed are shown and the pages are visited only once. However, the Web is not a tree, and generally there is more than one inlink to a page (occurrences of the page URL in other web pages). In fact, these inlinks are quite important when analyzing the web structure because they can be used as a measure of web page popularity or importance. Similar to the hubs, a web page with a large number of inlinks is also important and is called an *authority*. Finding good authorities is, however, not possible using the local crawls that we illustrated with the examples above and generally requires analyzing a much larger portion of the web (theoretically, the entire Web, if we want to find all inlinks).

Although there is more than one inlink to some of the pages in our example (e.g., the CCSU or the CCSU—Data Mining home pages are referred to in many other pages), these links come from the same site and are included basically for navigation

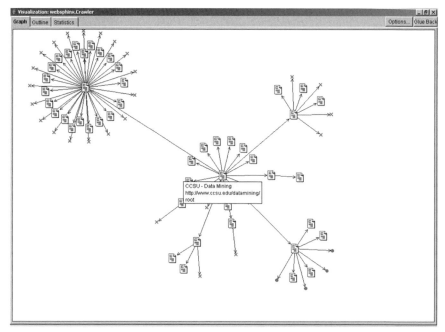

**Figure 1.2**   Breadth-first web crawling limited to depth 3.

purposes. Such links do not reflect the actual popularity of the web pages to which they point. This is a situation similar to self-citation in scientific literature, which is hardly considered as a good measure of authority. We discuss these issues in more depth later in the context of page ranking.

Although visualizing the web graph is a nice feature of web crawlers, it is not the most important. In fact, the basic role of a crawler that is part of a search engine is to collect information about web pages. This may be web page textual content, page titles, headers, tag structure, or web links structure. This information is organized properly for efficient access and stored in a local repository to be used for indexing and search (see the next section). Thus, a crawler is not only an implementation of a graph search algorithm, but also an HTML parser and analyzer, and much more. Some of the extended functionalities of web crawlers are discussed next.

The Web is far from an ideal graph structure such as the one shown in Figures 1.1 and 1.2. Crawling the Web involves interaction with hundreds of thousands of web servers, designed to meet different goals, provide different services such as database access and user interactions, generate dynamic pages, and so on. Another very important factor is the huge number of pages that have to be visited, analyzed, and stored. Therefore, a web crawler designed to crawl the entire Web is a sophisticated program that uses advanced programming technology to improve its time and space efficiency and usually runs on high-performance parallel computers. Hereafter we provide a brief account of common problems that large-scale crawlers are faced with and outline some solutions. We are not going into technical details because this is aside from our main goal: analyzing the web content.

- The process of fetching a web page involves some network latency (sometimes a "timeout"). To avoid waiting for the current page to load in order to continue with the next page, crawlers fetch multiple pages simultaneously. In turn, this requires connecting to multiple servers (usually thousands) at the same time, which is achieved by using parallel and distributed programming technology such as multithreading (running multiple clients concurrently) or nonblocking sockets and event handlers.

- The first step in fetching a web page is address resolution, converting the symbolic web address into an IP address. This is done by a DNS server that the crawler connects. Since multiple pages may be located at a single server, storing addresses already looked up in a local cache allows the crawler to avoid repeating DNS requests and consequently, improves its efficiency and minimizes the Internet traffic.

- After fetching a web page it is scanned and the URLs are extracted—these are the outlinks that will be followed next by the crawler. There are many ways to specify an URL in HTML. It may also be specified by using the IP address of the server. As the mapping between server names and IP addresses is many-to-many,[1] this may result in multiple URLs for a single web page. The problem is aggravated by the fact that browsers are tolerant of pages that have the wrong syntax. As a result, HTML documents are not designed with enough care and often include wrongly specified URLs as well as other malicious structures. All this makes parsing and extracting URLs from HTML documents not an easy task. The solution is to use a well-designed and robust parser and after extracting the URLs to convert them into a canonical form. Even so, there are traps that the crawler may fall into. The best policy is to collect statistics regularly about each crawl and use them in a special module called a *guard*. The purpose of the guard is to exclude outlinks that come from sites that dominate the crawler collection of pages. Also, it may filter out links to dynamic pages or forms as well as to nontextual pages (e.g., images, scripts).

- Following the web page links may bring the crawler back to pages already visited. There may also exist identical web pages at different web addresses (called *mirror sites*). To avoid following identical links and fetching identical pages multiple times, the crawler should keep caches for URLs and pages (this is another reason for putting URLs into canonical form). Various hashing techniques are used for this purpose.

- An important part of the web crawler system is the *text repository*. Yahoo! claimed that in August 2005 their index included 20 billion pages [2], 19.2 of them web documents. With an average of 10 kB for a web document, this

---

[1] A server may have more than one IP address, and different host names may be mapped onto a single IP address. The former is usually done for load balancing of servers that handle a large number of requests, and the latter, for organizing web pages into more logical host names than the number of IP addresses available (virtual hosting).

makes about 200,000 GB (gigabytes) of storage. Managing such a huge repository is a challenging task. Note that this is the crawler repository, not the indexed collection of web pages used to answer search queries. The latter is of comparable size, but even more complicated because of the need for fast access. The crawler repository is used to store pages, maintain the URL and document caches needed by the crawler, and provide access for building indices at the next stage. To minimize storage needs, the web pages are usually compressed, which reduces the storage requirements two- to threefold. For large-scale crawlers the text repository may be distributed over a number of storage servers.

- The purpose of a web crawler used by a search engine is to provide local access to the most recent versions of possibly all web pages. This means that the Web should be crawled regularly and the collection of pages updated accordingly. Having in mind the huge capacity of the text repository, the need for regular updates poses another challenge for the web crawler designers. The problem is the high cost of updating indices. A common solution is to append the new versions of web pages without deleting the old ones. This increases the storage requirements but also allows the crawler repository to be used for archival purposes. In fact, there are crawlers that are used just for the purposes of archiving the web. The most popular web archive is the Internet Archive at `http://www.archive.org/`.

- The Web is a live system, it is constantly changing—new features emerge and new services are offered. In many cases they are not known in advance, or even worse, web pages and servers may behave unpredictably as a result of bugs or malicious design. Thus, the web crawler should be a very robust system that is updated constantly in order to respond to the ever-changing Web.

- Crawling of the Web also involves interaction of web page developers. As Brin and Page [5] mention in a paper about their search engine Google, they were getting e-mail from people who noticed that somebody (or something) visited their pages. To facilitate this interaction there are standards that allow web servers and crawlers to exchange information. One of them is the *robot exclusion protocol*. A file named robots.txt that lists all path prefixes of pages that crawlers should not fetch is placed in the http root directory of the server and read by the crawlers before crawling of the server tree.

So far we discussed crawling based on the syntax of the web graph: that is, following links and visiting pages without taking into account their semantics. This is in a sense equivalent to *uninformed graph search*. However, let's not forget that we discuss web crawling in the context of web search. Thus, to improve its efficiency, or for specific purposes, crawling can also be done as a *guided (informed) search*. Usually, crawling precedes the phase of web page evaluation and ranking, as the latter comes after indexing and retrieval of web documents. However, web pages can be evaluated while being crawled. Thus, we get some type of enhanced crawling that uses page ranking methods to achieve focusing on interesting parts of the Web and avoiding fetching irrelevant or uninteresting pages.

# INDEXING AND KEYWORD SEARCH

Generally, there are two types of data: structured and unstructured. *Structured data* have keys (attributes, features) associated with each data item that reflect its content, meaning, or usage. A typical example of structured data is a relational table in a database. Given an attribute (column) name and its value, we can get a set of tuples (rows) that include this value. For example, consider a table that contains descriptions of departments in a school described by a number of attributes, such as subject, programs offered, areas of specialization, facilities, and courses. Then, by a simple query, we may get all departments that, for example, have computer labs. In SQL (Structured Query Language) this query is expressed as `select * from Departments where facilities=``computer lab´´`. A more common situation is, however, to have the same information specified as a one-paragraph text description for each department. Then looking for departments with computer labs would be more difficult and generally would require people to read and understand the text descriptions.

The problem with using structured data is the cost associated with the process of structuring them. The information that people use is available primarily in unstructured form. The largest part of it are text documents (books, magazines, newspapers) written in natural language. To have content-based access to these documents, we organize them in libraries, bibliography systems, and by other means. This process takes a lot of time and effort because it is done by people. There are attempts to use computers for this purpose, but the problem is that content-based access assumes understanding the meaning of documents, something that is still a research question, studied in the area of artificial intelligence and natural language processing in particular. One may argue that natural language texts are structured, which is true as long as the language syntax (grammatical structure) is concerned. However, the transition to meaning still requires semantic structuring or understanding. There exists a solution that avoids the problem of meaning but still provides some types of content-based access to unstructured data. This is the *keyword search* approach known from the area of *information retrieval* (IR). The idea of IR is to retrieve documents by using a simple Boolean criterion: the presence or absence of specific words (keywords, terms) in the documents (the question of meaning here is left to the user who formulates the query). Keywords may be combined in disjunctions and conjunctions, thus providing more expressiveness of the queries. A keyword-based query cannot identify the matching documents uniquely, and thus it usually returns a large number of documents. Therefore, in IR there is a need to rank documents by their relevance to the query. *Relevance ranking* is an important difference with querying structured data where the result of a query is a set (unordered collection) of data items.

IR approaches are applicable to bibliographic databases, collections of journal and newspaper articles, and other large text document collections that are not well structured (not organized by content), but require content-based access. In short, IR is about *finding relevant data using irrelevant keys*. The Web search engines rely heavily on IR technology. The web crawler text repository is very much like the document collection for which the IR approaches have been developed. Thus, having a web crawler, the implementation of IR-based keyword search for the Web is straightforward. Because of their internal HTML tag structure and external web link

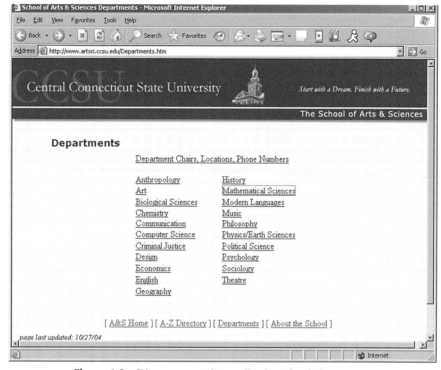

**Figure 1.3**　Directory page for a collection of web documents.

structure, the web documents are richer than simple text documents. This allows search engines to go further and provide more sophisticated methods for matching keyword queries with web documents and to do better relevance ranking. In this section we discuss standard IR techniques for text document processing. The enhancements that come from the Web structure are discussed in the next sections.

To illustrate the basic keyword search approach to the Web, we consider again the unstructured version of our example with the departments and make it more realistic by taking the web page that lists all departments in the school of Arts and Sciences at CCSU (Figure 1.3). The information about each department is provided in a separate web page linked to the department name listed on the main page. We include one of those pages in Figure 1.4 (the others have a similar format).

The first step is to fetch the documents from the Web, remove the HTML tags, and store the documents as plain text files. This can easily be done by a web crawler (the reader may want to try WebSPHINX) with proper parameter settings. Then the keyword search approach can be used to answer such queries as:

1. Find documents that contain the word *computer* and the word *programming*.

2. Find documents that contain the word *program*, but not the word *programming*.

3. Find documents where the words *computer* and *lab* are adjacent. This query is called *proximity query*, because it takes into account the lexical distance between words. Another way to do it is by searching for the phrase *computer lab*.

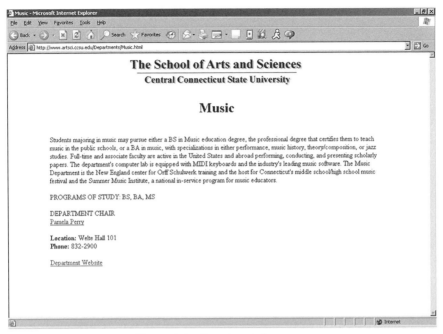

**Figure 1.4** Sample web document.

Answering such queries can be done by scanning the content of the documents and matching the keywords against the words in the documents. For example, the music department document shown in Figure 1.4 will be returned by the second and third queries.

## Document Representation

To facilitate the process of matching keywords and documents, some preprocessing steps are taken first:

1. Documents are *tokenized*; that is, all punctuation marks are removed and the character strings without spaces are considered as tokens (words, also called *terms*).

2. All characters in the documents and in the query are converted to upper or lower case.

3. Words are reduced to their canonical form (stem, base, or root). For example, variant forms such as *is* and *are* are replaced with *be*, various endings are removed, or the words are transformed into their root form, such as *programs* and *programming* into *program*. This process, called *stemming*, uses morphological information to allow matching different variants of words.

4. Articles, prepositions, and other common words that appear frequently in text documents but do not bring any meaning or help distinguish documents are

**TABLE 1.1  Basic Statistics for A&S Documents**

| Document ID | Document Name | Words | Terms |
|---|---|---|---|
| $d_1$ | Anthropology | 114 | 86 |
| $d_2$ | Art | 153 | 105 |
| $d_3$ | Biology | 123 | 91 |
| $d_4$ | Chemistry | 87 | 58 |
| $d_5$ | Communication | 124 | 88 |
| $d_6$ | Computer Science | 101 | 77 |
| $d_7$ | Criminal Justice | 85 | 60 |
| $d_8$ | Economics | 107 | 76 |
| $d_9$ | English | 116 | 80 |
| $d_{10}$ | Geography | 95 | 68 |
| $d_{11}$ | History | 108 | 78 |
| $d_{12}$ | Mathematics | 89 | 66 |
| $d_{13}$ | Modern Languages | 110 | 75 |
| $d_{14}$ | Music | 137 | 91 |
| $d_{15}$ | Philosophy | 85 | 54 |
| $d_{16}$ | Physics | 130 | 100 |
| $d_{17}$ | Political Science | 120 | 86 |
| $d_{18}$ | Psychology | 96 | 60 |
| $d_{19}$ | Sociology | 99 | 66 |
| $d_{20}$ | Theatre | 116 | 80 |
| Total number of words/terms | | 2195 | 1545 |
| Number of different words/terms | | 744 | 671 |

called *stopwords*. Examples are *a*, *an*, *the*, *on*, *in*, and *at*. These words are usually removed.

The collection of words that are left in the document after all those steps is different from the original document and may be considered as a *formal representation* of the document. To emphasize this difference, we call the words in this collection *terms*. The collection of words (terms) in the entire set of documents is called the *text corpus*.

Table 1.1 shows some statistics about documents from the school of Arts and Sciences (A&S) that illustrate this process (the design department is not included because the link points directly to the department web page). The words are counted after tokenizing the plain text versions of the documents (without the HTML structures). The term counts are taken after removing the stopwords but without stemming.

The terms that occur in a document are in fact the *parameters* (also called *features*, *attributes*, or *variables* in different contexts) of the document representation. The types of parameters determine the type of document representation:

- The simplest way to use a term as a feature in a document representation is to check whether or not the term occurs in the document. Thus, the term is considered as a Boolean attribute, so the representation is called *Boolean*.

- The value of a term as a feature in a document representation may be the number of occurrences of the term (*term frequency*) in the document or in the entire corpus. Document representation that includes the term frequencies but not the term positions is called a *bag-of-words representation* because formally it is a multiset or bag (a type of set in which each item may occur numerous times).

- Term positions may be included along with the frequency. This is a "complete" representation that preserves most of the information and may be used to generate the original document from its representation.

The purpose of the document representation is to help the process of keyword matching. However, it may also result in loss of information, which generally increases the number of documents in response to the keyword query. Thus, some irrelevant documents may also be returned. For example, stemming of *programming* would change the second query and allow the first one to return more documents (its original purpose is to identify the Computer Science department, but stemming would allow more documents to be returned, as they all include the word *program* or *programs* in the sense of "program of study"). Therefore, stemming should be applied with care and even avoided, especially for Web searches, where a lot of common words are used with specific technical meaning. This problem is also related to the issue of context (lexical or semantic), which is generally lost in keyword search. A partial solution to the latter problem is the use of proximity information or lexical context. For this purpose a richer document representation can be used that preserves term positions. Some punctuation marks can be replaced by placeholders (tokens that are left in a document but cannot be used for searching), so that part of the lexical structure of the document, such as sentence boundaries, can be preserved. This would allow answering queries such as "Find documents containing *computer* and *programming* in the same sentence." Another approach, called *part-of-speech tagging*, is to attach to words tags that reflect their part-of-speech roles (e.g., verb or noun). For example, the word *can* usually appears in the stopword list, but as a noun it may be important for a query.

For the purposes of searching small documents and document collections such as the CCSU Arts and Sciences directory, direct text scanning may work well. This approach cannot, however, be scaled up to large documents and/or collections of documents such as the Web, due to the prohibitive computational cost. The approach used for the latter purposes is called an *inverted index* and is central to IR. The idea is to switch the roles of document IDs and terms. Instead of accessing documents by IDs and then scanning their content for specific terms, the terms that documents contain are used as access keys. The simplest form of an inverted index is a *document–term matrix*, where the access is by terms (i.e., it is transposed to *term–document matrix*).

The term–document matrix for our department example has 20 rows, corresponding to documents, and 671 columns, corresponding to all the different terms that occur in the text corpus. In the *Boolean* form of this matrix, each cell contains 1 if the term occurs in the document, and 0 otherwise. We assign the documents as rows because this representation is also used in later sections, but in fact, the table is accessed by columns. A small part of the matrix is shown in Table 1.2 (instead of names, document IDs are used).

**TABLE 1.2  Boolean Term–Document Matrix**

| Document ID | *lab* | *laboratory* | *programming* | *computer* | *program* |
|:---:|:---:|:---:|:---:|:---:|:---:|
| $d_1$ | 0 | 0 | 0 | 0 | 1 |
| $d_2$ | 0 | 0 | 0 | 0 | 1 |
| $d_3$ | 0 | 1 | 0 | 1 | 0 |
| $d_4$ | 0 | 0 | 0 | 1 | 1 |
| $d_5$ | 0 | 0 | 0 | 0 | 0 |
| $d_6$ | 0 | 0 | 1 | 1 | 1 |
| $d_7$ | 0 | 0 | 0 | 0 | 1 |
| $d_8$ | 0 | 0 | 0 | 0 | 1 |
| $d_9$ | 0 | 0 | 0 | 0 | 0 |
| $d_{10}$ | 0 | 0 | 0 | 0 | 0 |
| $d_{11}$ | 0 | 0 | 0 | 0 | 0 |
| $d_{12}$ | 0 | 0 | 0 | 1 | 0 |
| $d_{13}$ | 0 | 0 | 0 | 0 | 0 |
| $d_{14}$ | 1 | 0 | 0 | 1 | 1 |
| $d_{15}$ | 0 | 0 | 0 | 0 | 1 |
| $d_{16}$ | 0 | 0 | 0 | 0 | 1 |
| $d_{17}$ | 0 | 0 | 0 | 0 | 1 |
| $d_{18}$ | 0 | 0 | 0 | 0 | 0 |
| $d_{19}$ | 0 | 0 | 0 | 0 | 1 |
| $d_{20}$ | 0 | 0 | 0 | 0 | 0 |

Using the term–document matrix, answering the keyword search queries is straightforward. For example, query 1 returns only $d_6$ (Computer Science document), because it has 1's in the columns *programming* and *computer*, while query 2 returns all documents with 1's in the column *program*, excluding $d_6$, because the latter has 1 in the column *programming*. The proximity query (number 3), however, cannot be answered using a Boolean representation. This is because information about the term positions (offsets) in the document is lost. The problem can be solved by using a richer representation that includes the position for each occurrence of a term. In this case, each cell of the term–document matrix contains a list of integers that represent the term offsets for each of its occurrences in the corresponding document. Table 1.3 shows the version of the term–document matrix from Table 1.2 that includes term positions. Having this representation, the proximity query can also be answered. For document $d_{14}$ (Music department) the matrix shows the following position lists: [42] for *lab* and [41] for *computer*. This clearly shows that the two terms are adjacent and appear in the phrase *computer lab*.

The term position lists also show the term frequencies (the length of these lists). For example, the term *computer* occurs six times in the Computer Science document and once in the Biology, Chemistry, Mathematics, and Music documents. Obviously, this is a piece of information that shows the importance of this particular feature for those documents. Thus, if *computer* is the query term, clearly the most relevant document returned would be Computer Science. For the other four documents, additional keywords may be needed to get a more precise *relevance ranking*. These issues are further discussed in the next sections.

**TABLE 1.3    Term–Document Matrix with Term Positions**

| Document ID | lab | laboratory | programming | computer | program |
|---|---|---|---|---|---|
| $d_1$ | 0 | 0 | 0 | 0 | [71] |
| $d_2$ | 0 | 0 | 0 | 0 | [7] |
| $d_3$ | 0 | [65,69] | 0 | [68] | 0 |
| $d_4$ | 0 | 0 | 0 | [26] | [30,43] |
| $d_5$ | 0 | 0 | 0 | 0 | 0 |
| $d_6$ | 0 | 0 | [40,42] | [1,3,7,13,26,34] | [11,18,61] |
| $d_7$ | 0 | 0 | 0 | 0 | [9,42] |
| $d_8$ | 0 | 0 | 0 | 0 | [57] |
| $d_9$ | 0 | 0 | 0 | 0 | 0 |
| $d_{10}$ | 0 | 0 | 0 | 0 | 0 |
| $d_{11}$ | 0 | 0 | 0 | 0 | 0 |
| $d_{12}$ | 0 | 0 | 0 | [17] | 0 |
| $d_{13}$ | 0 | 0 | 0 | 0 | 0 |
| $d_{14}$ | [42] | 0 | 0 | [41] | [71] |
| $d_{15}$ | 0 | 0 | 0 | 0 | [37,38] |
| $d_{16}$ | 0 | 0 | 0 | 0 | [81] |
| $d_{17}$ | 0 | 0 | 0 | 0 | [68] |
| $d_{18}$ | 0 | 0 | 0 | 0 | 0 |
| $d_{19}$ | 0 | 0 | 0 | 0 | [51] |
| $d_{20}$ | 0 | 0 | 0 | 0 | 0 |

## Implementation Considerations

The Boolean representation of a term–document matrix is simple and can easily be implemented as a relational table. We use this representation later in the book for the purposes of document classification and clustering. However, for large document collections (such as those used by search engines) and for incorporating term positions, the amount of space needed is too large and does not allow straightforward implementation using a relational database. In these cases more advanced methods such as *B-trees* and *hash tables* are used. The idea is to implement the mappings directly from terms to documents and term positions. For example, the following structures can be used for this purpose:

$$lab \rightarrow d_{14}/42$$
$$laboratory \rightarrow d_3/65, 69$$
$$programming \rightarrow d_6/40, 42$$
$$computer \rightarrow d_3/68; d_4/26; d_6/1, 3, 7, 13, 26, 34; d_{12}/17; d_{14}/41$$

There are two problems associated with this representation:

1. The efficiency of creating the data structure implementing the index
2. The efficiency of updating the index

Both issues are critical, especially for the indices used by web search engines. To get an idea of the magnitude of the problem, we provide here some figures from experiments performed with the GOV2 collection reported at the Text Retrieval Conference 2004-terabyte (TB) track. The GOV2 document collection is 426 GB and contains 25 million documents taken from the .gov web domain, including HTML and text, plus the extracted text of PDF, Word, and postscript files. For one of the submissions to this track (Indri), the index size was 224 GB and took 6 hours to build on a cluster of six computers. Given these figures, we can also get an idea about the indices build by web search engines. Assuming a web document collection of 20 billion documents (the size of the document collection that Yahoo! claimed to index in August 2005), its size can be estimated to be 500 TB (for comparison, the books in the U.S. Library of Congress contain approximately 20 TB of text). Simple projection suggests an index size of about 200 TB and an indexing time of 6000 hours (!). This amount of memory can be managed by recent technology. Moreover, there exist compression techniques that can substantially reduce the memory requirements. This indexing time is, however, prohibitive for search engines because the web pages change at a much quicker rate. The web indices should be built quickly and, most important, updated at a rate equal to the average rate of updating web pages.

There is another important parameter in indexing and search: the *query time*. It is assumed that this time should be in the range of seconds (typically, less than a second). The problem is that when the index is compressed, the time to update it and the access time (query time) both increase. Thus, the concern is to find the right balance between memory and time requirements (a version of the time–space complexity trade-off well known in computing).

## Relevance Ranking

The Boolean keyword search is simple and efficient, but it returns a set (unordered collection) of documents. As we mentioned earlier, information retrieval queries are not well defined and cannot uniquely identify the resulting documents. The average size of a web search query is two terms. Obviously, such a short query cannot specify precisely the information needs of web users, and as a result, the response set is large and therefore useless (imagine getting a list of a million documents from a web search engine in random order). One may argue that users have to make their queries specific enough to get a small set of all relevant documents, but this is impractical. The solution is to rank documents in the response set by relevance to the query and present to the user an ordered list with the top-ranking documents first. The Boolean term–document matrix cannot, however, provide ordering within the documents matching the set of keywords. Therefore, additional information about terms is needed, such as counts, positions, and other context information. One straightforward approach is to incorporate the term count (frequencies). This is done in the term frequency–inverse document frequency (TFIDF) framework used widely in IR and Web search. Other approaches using positions and lexical and web context are discussed in later sections.

### *Vector Space Model*

The *vector space model* defines documents as vectors (or points) in a multidimensional Euclidean space where the axes (dimensions) are represented by terms. Depending on the type of vector components (coordinates), there are three basic versions of this representation: Boolean, term frequency (TF), and term frequency–inverse document frequency (TFIDF).

Assume that there are $n$ documents $d_1, d_2, \ldots, d_n$ and $m$ terms $t_1, t_2, \ldots, t_m$. Let us denote as $n_{ij}$ the number of times that term $t_i$ occurs in document $d_j$. In a *Boolean representation*, document $d_j$ is represented as an $m$-component vector $\vec{d}_j = (d_j^1 \, d_j^2 \cdots d_j^m)$, where[2]

$$d_j^i = \begin{cases} 0 & \text{if } n_{ij} = 0 \\ 1 & \text{if } n_{ij} > 0 \end{cases}$$

For example, in Table 1.2 the documents from our department collection are represented in five-dimensional space, where the axes are *lab*, *laboratory*, *programming*, *computer*, and *program*. In this space the Computer Science document is represented by the Boolean vector

$$\vec{d}_6 = (0\ 0\ 1\ 1\ 1)$$

As we mentioned earlier, the Boolean representation is simple, easy to compute, and works well for document classification and clustering. However, it is not suitable for keyword search because it does not allow document ranking. Therefore, we focus here on the TFIDF representation.

In the *term frequency* (TF) approach, the coordinates of the document vector $\vec{d}_j$ are represented as a function of the term counts, usually normalized with the document length. For each term $t_i$ and each document $d_j$, the TF $(t_i, d_j)$ measure is computed. This can be done in different ways; for example:

- Using the sum of term counts over all terms (the total number of terms in the document):

$$\text{TF}(t_i, d_j) = \begin{cases} 0 & \text{if } n_{ij} = 0 \\ \dfrac{n_{ij}}{\sum_{k=1}^{m} n_{kj}} & \text{if } n_{ij} > 0 \end{cases}$$

- Using the maximum of the term count over all terms in the document:

$$\text{TF}(t_i, d_j) = \begin{cases} 0 & \text{if } n_{ij} = 0 \\ \dfrac{n_{ij}}{\max_k n_{kj}} & \text{if } n_{ij} > 0 \end{cases}$$

- Using a log scale to condition the term count (this approach is used in the Cornell SMART system [3]):

$$\text{TF}(t_i, d_j) = \begin{cases} 0 & \text{if } n_{ij} = 0 \\ 1 + \log(1 + \log n_{ij}) & \text{if } n_{ij} > 0 \end{cases}$$

---

[2] For compactness of presentation here and throughout the book, we interchange the row and column notation for vectors where appropriate.

This approach does not use the document length; rather, the counts are just smoothed by the log function.

In the Boolean and TF representations, each coordinate of a document vector is computed locally, taking into account only the particular term and document. This means that all axes are considered to be equally important. However, terms that occur frequently in documents may not be related to the content of the document. This is the case with the term *program* in our department example. Too many vectors have 1's (in the Boolean case) or large values (in TF) along this axis. This in turn increases the size of the resulting set and makes document ranking difficult if this term is used in the query. The same effect is caused by stopwords such as *a*, *an*, *the*, *on*, *in*, and *at* and is one reason to eliminate them from the corpus.

The basic idea of the *inverse document frequency* (IDF) approach is to scale down the coordinates for some axes, corresponding to terms that occur in many documents. For each term $t_i$ the IDF measure is computed as a proportion of documents where $t_i$ occurs with respect to the total number of documents in the collection. Let $D = \bigcup_1^n d_j$ be the document collection and $D_{t_i}$ the set of documents where term $t_i$ occurs. That is, $D_{t_i} = \{d_j | n_{ij} > 0\}$. As with TF, there are a variety of ways to compute IDF; some take a simple fraction $|D|/|D_{t_i}|$, others use a log function such as

$$\mathrm{IDF}(t_i) = \log \frac{1 + |D|}{|D_{t_i}|}$$

In the TFIDF representation each coordinate of the document vector is computed as a product of its TF and IDF components:

$$d_j^i = \mathrm{TF}(t_i, d_j)\mathrm{IDF}(t_i)$$

To illustrate the approach we represent our department documents in the TFIDF framework. First we need to compute the TF component for each term and each document. For this purpose we use a term–document matrix with term positions (Table 1.3) to get the counts $n_{ij}$, which are equal to the length of the lists with positions. These counts then have to be scaled with the document lengths (the number of terms taken from Table 1.1). The result of this is shown in Table 1.4, where the vectors are rows in the table (the first column is the vector name and the rest are its coordinates).

Note that the coordinates of the document vectors changed their scale, but relative to each other they are more or less the same. This is because the factors used for scaling down the term frequencies are similar (documents are similar in length). In the next step, IDF will, however, change the coordinates substantially.

Using the log version of the IDF measure, we get the following factors for each term (in decreasing order):

| *lab* | *laboratory* | *programming* | *computer* | *program* |
|---|---|---|---|---|
| 3.04452 | 3.04452 | 3.04452 | 1.43508 | 0.559616 |

These numbers reflect the specificity of each term with respect to the document collection. The first three get the biggest value, as they occur in only one document each. The term *computer* occurs in five documents and *program* in 11. The document vector

**TABLE 1.4    Document Vectors with TF Coordinates**

| Document ID | TF Coordinates | | | | |
|---|---|---|---|---|---|
| $\vec{d}_1$ | 0 | 0 | 0 | 0 | 0.012 |
| $\vec{d}_2$ | 0 | 0 | 0 | 0 | 0.010 |
| $\vec{d}_3$ | 0 | 0.022 | 0 | 0.011 | 0 |
| $\vec{d}_4$ | 0 | 0 | 0 | 0.017 | 0.034 |
| $\vec{d}_5$ | 0 | 0 | 0 | 0 | 0.011 |
| $\vec{d}_6$ | 0 | 0 | 0.026 | 0.078 | 0.039 |
| $\vec{d}_7$ | 0 | 0 | 0 | 0 | 0.033 |
| $\vec{d}_8$ | 0 | 0 | 0 | 0 | 0.013 |
| $\vec{d}_9$ | 0 | 0 | 0 | 0 | 0 |
| $\vec{d}_{10}$ | 0 | 0 | 0 | 0 | 0 |
| $\vec{d}_{11}$ | 0 | 0 | 0 | 0 | 0 |
| $\vec{d}_{12}$ | 0 | 0 | 0 | 0.015 | 0 |
| $\vec{d}_{13}$ | 0 | 0 | 0 | 0 | 0 |
| $\vec{d}_{14}$ | 0.011 | 0 | 0 | 0.011 | 0.011 |
| $\vec{d}_{15}$ | 0 | 0 | 0 | 0 | 0.037 |
| $\vec{d}_{16}$ | 0 | 0 | 0 | 0 | 0.010 |
| $\vec{d}_{17}$ | 0 | 0 | 0 | 0 | 0.012 |
| $\vec{d}_{18}$ | 0 | 0 | 0 | 0 | 0 |
| $\vec{d}_{19}$ | 0 | 0 | 0 | 0 | 0.015 |
| $\vec{d}_{20}$ | 0 | 0 | 0 | 0 | 0 |

TF components are now multiplied by the IDF factors. In this way the vector coordinates corresponding to rare terms (*lab*, *laboratory*, and *programming*) increase, and those corresponding to frequent ones (*computer* and *program*) decrease. For example, the Computer Science (CS) document vector with TF only is

$$\vec{d}_6 = (0 \;\; 0 \;\; 0.026 \;\; 0.078 \;\; 0.039)$$

whereas after applying IDF, it becomes

$$\vec{d}_6 = (0 \;\; 0 \;\; 0.079 \;\; 0.112 \;\; 0.022)$$

In this vector the term *computer* is still the winner (obviously, the most important term for CS), but the vector is now stretched out along the *programming* axis, which means that the term *programming* is more relevant to identifying the document than the term *program* (quite true for CS, having in mind that *program* also has other non-CS meanings).

## Document Ranking

In the Boolean model the query terms are simply matched against the document vectors, and the documents that match the query exactly are returned. In the TFIDF model, exact matching is not possible; therefore, we need some *proximity measure* between the query and the documents in the collection. The basic idea is to represent the query as a vector (called a *query vector*) in the document vector space and then to use the metric properties of vector spaces. For this purpose we first consider the keyword query as a document. For example, the query that is supposed to return all documents containing the terms *computer* and *program* is represented as a document $q = \{computer, program\}$. As each term occurs once, its TF component is $\frac{1}{2}$ (normalized with the document length of 2). Thus, the TF vector in five-dimensional space is

$$\vec{q} = (0 \ \ 0 \ \ 0 \ \ 0.5 \ \ 0.5)$$

which after scaling with IDF becomes

$$\vec{q} = (0 \ \ 0 \ \ 0 \ \ 0.718 \ \ 0.28)$$

When we specify a Boolean query we usually assume that the terms are equally important for the document we are looking for. However, it appears that the *importance of the keywords depends on the document collection*. Thus, the search engine automatically adjusts the importance of each term in the query. For example, the term *computer* seems to be more important than *program* simply because *program* is a more common term (occurs in more documents) in this particular collection. The situation may change if we search a different collection of documents (e.g., in the area of CS only).

Given a query vector $\vec{q}$ and document vectors $\vec{d}_j, j = 1, 2, \ldots, 20$, the objective of a search engine is to order (rank) the documents with respect to their proximity to $\vec{q}$. The result list should include a number of top-ranked documents. There are several approaches to this type of ranking. One option is to use the *Euclidean norm of the vector difference* $\|\vec{q} - \vec{d}_j\|$, defined as

$$\|\vec{q} - \vec{d}_j\| = \sqrt{\sum_{i=1}^{m} \left(q^i - d_j^i\right)^2}$$

This measure is, in fact, the *Euclidian distance* between the vectors considered as points in Euclidean space, and being a *metric function*, it has some nice properties, such as the triangle inequality. However, it depends greatly on the length of the vectors to be compared. This property is not in agreement with one of the basic assumptions in IR: that similar documents (in terms of their relevance to the query) also have to be close in the vector space. For example, a large and a small document will be at a great distance even though they may both be relevant to the same query. To avoid this, the document and the query vectors are normalized to unit length before taking the vector difference. This approach still has a drawback because queries are very short and when scaled down with the query length (typically, 2), their vectors tend to be at a great distance from large documents.

Another approach is to use the cosine of the angle between the query vector and the document vectors. When the vectors are normalized, this measure is equivalent to the *dot product* $\vec{q} \cdot \vec{d}_j$, defined as

$$\vec{q} \cdot \vec{d}_j = \sum_{i=1}^{m} q^i d_j^i$$

This measure, known as *cosine similarity*, is the one used primarily in IR and web search.

**TABLE 1.5  Cosine Similarity and Distances with $\vec{q} = (0\ 0\ 0\ 0.932\ 0.363)$**

| Document ID | TFIDF Coordinates (Normalized) | | | | | $\vec{q} \cdot \vec{d_j}$ (rank)[a] | $|\vec{q} - \vec{d_j}|$ (rank)[a] |
|---|---|---|---|---|---|---|---|
| $\vec{d_1}$ | 0 | 0 | 0 | 0 | 1 | 0.363 | 1.129 |
| $\vec{d_2}$ | 0 | 0 | 0 | 0 | 1 | 0.363 | 1.129 |
| $\vec{d_3}$ | 0 | **0.972** | 0 | 0.234 | 0 | 0.218 | 1.250 |
| $\vec{d_4}$ | **0** | **0** | **0** | **0.783** | **0.622** | **0.956 (1)** | **0.298 (1)** |
| $\vec{d_5}$ | 0 | 0 | 0 | 0 | 1 | 0.363 | 1.129 |
| $\vec{d_6}$ | **0** | **0** | **0.559** | **0.811** | **0.172** | **0.819 (2)** | **0.603 (2)** |
| $\vec{d_7}$ | 0 | 0 | 0 | 0 | 1 | 0.363 | 1.129 |
| $\vec{d_8}$ | 0 | 0 | 0 | 0 | 1 | 0.363 | 1.129 |
| $\vec{d_9}$ | 0 | 0 | 0 | 0 | 0 | 0 | 1 |
| $\vec{d_{10}}$ | 0 | 0 | 0 | 0 | 0 | 0 | 1 |
| $\vec{d_{11}}$ | 0 | 0 | 0 | 0 | 0 | 0 | 1 |
| $\vec{d_{12}}$ | 0 | 0 | 0 | 1 | 0 | 0.932 | 0.369 |
| $\vec{d_{13}}$ | 0 | 0 | 0 | 0 | 0 | 0 | 1 |
| $\vec{d_{14}}$ | **0.890** | **0** | **0** | **0.424** | **0.167** | **0.456 (3)** | **1.043 (3)** |
| $\vec{d_{15}}$ | 0 | 0 | 0 | 0 | 1 | 0.363 | 1.129 |
| $\vec{d_{16}}$ | 0 | 0 | 0 | 0 | 1 | 0.363 | 1.129 |
| $\vec{d_{17}}$ | 0 | 0 | 0 | 0 | 1 | 0.363 | 1.129 |
| $\vec{d_{18}}$ | 0 | 0 | 0 | 0 | 0 | 0 | 1 |
| $\vec{d_{19}}$ | 0 | 0 | 0 | 0 | 1 | 0.363 | 1.129 |
| $\vec{d_{20}}$ | 0 | 0 | 0 | 0 | 0 | 0 | 1 |

[a] The rank is shown only for documents that include both terms (*computer* and *program*)

Table 1.5 illustrates the query processing and document ranking approach discussed so far with the department example. The query is "*computer* AND *program*," represented by the normalized query vector $\vec{q} = (0\ 0\ 0\ 0.932\ 0.363)$. The document vectors are generated from those shown in Table 1.4 by applying IDF scaling and normalization. The last two columns show the cosine similarity (dot product) and the distance (norm of the vector difference) between those vectors and the query vector. The documents that include both terms (*computer* and *program*) are emphasized and their ranking is shown in parentheses.

First let us look at the document vectors. Those with just one nonzero coordinate look like Boolean vectors. This is because of the normalization step, which scales the coordinates so that the vector norm is equal to 1. Another interesting effect due to normalization is demonstrated by vectors $\vec{d_6}$ and $\vec{d_{12}}$. Both documents include the term *computer*, but the TFIDF component for *computer* in $\vec{d_6}$ is lower than the one in $\vec{d_{12}}$. The explanation is that the normalization step scaled up the *computer* coordinate of $\vec{d_{12}}$ to 1 because that was the only nonzero coordinate, whereas the same coordinate of $\vec{d_6}$ was scaled down due to the presence of two other nonzero coordinates. Generally, this shows the *importance of the choice of terms to represent documents*. In this particular case the problem is caused by the limited number of terms used (only five). One straightforward solution is to use all 671 terms that occur in the entire document collection. However, in large collections the number of terms is usually tens of thousands, and most important, they are not distributed uniformly over the documents. Moreover, the documents are of different lengths, which again may cause a lot of 0's in the document vectors. All this results in *extremely sparse distribution* of the document vectors, especially those collected from the Web. In this respect the sparsely populated Table 1.5 seems to represent well the general situation with document vector space.

Table 1.5 shows the similarity of all document vectors with the query vector. However, to answer the query (*computer* AND *program*), only the documents that include both keywords need to be considered. They are $\vec{d}_4$ (Chemistry), $\vec{d}_6$ (Computer Science), and $\vec{d}_{14}$ (Music), in the order of their ranking. Interestingly, both measures, maximum dot product and minimum distance, agree on the relevance of these documents to the query. We would also like to have these three documents ranked at the top among all documents. Another desired property would be the existence of a cutoff value that would allow us to distinguish the exact Boolean match with all keywords. However, this is not the case here. The ordering of documents that do not match both keywords is indicative for the differences between the two proximity measures. The cosine similarity ordering seems more natural, while the distance ranking looks peculiar. For example, at distance 1 to the query the documents are represented by all-zero vectors [i.e., none of the terms used in the representation (the dimensions) occur in those documents]. Strangely, one of the matches with the query ($\vec{d}_{14}$) is farther from the query than the all-zero vectors. There is a similar situation with cosine similarity: Document vector $\vec{d}_{12}$, with just one nonzero component (the one that matches one of the keywords), has the second-highest score among all the documents, but obviously this is an exception. In general, the cosine similarity measure seems more stable with respect to the choice of terms, which in turn may explain why it is the preferred proximity measure for IR systems.

The results above suggest that terms have to be chosen such that the zero-valued coordinates of the vectors are minimized. One approach to achieving this is to use terms with high TF scores. For example, the term counts may be taken on the entire corpus and then the top frequency terms chosen as dimensions of the vector space. In this way we can have more nonzero components in each vector. However, as we have already seen, these frequent terms do not reflect the content and meaning of a document. In fact, the important terms are the more document-specific terms (i.e., those with high IDF scores). Thus, the question is how to balance the TF and IDF contributions when we choose terms (features) to represent documents. In a more general context, this problem, called *feature selection*, plays an important role in document classification and clustering. In later chapters we shall discuss it in more detail.

### *Relevance Feedback*

Keyword queries are often incomplete or ambiguous. The response from such queries may not return the relevant documents that match user information needs or may include many irrelevant documents. So queries have to be specialized and refined, which is usually done through advanced search options, available in most search engines. This means, however, that the user needs to know more about the document searched, which contradicts the basic philosophy of information retrieval, which is about search for information, not documents. The relevance feedback approach refines the query automatically using user feedback as to the relevance of the result. This can be done by providing some type of rating for each document in the result list. In the initial response these ratings may be the document ranks or simply binary labels indicating the relevance or irrelevance for each document. For example, the top 10 documents in the ranked list may be considered as relevant and the rest as irrelevant.

After the initial response the user evaluates the actual relevance of each document (e.g., by reading its content) and is provided with the option to change the relevance suggested by the system. This information, called *relevance feedback*, is then sent back to the search engine and the query is repeated. At this point the relevance feedback is used to adjust the original query vector. This can be done using *Rocchio's method*, a simple and popular technique known from early IR systems and used recently in related areas, such as machine learning. The idea is to update the query vector using a linear combination of the previous query vector $\vec{q}$ and the document vectors $\vec{d}_j$ of relevant and irrelevant documents. That is,

$$\vec{q}' = \alpha \vec{q} + \beta \sum_{d_j \in D_+} \vec{d}_j - \gamma \sum_{d_j \in D_-} \vec{d}_j$$

where $\alpha$, $\beta$, and $\gamma$ are adjustable parameters and $D_+$ and $D_-$ are the sets of relevant and irrelevant documents provided by the user. These sets can also be determined automatically (the approach is then called *pseudorelevance feedback*): for example, by assuming that the top 10 documents returned by the original query belong to $D_+$ and the rest to $D_-$. Because the set of irrelevant documents is usually much larger, we may want not to use $D_-$ (i.e., set $\gamma = 0$). Also, not all terms have to be included in the equation. The reason is that terms with high TF may occur in many documents and thus contribute too much to the corresponding component of the query vector. This would shift the focus to unimportant terms and may call up documents that are more irrelevant. To avoid this, terms are ordered in decreasing order by their IDF score, and a given number of terms from the top of the list (e.g., 10) are chosen.

To illustrate the approach, let us try to improve the search results shown in Table 1.5. Let $\alpha = 1$, $\beta = 0.5$, $\gamma = 0$, and $D_+$ be the set of three relevant documents returned by the original query. Let us also use only the top three terms from the list sorted by IDF score (*lab*, *laboratory*, and *programming*), thus excluding *computer* and *program*, which occur in more documents and have lower IDF scores (see the earlier table showing the IDF scores). The new query vector is computed as

$$\vec{q}' = \vec{q} + 0.5 (\vec{d}_4 + \vec{d}_6 + \vec{d}_{14})$$

$$= \begin{pmatrix} 0 \\ 0 \\ 0 \\ 0.932 \\ 0.363 \end{pmatrix} + 0.5 \left[ \begin{pmatrix} 0. \\ 0 \\ 0 \\ 0 \\ 0 \end{pmatrix} + \begin{pmatrix} 0 \\ 0 \\ 0.559 \\ 0 \\ 0 \end{pmatrix} + \begin{pmatrix} 0.89 \\ 0 \\ 0 \\ 0 \\ 0 \end{pmatrix} \right] = \begin{pmatrix} 0.445 \\ 0 \\ 0.28 \\ 0 \\ 0.363 \end{pmatrix}$$

Note that the last two coordinates of the document vectors are replaced with 0's, as we decided to exclude these terms due to low IDF scores. Before the second run the query vector is normalized to $\vec{q}' = (0.394\ 0\ 0.248\ 0.824\ 0.321)$. The resulting list of documents ranked by cosine similarity (shown in parentheses in Table 1.5) is now $d_6(0.863)$, $d_4(0.846)$, and $d_{14}(0.754)$. This ranking seems a little more natural because the Computer Science document ($d_6$), which has a higher count for the term *computer* (the more important query term), is now ranked before the Chemistry document ($d_4$), which has a smaller count for the same term. Also, the incorrectly ranked document from the original query $d_{12}$ (now with cosine similarity 0.824) is one position down.

The general effect of pseudorelevance feedback is that the query becomes more similar to the relevant documents returned from the original query. Consequently, on the second run the relevant documents' vectors are grouped around bigger and more homogeneous vectors (with more uniform distribution of terms, such as $d_6$ in the example), and those with scattered terms (e.g., $d_{12}$) are pushed away. When the user provides the feedback, the group of relevant vectors may be moved toward a user-specified set of relevant vectors.

Relevance feedback is a standard technique in classical IR. However, it is not popular for web search mainly because web users generally expect instant results from their queries. Also, user feedback would increase the computational cost for handling the millions of queries that search engines have to deal with every second. The reason we include the discussion of relevance feedback here is that it contributes further to better understanding the vector space model and the TFIDF framework.

There also exist probabilistic approaches to relevance feedback that try to model the mapping between queries and relevant documents using statistical techniques. Basically, these techniques assume term independence (with respect to other terms, queries, and document relevance) and calculate conditional probabilities for document relevance. We are not discussing these approaches here because similar ones exist in the more general context of document classification, where the document relevance can be seen as a category (class) label of a document and *machine learning* techniques can be used to learn mappings between queries and documents, considering user feedback as a training set of examples. We discuss some of these techniques in later chapters.

## Advanced Text Search

The commonly used text search queries include only individual terms, and by default most search engines assume that all of the terms specified must occur in the documents returned (they are implicitly AND-ed). Advanced search options also allow the use of "OR" or "NOT" Boolean operators. All these constraints can be implemented easily during the retrieval phase, when documents are looked up in the inverted index. After (or while) obtaining a set of documents that satisfy the Boolean Query, the TFIDF measure is used to compute the proximity of the document vectors to the query vector. This allows the documents retrieved to be ordered by relevance to the query.

Another advanced search option is *phrase search*. Documents that include given phrases can be retrieved using the standard term-based inverted index, as it also contains term position information. We have illustrated this with the phrase *computer lab* (see Table 1.3) found in the Music document ($d_{14}$) because *computer* and *lab* occurred in successive positions (41 and 42) in that particular document.

Ranking documents retrieved by phrase search is, however, more difficult. Using combinations of the TFIDF measures of the terms that occur in the phrase is not appropriate because these measures are computed independently for the individual terms. So we need the TF and IDF values for the phrase itself. Once we have those measures, phrases can be added as new dimensions to the document vector space, and cosine similarity can be used for relevance ranking. Thus, the question is how to identify potentially useful phrases from a given corpus. A collection of phrases that occur in a corpus is called a *phrase dictionary*.

The phrase dictionary may be built manually or derived from the corpus automatically. Most approaches use statistical methods first to extract possible phrases and then linguistic tools or manual editing to refine the phrase dictionary. Phrases typically consist of two or three words. In a large corpus two or three words may occur together by chance or they may be a pattern (i.e., a phrase). The statistical approach tries to answer this question by estimating the probabilities of occurrences of the terms individually and as a phrase. For example, if two terms $t_1$ and $t_2$ are independent, the probability of their cooccurrence is $P(t_1 t_2) = P(t_1)P(t_2)$. However if "$t_1 t_2$" is a phrase, the probability $P(t_1 t_2)$ would significantly differ from the product $P(t_1)P(t_2)$. Statistical tests such as likelihood ratio are used to determine this.

Phrases provide context for terms, but they play the same role as that played by individual terms: They add new features to the document model (dimensions in vector space). Another, richer context for terms is provided by *tagging*. We have already mentioned part-of-speech tagging, where words are associated with their role in the sentence and the same words with different tags are used as dimensions in vector space. This approach allows queries to be more specific and unambiguous.

So far we have assumed that keywords in queries can match exactly words that occur in documents. In practice, however, various languages and dialects are used and words are often misspelled. Thus, if only exact matching is used, many relevant documents may be missed. Generally, there are two approaches to solving this problem. One is to extend the process of stemming with some conflation mechanism that may handle misspelling and dialects. The difficulties with this approach are that such mechanisms are developed mostly for English and other Western languages. Also, a lot of common words are used with specific technical meaning.

The other approach is to try to find the closest match of the query term to terms in the inverted index. This can be done by *approximate string matching*. One popular approach for this is to decompose words into subsequences of characters with fixed length called *n-grams* (or *q-grams*). For example, the word *program* may be represented by a sequence of 2-grams as {pr, ro, og, gr, ra, am} and its misspelling *prorgam* as {pr, ro, or, rg, ga, am}. So they overlap in three of the six 2-grams and may be considered close.

To use *n*-grams in keyword search, the query term is first looked up in a index of *n*-grams (*n* is usually 2 to 4) and is slightly modified so that a set of variant terms is obtained. Then the inverted index is used with each one those terms. The closest match is determined by comparing the relevance of the documents retrieved.

## Using the HTML Structure in Keyword Search

So far we have ignored the rich HTML structure of web documents. However, HTML tags provide a lot of context information that may be very useful in keyword search. Basically, the tags that add to or modify the meaning of web page text are important for this purpose. These are:

- *Titles and metatags that provide meta information about the web page.* For example, the following fragments from the Music page (Figure 1.4) provide information about the title of the page, its authors, and the software used to create it:

```
<title>Music</title>
<meta name="Author" content="John Smith ">
<meta name="GENERATOR" content="Microsoft FrontPage 5.0">
```

This information is included in the "head" area of the web page, and with the exception of the title is not displayed by the browser.

- *Headings and font modifiers used to separate or emphasize parts of the text* (e.g., <h2>···</h2>, ···, <font>···</font>, <p>, <br>). For example, the title of the web page is generated with the following structure:

```
<h2 align="center">
<font color="#000080"><big>Music</big></font>
</h2>
```

- *Anchor text.* For example, the following anchor occurs in the department directory page (Figure 1.3):

```
<a href="ASLinks/Chairs.html" target="_top">
<font color="#000000">
Department Chairs, Locations, Phone Numbers<br>
</font></a>
```

The anchor text here explains briefly the content of the page to which it links.

HTML tags have two basic uses in web search. First, the terms that occur in their context may be tagged and indexed accordingly. For this purpose the main index can be extended with tagged terms, or separate indices can be built for faster access. This will allow web documents to be retrieved by specific parts of their HTML structure. For example, Google advanced search options allow specifying exactly where the terms should occur in the page: in the title, in the text (excluding the title), in the page URL, or in links (anchor text) pointing to the page. Some of these HTML structures may even replace full text indexing. For example, one of the early versions of Google built at Stanford University indexed only the titles of 16 million web pages and was very successful because of the small and efficient index (and also because of the use of hyperlink-based ranking, which we discuss later). However, the lack of authority and editorial control on web publishing allows many web pages to have no titles, or titles that are irrelevant to the page content. The same is true for other tags generally supposed to provide metainformation about the web page. All this made the designers of web search engines take the full-text indexing approach.

The other use of HTML tags is for relevance ranking. The specific HTML scope where keyword terms occur in a document may affect its ranking. This can be achieved by assigning different weights to terms occurring in different HTML structures. These weights are then used to modify the corresponding TFIDF components of the query and document vectors, which in turn affect their cosine similarity and consequently the relevance ranking of the documents in the response. Typically, words in titles, emphasized text, heading, and anchors may get higher scores and thus increase the relevance score of the documents in which they occur. This approach was popular in the early search engines and worked well for providing more natural relevance ranking. The reason for this is that these are techniques used in traditional typesetting and, more recently, in web page design to emphasize important words and phrases that have high relevance to the document content and meaning.

With the appearance of spam, however, HTML tags became a tool for making search engines index web pages with content irrelevant to the indexed terms or for getting top ranking in search engines. One popular way to achieve this was to include in the web page invisible words (text with the same foreground and background color) that will be indexed by search engines but will not be seen by web users. Metatags were also used by spammers to get top ranking in search engines because the metainformation they include is not displayed by browsers but is taken into account for relevance ranking. All this shifted the emphasis of search engines from the HTML tags to the page hyperlink structure. We discuss link-based ranking in detail in Chapter 2.

Still, one HTML structure plays a significant role in web page indexing and search. This is the *anchor tag*, which actually implements the main feature of the web pages, the hyperlinks. As we mentioned earlier, the purpose of web search is to access unstructured data by content. The discussion so far was focused on the approaches to model the web page content. Hyperlinks and especially, *anchor text* provide additional content description of web pages. For example, the anchor text "Department Chairs, Locations, Phone Numbers" (from the A&S directory page shown in Figure 1.4) includes the term *phone*, which in fact is not present in the content of the page to which it points (`http://www.artsci.ccsu.edu/ASLinks/Chairs.html`). The latter contains a table in which the phone numbers are listed in a column named "Ext." Obviously, when crawled and indexed, this page will not be included in the index entry for the term *phone* and consequently cannot be retrieved by keyword search with the term *phone*. However, this term may be taken from the anchor text that points to the page and is included in the set of terms representing the document. Weight that would increase the TFIDF score of the document vector along this dimension may also be assigned to such external terms, because they are often more relevant to the page content than are terms from the original page. The reason for this is that the pages that link to a particular page provide independent and authoritative judgment about its content. In some cases the anchor text may be used for indexing instead of the actual page content. For example, the web page with the phone numbers mentioned above can be indexed by all the terms that occur in the anchor text pointing to it: *department*, *chairs*, *locations*, *phone*, and *numbers*. More terms may be collected from other pages pointing to it. This idea was implemented in one of the first search engines, the World Wide Web Worm system [4], and later used by Lycos and Google. This allows search engines to increase their indices with pages that have never been crawled, are unavailable, or include nontextual content that cannot be indexed, such as images and programs. As reported by Brin and Page [5] in 1998, Google indexed 24 million pages and over 259 million anchors.

## EVALUATING SEARCH QUALITY

Information retrieval systems do not have formal semantics (such as that of databases), and consequently, the query and the set of documents retrieved (the response of the IR system) cannot be mapped one to one. Therefore, some measures are used to evaluate the degree of fitness (accuracy) of the response. A standard benchmark for this purpose is the recall-precision measure, which is also used in related areas (such as machine learning and data mining).

Assume that there is a set of queries $Q$ and a set of documents $D$, and for each query $q \in Q$ submitted to the system we have:

- The response set of documents (retrieved documents) $R_q \subseteq D$
- The set of relevant documents $D_q$ selected manually from the entire collection of documents $D$ (i.e., $D_q \subseteq D$)

The proportion of retrieved relevant documents to all retrieved documents is called *precision* and is defined as

$$\text{precision} = \frac{\left| D_q \cap R_q \right|}{\left| R_q \right|}$$

Clearly, the value of the precision is between 0 and 1: where 0 is the worst case—no relevant documents are retrieved—and 1 is the best case—all documents retrieved are relevant. Precision 1 is not, however, all that an ideal IR system should provide, because there may be relevant documents that are not retrieved. *Recall* is the measure that accounts for this. It represents the proportion of relevant documents retrieved to all relevant documents. Formally,

$$\text{recall} = \frac{\left| D_q \cap R_q \right|}{\left| D_q \right|}$$

Again, the best case is 1—all relevant documents are retrieved—and the worst case is 0—no relevant documents are retrieved.

Recall and precision determine the relationship between two sets of documents: relevant ($D_q$) and retrieved ($R_q$). Ideally, these sets coincide (precision and recall are both 1), but this never happens in real systems. Generally, there is some overlap ($D_q \cap R_q \subset D_q$) which we would like to maximize, or the set retrieved is too large ($D_q \subset R_q$) and we want to exclude from it documents that are irrelevant. Interestingly, achieving the maximum value for each of the two measures individually is trivial. By using a very general query (e.g., a query including terms that occur in all documents), the response set will be the entire collection of documents $D$, and thus the recall will be 1. However, the precision will be low because all irrelevant documents will also be included in the response. Inversely, with a very restrictive query, a small subset of relevant-only documents may be retrieved easily. For example, one of the relevant documents may be used as a query, and then the precision will be 1. These observations suggest that there is an important trade-off between precision and recall. A plot of precision against recall generally slopes down with increasing recall. Thus, a better IR system will have its recall–precision curve above that of a poorer system.

The set-valued recall–precision framework is oversimplified and is commonly used only to illustrate the general idea or in areas where ranking is not possible. Real IR systems, such as web search engines, return thousands of documents. Considering them as a set as well as computing the set $D_q$ is practically impossible. Obviously, the document ranks have to be taken into consideration. For this purpose we modify the setting as follows. Consider that the response to a query $q$ is now not a set but a *list* $R_q = (d_1, d_2, \ldots, d_m)$ of *ranked documents* (highest ranks first). Then using the set of relevant documents $D_q$, for each document $d_i \in R_q$ we can compute its relevance $r_i$ as a Boolean value. That is,

$$r_i = \begin{cases} 1 & \text{if } d_i \in D_q \\ 0 & \text{otherwise} \end{cases}$$

We also add a parameter $k \geq 0$ that represents the number of documents from the top of the list $R_q$ that we consider. Thus, we define *precision* at rank $k$ as

$$\text{precision}(k) = \frac{1}{k} \sum_{i=1}^{k} r_i$$

and *recall* at rank $k$ as

$$\text{recall}(k) = \frac{1}{|D_q|} \sum_{i=1}^{k} r_i$$

If we fix $k$ and consider the top $k$ elements from $R_q$ as a set, the new measures work exactly the same as the set-based measures. The parameter $k$ allows us to see how recall and precision change with increasing $k$ (i.e., decreasing rank). The *average precision* is the measure that accounts for this:

$$\text{average precision} = \frac{1}{|D_q|} \sum_{k=1}^{|D|} r_k \times \text{precision}(k)$$

The average precision is a useful measure that combines precision and recall and also evaluates document ranking. The maximal value of average precision is 1, reached when all relevant documents are retrieved and ranked in the response list before any irrelevant documents. Note that the sum goes over all documents in the collection $D$. Although the system provides ranking only for the documents in the response list $R_q$, we assume that all documents in $D$ are ordered by their rank. In practice, to compute the average precision we first go over the ranked documents from the response list $R_q$ and then continue with the rest of the documents from $D$. Also, we assume that $r_i$'s are computed for all documents in $D$. Thus, the maximum of 1 is reached when $R_q$

TABLE 1.6   Document Ranking, Relevance, Recall, and Precision

| $k$ | Document Index | $r_k$ | recall $(k)$ | precision $(k)$ |
|---|---|---|---|---|
| 1 | 4 | 1 | 0.333 | 1 |
| 2 | 12 | 0 | 0.333 | 0.5 |
| 3 | 6 | 1 | 0.667 | 0.667 |
| 4 | 14 | 1 | 1 | 0.75 |
| 5 | 1 | 0 | 1 | 0.6 |
| 6 | 2 | 0 | 1 | 0.5 |
| 7 | 3 | 0 | 1 | 0.429 |
| 8 | 5 | 0 | 1 | 0.375 |
| 9 | 7 | 0 | 1 | 0.333 |
| 10 | 8 | 0 | 1 | 0.3 |
| 11 | 15 | 0 | 1 | 0.273 |
| 12 | 16 | 0 | 1 | 0.25 |
| 13 | 17 | 0 | 1 | 0.231 |
| 14 | 19 | 0 | 1 | 0.214 |
| 15 | 9 | 0 | 1 | 0.2 |
| 16 | 10 | 0 | 1 | 0.188 |
| 17 | 11 | 0 | 1 | 0.176 |
| 18 | 13 | 0 | 1 | 0.167 |
| 19 | 18 | 0 | 1 | 0.158 |
| 20 | 20 | 0 | 1 | 0.15 |

includes *all* relevant documents. It may also include irrelevant ones, but they should occur after the relevant documents.

To generate a plot of precision against recall, *interpolated precision* is used. First, the actual recall levels *recall(k)* are computed for each $k$ corresponding to a relevant document from set $D_q$, that is, for those $k$'s for which $r_k = 1$. Then for each standard value of recall $\rho$ (e.g., $\rho = 0, 0.1, 0.2, \ldots, 1$) the interpolated precision is the maximum precision computed for recall levels greater than or equal to $\rho$ (interpolated precision is defined as 0 for recall 0). To get the average performance of an IR system on a set of queries $Q$ at each level of recall, the interpolated precision is averaged over all $q \in Q$.

Let us illustrate the recall–precision evaluation technique with our department example. The initial data needed for this purpose include the ranking of all documents and the corresponding $r_k$'s. As the ranking shown in Table 1.5 is nearly perfect, we modify it a bit to get a more interesting situation. The new ranking that we are going to evaluate here is based purely on the cosine similarity (the original ranking was done only on documents that include both keywords). The relevant documents that form the list $R_q$ (determined manually) are $d_4$ (Chemistry), $d_6$ (Computer Science), and $d_{14}$ (Music): that is, those that include both *computer* and *program*. Thus, we rank all documents in the collection as shown in Table 1.6.

As the recall values increase with $k$, the precision interpolated at each standard recall level $\rho$ is computed as the maximum precision in all rows, starting with the first one (from the top) in which the actual recall value is greater than or equal to $\rho$. Thus,

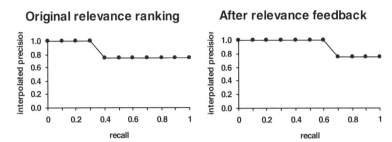

**Figure 1.5**    Interpolated precision against recall before and after relevance feedback.

for recall levels of 0, 0.1, 0.2, and 0.3, the interpolated precision of 1 is computed as the maximum precision on rows 1 to 20. For recall levels 0.4, 0.5, and 0.6, the interpolated precision is 0.75 (maximum precision on rows 3 to 20), and it is also 0.75 for levels 0.7 to 1 (maximum precision on rows 4 to 20). The plot of the precision interpolated against recall computed as described is shown on the left in Figure 1.5. For comparison the right side of the figure shows the precision against recall for the ranking produced by Rocchio's method as described in the section "Relevance Feedback" (the sequence of $r_k$'s starts with $1, 1, 0, 1, 0, \dots$). The curve on the right of the figure is above that on the left, which indicates that relevance feedback improves the performance of an IR system.

Let us also compute the average precision for the two rankings shown in Figure 1.5. We use Table 1.6 and average the precision in the rows where $r_k = 1$(rows 1, 3, and 4). Thus, for the original ranking we have

$$\text{average precision} = \tfrac{1}{3}(1 + 0.667 + 0.75) = 0.806$$

The relevance feedback swaps the values of $r_2$ and $r_3$ and changes the precisions accordingly. Thus, we have

$$\text{average precision} = \tfrac{1}{3}(1 + 1 + 0.75) = 0.917$$

Clearly, the average precision also indicates that the relevance feedback improves document ranking.

The recall–precision framework is a useful method for evaluating IR system performance. It is, however, important to note that it has its limitations. As we already mentioned for large document collections such as the Web, it is not possible to use the response set $R_q$ explicitly. For example, a Web search with the query that we have used for our small collection of 20 documents, *computer program*, submitted to Google returns about 504 million documents (!). Of course, the recall and precision can be computed on the first 10 or 20 documents, which is still useful. There is another critical issue, however, that may require a different approach. The classical IR recall–precision evaluation is based entirely on the document content (the TFIDF vector space model). As we shall see in Chapter 2, other measures, such as popularity and authority, are also important and have to be taken into account.

## SIMILARITY SEARCH

We have assumed that web user information needs are represented by keyword queries, and thus document relevance is defined in terms of how close a query is to documents found by the search engine. Because web search queries are usually incomplete and ambiguous, many of the documents returned may not be relevant to the query. However, once a relevant document is found, a larger collection of possibly relevant documents may be found by retrieving documents similar to the relevant document. This process, called *similarity search*, is implemented in some search engines (e.g., Google) as an option to find pages similar or related to a given page. The intuition behind similarity search is the *cluster hypothesis* in IR, stating that documents similar to relevant documents are also likely to be relevant. In this section we discuss mostly approaches to similarity search based on the content of the web documents. Document similarity can also be considered in the context of the web link structure. The latter approach is discussed briefly in the section "Authorities and Hubs" in Chapter 2.

### Cosine Similarity

The query-to-document similarity which we have explored so far is based on the vector space model. Both queries and documents are represented by TFIDF vectors, and similarity is computed using the metric properties of vector space. It is also straightforward to compute similarity between documents. Moreover, we may expect that document-to-document similarity would be more accurate than query-to-document similarity because queries are usually too short, so their vectors are extremely sparse in the highly dimensional vector space. Thus, given a document $d$ and a collection $D$, the problem is to find a number (usually, 10 or 20) of documents $d_i \in D$ which have the largest value of cosine similarity to $d$: that is, the maximum value of the dot product $\vec{d}.\vec{d_i}$.

In similarity search we are not concerned with a small query vector, so we are free to use more (or all) dimensions of the vector space to represent our documents. In this respect it will be interesting to investigate how the dimensionality of vector space affects the similarity search results. This issue is related to *feature selection*, a problem that we mentioned earlier and will revisit later. Generally, several options can be explored:

- *Using all terms from the corpus.* This is the easiest option but may cause problems if the corpus is too large (such as the document repository of a web search engine).
- *Selecting terms with high TF scores* (usually based on the entire corpus). This approach prefers terms that occur frequently in many documents and thus makes documents look more similar. However, this similarity is not indicative of document content.
- *Selecting terms with high IDF scores.* This approach prefers more document-specific terms and thus better differentiates documents in vector space. However,

it results in extremely sparse document vectors, so that similarity search is too restricted to closely related documents.

- *Combining the TF and IDF criteria.* For example, a preference may be given to terms that maximize the product of their TF (on the entire corpus) and TDF scores. As this is the same type of measure used in the vector coordinates (the difference is that the TF score in the vector is taken on the particular document), the vectors will be better populated with nonzero coordinates. We explore this option when we discuss document clustering and classification later in the book.

Let us illustrate the similarity search basics with our department example. We shall represent all documents as TFIDF vectors with different dimensionality (to examine the effect of feature selection). For this purpose we create two lists, including all 671 terms in the corpus (see the basic statistics in Table 1.1), one ordered by their global (for the corpus) frequency scores and another ordered by their IDF scores. The two halves of Table 1.7 give us an idea of what these lists look like. The left half shows the 10 most frequent terms along with their frequencies, IDF scores, and the number of documents in which they occur. The right half shows the terms with the top 10 IDF scores, their frequency counts, and the number of documents in which they occur.

In fact, the table shows the beginning and end of the frequency-ordered list of terms and illustrates nicely the basic properties of the IDF measure. The highest-frequency terms usually occur in many documents and have low IDF scores. Using these terms as dimensions of vector space would make all documents too similar. On the other hand, each of the top IDF-scored terms occurs in one document only (these are, in fact, the department names). Obviously, in a 20-dimensional vector space created with the top 20 terms from this list, the documents will be represented by orthogonal vectors and thus will be perfectly differentiated. However, in such a space all vectors will be equally dissimilar one to another (with cosine similarity 0).

To further illustrate the observations above, increasingly large samples are taken from the top of the TF list, the IDF list, and the TF*IDF list (ordered by the product of TF and IDF) and the documents are ordered by their cosine similarity to the Computer

**TABLE 1.7  Term Frequencies and IDF Scores**

| Term | Count | IDF | Docs. | Term | IDF | Count | Docs. |
|------|-------|-----|-------|------|-----|-------|-------|
| *department* | 65 | 0.049 | 20 | *english* | 3.045 | 5 | 1 |
| *study* | 28 | 0.049 | 20 | *psychology* | 3.045 | 5 | 1 |
| *students* | 26 | 0.336 | 15 | *chemistry* | 3.045 | 6 | 1 |
| *ba* | 22 | 0.272 | 16 | *communication* | 3.045 | 6 | 1 |
| *website* | 21 | 0.049 | 20 | *justice* | 3.045 | 7 | 1 |
| *location* | 21 | 0.049 | 20 | *criminal* | 3.045 | 8 | 1 |
| *programs* | 21 | 0.405 | 14 | *theatre* | 3.045 | 8 | 1 |
| 832 | 20 | 0.100 | 19 | *anthropology* | 3.045 | 9 | 1 |
| *phone* | 20 | 0.049 | 20 | *sociology* | 3.045 | 10 | 1 |
| *chair* | 20 | 0.049 | 20 | *music* | 3.045 | 12 | 1 |

TABLE 1.8 Experiments with Cosine Similarity

| Sample | $i/\vec{d}_i \cdot \vec{d}_6$ (Indices of Documents Ordered by $\vec{d}_i \cdot \vec{d}_6$) | | | | |
|---|---|---|---|---|---|
| 100 TF | 17/0.23, | 3/0.20, | 4/0.18, | 12/0.17, | 14/0.05 |
| 200 TF | 12/0.19, | 17/0.19, | 4/0.16, | 3/0.13, | 14/0.08 |
| 300 TF | 17/0.21, | 12/0.19, | 4/0.17, | 3/0.13, | 14/0.08 |
| 400 TF | 17/0.21, | 12/0.19, | 4/0.17, | 3/0.13, | 14/0.13 |
| 500 TF | 17/0.21, | 12/0.20, | 4/0.17, | 3/0.13, | 14/0.13 |
| 600 TF | 17/0.24, | 4/0.22, | 12/0.2, | 3/0.16, | 14/0.13 |
| 100–500 IDF | 20/0, | 19/0, | 18/0, | 17/0, | 16/0 |
| 600 IDF | 12/0.08, | 14/0.05, | 2/0.03, | 15/0.03, | 17/0.02 |
| 100 TF*IDF | **17/0.42,** | **12/0.22,** | **4/0.20,** | **3/0.09,** | **1/0.07** |
| 200 TF*IDF | 17/0.26, | 12/0.14, | 4/0.14, | 1/0.06, | 2/0.05 |
| 300 TF*IDF | 17/0.16, | 4/0.13, | 12/0.12, | 1/0.06, | 2/0.05 |
| 400 TF*IDF | 17/0.16, | 4/0.13, | 12/0.08, | 1/0.06, | 2/0.04 |
| 500 TF*IDF | 17/0.17, | 12/0.13, | 4/0.12, | 1/0.06, | 3/0.05 |
| 600 TF*IDF | 17/0.19, | 12/0.19, | 4/0.18, | 3/0.14, | 14/0.10 |
| 671 ALL | 17/0.24, | 4/0.22, | 12/0.20, | 3/0.16, | 14/0.13 |

Science document ($\vec{d}_6$). Table 1.8 summarizes the results. The results from TF and TF*IDF sampling generally look more stable with increasing sample size and tend toward the results obtained from the complete set of features. This comes as no surprise, because with many frequent terms the document vectors are well populated with nonzero coordinates, so that adding new features does not change similarity values very much. The situation with IDF sampling is different. With 100 to 500 features, all vectors are orthogonal (the dot product with $\vec{d}_6$ is 0). With 600 features the vectors are somewhat more populated, but many are still orthogonal. They are also very sparsely populated; for example, the 600-dimensional IDF query vector $\vec{d}_6$ has only 43 nonzero coordinates.

Another interesting observation is based on the similarity values. Because all vectors are normalized to unit length, the dot product values can be compared directly, even for vectors with different number of coordinates. Thus, the similarity values may be used as an objective measure of the *quality of feature selection*. Not surprisingly, the highest values are achieved with the 100 TF*IDF sample (shown in boldface). This is an additional argument that a good balance between TF and IDF measures could bring the best results.

## Jaccard Similarity

There is an alternative to cosine similarity, which appears to be more popular in the context of similarity search (we discuss the reason for this later). It takes all terms that occur in the documents but uses the simpler Boolean document representation. The idea is to consider only the nonzero coordinates (i.e., those that are 1) of the Boolean vectors. The approach uses the *Jaccard coefficient*, which is generally defined (not only for Boolean vectors) as the percentage of nonzero coordinates that are different in the two vectors. In our particular case the similarity between two Boolean document vectors sim($\vec{d}_1$, $\vec{d}_2$) is defined as the proportion of coordinates that are 1 in both $\vec{d}_1$ and $\vec{d}_2$ to those that are 1 in $\vec{d}_1$ or $\vec{d}_2$. Thus, formally,

$$\text{sim}(\vec{d}_1, \vec{d}_2) = \frac{\left|\{j | d_1^j = 1 \wedge d_2^j = 1\}\right|}{\left|\{j | d_1^j = 1 \vee d_2^j = 1\}\right|}$$

As each 1 in the document vector represents a term that occurs in the document, this formula can be rewritten using sets of terms. Thus, we arrive at an alternative formulation of the Jaccard coefficient defined on *sets*. Let us denote the set of terms that occur in document $d$ as $T(d)$. Then the similarity between two documents sim ($d_1$, $d_2$) is defined as

$$\text{sim}(d_1, d_2) = \frac{|T(d_1) \cap T(d_2)|}{|T(d_1) \cup T(d_2)|}$$

sim ($d_1$, $d_2$) has some nice properties that are important in the context of a similarity search. For example, the similarity reaches its maximum (1) if the two documents are identical [i.e., sim ($d$, $d$) = 1] and is symmetrical [i.e., sim ($d_1$, $d_2$) = sim ($d_2$, $d_1$)]. However, it is not a formal metric (distance function), as it does not satisfy the triangle equality. Note, however, that $1 - \text{sim}(d_1, d_2)$ is a metric called the *Jaccard metric*.

Direct computation of the Jaccard coefficient is straightforward, but with large documents and collections it may lead to a very inefficient similarity search. Also, finding similar documents at query time is impractical because it may take quite a long time. Therefore, some optimization techniques are used and most of the similarity computation is done offline (i.e., for each document from the collection, a number of nearest documents are precomputed). The inverted index provides a good deal of information that may be used for this purpose. The idea is to create a list of all document pairs sorted by the similarity of the documents in each pair. Then the $k$ most similar documents to a given document $d$ are those that are paired with $d$ in the first $k$ pairs from the list. Theoretically, the number of document pairs is $n(n-1)/2$ for $n$ documents. However, two simple heuristics may drastically reduce the number of candidate pairs:

1. Frequent terms that occur in many documents (say, more than 50% of the collection) are eliminated because they cause even loosely related documents to look similar.

2. Only documents that share at least one term are used to form a pair.

Let us illustrate the basic steps of precomputing document similarity with our department collection. To simplify the discussion, in the first two steps we use the five-column term–document matrix shown in Table 1.2. In step 3, however, we compute the Jaccard coefficient using the complete set of terms for each document.

1. For each term, create a set of documents that includes the term. At this point we eliminate three terms (*lab*, *laboratory*, and *programming*) because their respective sets include only one document (no document pair can be created).

Thus, we end up with (for brevity, only the document indices are shown)

[(*program*, {1,2,4,6,7,8,14,15,16,17,19}), (*computer*, {3,4,6,12,14})]

(One may decide to eliminate *program*, due to its high frequency, but we leave it, because otherwise the example would be trivial.)

2. Create pairs of documents from each set in item 1, store them in a single file, and sort the file by the frequency counts of the pairs. The result of this step is a list of 78 pairs (counts follow the slash): [(4,6)/2, (4,14)/2, (6,14)/2, (1,2)/1, (1,4)/1, (1,6)/1, . . . ]. Thus, counts represent the number of terms shared by the documents in the pair. At this point more candidate pairs can be eliminated by setting a threshold for the minimal number of shared terms.

3. Compute the similarity between the documents in each pair and sort the list of pairs accordingly. The beginning of the sorted list is as follows:

[(7,15)/0.208, (1,17)/0.196, (15,19)/0.192, (8,17)/0.189, (3,12)/0.186, (17,19)/0.185, (12,15)/0.185, (12,17)/0.18, (1,19)/0.178, (4,14)/0.176, (**6**,**12**)/**0.175**, (3,4)/0.173, (12,19)/0.170, (4,19)/0.168, (7,17)/0.159, (8,19)/0.158, (8,7)/0.156, (8,12)/0.153, (1,14)/0.145, (1,15)/0.142, (7,12)/0.141, (1,12)/0.140, (4,7)/0.137, (15,17)/0.136, (**4**,**6**)/**0.136**, (4,12)/0.136, (7,14)/0.136, (**6**,**14**)/**0.135**, (12,14)/0.135, . . .]

Having done this computation, we are now able to answer similarity search queries very quickly. For example, to find the documents most similar to document 6 (computer science), we go through the list from left to right and report (in the order of occurrence) the other document in each pair that contains 6. Thus, we get 12 (Mathematics), 4 (Chemistry), and 14 (Music) for the part of the list that is shown above (the corresponding pairs are shown in boldface). The complete list of documents most similar to document 6 is [12,4,14,17,3,15,19,7,2,1,16,8].

It is interesting to compare these results with the TFIDF similarity results shown in Table 1.7. The closest match is with the list produced with all features, where the five most similar documents are the same but are ranked differently ([17,4,12,3,14]). Which of the two rankings is more trustworthy? The ranking produced by the cosine similarity may look a bit strange, because it picks the Political Science document (17), whereas generally, Computer Science as a subject may be considered closer to Mathematics (12). Obviously, the documents in both pairs, (6,17) and (6,12), share a lot of terms, but in TFIDF ranking not only is the term overlap taken into account but the TF and IDF measures as well. They bring more information into the similarity ranking process, which allows more accurate computation of similarity to be done, For example, both the Computer Science and Political Science documents have five occurrences of the term *science*, while Computer Science and Mathematics have one occurrence of the term *sciences*. Also, the term *science* has a relatively high IDF score. All this is taken into account by the cosine similarity measure but is simply ignored by the Jaccard measure.

There have been studies that compare the two measures for various tasks and in various domains. In many areas the two measures show comparable results (see, e.g., [6]). It seems, however, that for the purpose of document similarity search, the Jaccard measure is preferable. The reason for this is primarily scalability, which is an issue in large document collections such as the Web. There exist methods for approximate computation of the Jaccard coefficient that work quite well in these cases. Broder [7] proposed a method for estimating the resemblance between two documents using a set representation of document subsequences called shingles (see the next section). In fact, his method estimates the Jaccard coefficient on two sets by representing them as smaller sets called *sketches*, which are then used instead of the original documents to compute the Jaccard coefficient. Sketches are created by choosing a random permutation, which is used to generate a sample for each document. Most important, sketches have a fixed size for all documents. In a large document collection each document can be represented by its sketch, thus substantially reducing the storage requirements as well as the running time for precomputing similarity between document pairs. The method was evaluated by large-scale experiments with clustering of all documents on the Web [8]. Used originally in a clustering framework, the method also suits very well the similarity search setting.

## Document Resemblance

So far we have discussed two approaches to document modeling: the TFIDF vector and set representations. Both approaches try to capture document semantics using the terms that documents contain as descriptive features and ignoring any information related to term positions, ordering, or structure. The only relevant information used for this purpose is whether or not a particular term occurs in the documents (the *set-of-words approach*) and the frequency of its occurrence (the *bag-of-words approach*). For example, the documents "Mary loves John" and "John loves Mary" are identical, because they include the same words with the same counts, although they have different meanings. The idea behind this representation is that *content* is identified with *topic* or *area* but not with *meaning* (that is why these approaches are also called *syntactic*). Thus, we can say that the topic of both documents is people and love, which is the meaning of the terms that occur in the documents.

Assume, however, that the task is to find identical or nearly identical documents, or documents that share phrases, sentences, or paragraphs. Obviously, set-based representation is not appropriate for such tasks. In a similarity search a query may return many copies of the same document (sometimes with slight modifications) that are stored at different web locations (mirror sites). Such pages may also be fetched multiple times by the web crawler if it keeps track only of the URLs of pages that have been visited. To avoid such situations, some mechanism for detecting duplicates or near duplicates of documents is needed. Detecting shared sentences, paragraphs, or other structures of text is a useful technique for identifying cases of plagiarism or studying stylistic properties of texts. Some figures obtained in the clustering study of the Web that we mentioned earlier [8] illustrate the magnitude of the problem. Among the 30 million web pages that were analyzed, there were 2.1 million clusters containing only identical documents (5.3 million documents).

There is a technique that extends the set-of-words approach to sequences of words. The idea is to consider the document as a sequence of words (terms) and extract from this sequence short subsequences of fixed length called *n-grams* or *shingles*. The document is then represented as a set of such *n*-grams. For example, the document "Mary loves John" can be represented by the set of 2-grams {[Mary, loves], [loves, John]} and "John loves Mary" by {[John, loves], [loves, Mary]}. Now these four 2-grams are the features that represent our documents. In this representation the documents do not have any overlap. We have already mentioned *n*-grams as a technique for approximate string matching but they are also popular in many other areas where the task is detecting subsequences such as spelling correction, speech recognition, and character recognition.

Shingled document representation can be used for estimating document *resemblance*. Let us denote the set of shingles of size $w$ contained in document $d$ as $S(d,w)$. That is, the set $S(d,w)$ contains all $w$-grams obtained from document $d$. Note that $T(d) = S(d,1)$, because terms are in fact 1-grams. Also, $S(d,|d|) = d$ (i.e., the document itself is a $w$-gram, where $w$ is equal to the size of the document). The *resemblance* between documents $d_1$ and $d_2$ is defined by the Jaccard coefficient computed with shingled documents:

$$r_w(d_1,d_2) = \frac{|S(d_1,w) \cap S(d_2,w)|}{|S(d_1,w) \cup S(d_2,w)|}$$

The same technique for precomputing document similarity can be used with the shingled document representation. The advantage here is that after obtaining document pairs along with those that are too dissimilar, we can also eliminate those that are too similar in terms of resemblance [with large values of $r_w(d_1,d_2)$]. In this way, duplicates or near duplicates can be eliminated from the similarity search results.

Although the number of shingles needed to represent each document is roughly the same as the number of terms needed for this purpose, the storage requirements for shingled document representation increase substantially. A straightforward representation of $w$-word shingles as integers with a fixed number of bits results in a $w$-fold increase in storage. For example, if the term IDs are represented by 32-bit numbers, a four-word shingle will take 128 bits. There are, however, hashing (or fingerprinting) techniques that can be used to reduce the storage requirements. Each shingle may be hashed into a number with a fixed number of bits using a fingerprinting function (see [7]). Then instead of the complete set of shingles $S(d,w)$ for each document, only shingles with 0 modulo $p$ (some suitable prime number) are kept. Let $L(d)$ be the set of shingles that are $S(d,w)$ that are 0 modulo $p$. Then the estimated value of the resemblance between documents $d_1$ and $d_2$ is

$$r_e(d_1,d_2) = \frac{|L(d) \cap L(d_2)|}{|L(d_1) \cup L(d_2)|}$$

$L(d)$ is a smaller set of shingles called a *sketch* of document $d$. By choosing a proper value for $p$, the storage for $L(d)$, and consequently the storage needed for precomputing resemblance for pairs of documents, can be reduced. Of course, this comes at the expense of less accurate estimation of resemblance.

# REFERENCES

1. Tim Berners-Lee, *Information Management: A Proposal*, CERN, Geneva, Switzerland, 1989–1990, `http://www.w3.org/History/1989/proposal.html`.
2. Tim Mayer, Our blog is growing up—and so has our index, *Yahoo! Search Blog*, Aug. 2005, `http://www.ysearchblog.com/archives/000172.html`.
3. C. Buckley, Implementation of the SMART information retrieval system, Technical Report 85-686, Cornell University, Ithaca, NY, 1985.
4. Oliver A. McBryan, GENVL and WWW: tools for taming the Web, presented at the First International Conference on the World Wide Web, CERN, Geneva, Switzerland, May 25–27, 1994, `http://www.cs.colorado.edu/home/mcbryan/mypapers/www94.ps`.
5. Sergey Brin and Lawrence Page, The anatomy of a large-scale hypertextual Web search engine, in *Proceedings of the 7th World Wide Web Conference* (WWW7), 1998, `http://www7.scu.edu.au/1921/com1921.htm`.
6. L. Lee, Measures of distributional similarity. *Proc. ACL*, 1999.
7. A. Broder, On the resemblance and containment of documents, in *Proceedings on Compression and Complexity of Sequences* (SEQUENCES'97), pp. 21–29, IEEE Computer Society, Los Alamitos, CA, 1998.
8. A. Broder, S. Glassman, M. Manasse, and G. Zweig, Syntactic clustering of the Web, in *Proceedings of the 6th International World Wide Web Conference*, Apr. 1997, pp. 393–404.

# EXERCISES

1. Use the WebSPHINX crawler (`http://www.cs.cmu.edu/~rcm/websphinx/`, also available from the book series Web site `www.dataminingconsultant.com`), to collect the department web pages listed in the department directory page (Figure 1.3). Use the following parameters:

   - *Starting URL:* `http://www.artsci.ccsu.edu/Departments.htm`
   - *Crawl:* the Web (or the server)
   - Depth: 1 hop

   **a.** Save the pages as separate files in a directory (action: save, on pages: text). The crawler creates a directory tree automatically and saves the web pages as HTML documents. See how the directory structure matches the URL structure of the corresponding pages.

   **b.** Convert the web documents into text documents. For example, use the "Save As . . . " option of the Internet Explorer with "Save as type: Text File (*.txt)."

   **c.** Save all documents in a single file (action: concatenate, on pages: text). Convert it to text format [as done in part (b)] and examine its content.

2. Download and install the Weka data mining system (`http://www.cs.waikato.ac.nz/~ml/weka/`). Read the documentation and try some examples to familiarize yourself with its use (e.g., the weather data provided with the installation).

3. Create a data file in ARFF format (see a description of the format at `http://www.cs.waikato.ac.nz/~ml/weka/`). Follow the steps below.

   **a.** Use the concatenation of the web documents (Exercise 1c) and create a text file where each document is represented on a separate line in plain text format. For example, this can be done by loading the concatenation in MS Word and then saving the file in plain text format without line breaks.

**b.** Enclose the document content in quotation marks (") and add the document name at the beginning of each line and a file header at the beginning of the file:

```
@relation departments_string

@attribute document_name string
@attribute document_content string

@data
Anthropology, " Anthropology consists of four ...
...
```

This representation uses two attributes: `document_name` and `document_content`, both of type string. An example of such a data file is "Departments-string.arff," available from the book series Web site, `www.dataminingconsultant.com`. Note that the representation in "Departments-string.arff" uses an additional class attribute (see Chapter 5), which is defined in the file header, and its values are added at the end of each line in the data section (after @data).

**c.** Load the file in the Weka system using the "Open file" button in "Preprocess" mode. After successful loading the system shows some statistics about the number of attributes, their type, and the number of instances (rows in the data section or documents).

**d.** Choose the StringToNominal filter and apply it to the first attribute, document_name. Then choose the StringToWordVector filter and apply it with "outputWordCounts = true" (you may also change the setting of "onlyAlphabeticTokens" and "useStoplist" to see how the results change).

**e.** Now you have a document–term matrix loaded in Weka. Use the "Edit" option to see it in a tabular format, where you can also change its content or copy it to other applications (e.g., MS Excel). Once created in Weka the table can be stored in an ARFF file through the "Save" option. Figure E1.3e shows a screenshot of a part of the document–term table.

**f.** Weka can also show some interesting statistics about the terms. In the visualization area (preprocess mode), change the class to document_name. Then you will see the distribution of terms over documents as bar diagrams. The screenshot in Figure E1.3f shows some of these diagrams.

**g.** Examine the diagrams (the color indicates the document) and find the most specific terms for each document. For example, compare the diagrams of *anthropology* and *chair* and explain the difference. Which one is more representative, and for which document?

4. Similar to Exercise 3, create the Boolean and TFIDF representation of the document collection. Examples of these representations are provided in the files "Departments-binary.arff" and "Departments-TFIDF.arff," available from the book Web site, `www.dataminingconsultant.com`.

**a.** To obtain the Boolean representation, apply the NumericToBinary filter to the word-count representation. What changed in the diagrams?

**b.** For the TFIDF representation, use the original string representation and apply the StringToWordVector filter with IDFTransform = true. Examine the document–term table and the diagrams. Explain why some columns (e.g., *chair* and *website*) are all zero. See these columns in the book versions of the same document collection:

**Viewer**

Relation: departments_string-weka.filters.unsupervised.attribute.Remove-R3-weka.filters.unsupervised.attribute.Stri...

| No. | document_name Nominal | anthropology Numeric | applied Numeric | archaeology Numeric | attend Numeric | ba Numeric | background Numeric | behavioral Numeric |
|---|---|---|---|---|---|---|---|---|
| 1 | Anthropology | 9.0 | 1.0 | 2.0 | 1.0 | 1.0 | 1.0 | 1.0 |
| 2 | Art | 0.0 | 0.0 | 0.0 | 0.0 | 1.0 | 0.0 | 0.0 |
| 3 | Biology | 0.0 | 0.0 | 0.0 | 0.0 | 0.0 | 0.0 | 0.0 |
| 4 | Chemistry | 0.0 | 0.0 | 0.0 | 0.0 | 0.0 | 0.0 | 0.0 |
| 5 | Communication | 0.0 | 0.0 | 0.0 | 0.0 | 1.0 | 0.0 | 0.0 |
| 6 | Computer | 0.0 | 0.0 | 0.0 | 0.0 | 0.0 | 0.0 | 0.0 |
| 7 | Justice | 0.0 | 0.0 | 0.0 | 0.0 | 1.0 | 0.0 | 0.0 |
| 8 | Economics | 0.0 | 0.0 | 0.0 | 0.0 | 1.0 | 0.0 | 0.0 |
| 9 | English | 0.0 | 1.0 | 0.0 | 0.0 | 1.0 | 0.0 | 0.0 |
| 10 | Geography | 0.0 | 0.0 | 0.0 | 0.0 | 1.0 | 0.0 | 0.0 |
| 11 | History | 0.0 | 0.0 | 0.0 | 0.0 | 1.0 | 0.0 | 0.0 |
| 12 | Math | 0.0 | 0.0 | 0.0 | 0.0 | 2.0 | 0.0 | 0.0 |
| 13 | Languages | 0.0 | 0.0 | 0.0 | 0.0 | 2.0 | 0.0 | 0.0 |
| 14 | Music | 0.0 | 0.0 | 0.0 | 0.0 | 2.0 | 0.0 | 0.0 |
| 15 | Philosophy | 0.0 | 1.0 | 0.0 | 0.0 | 1.0 | 0.0 | 0.0 |
| 16 | Physics | 0.0 | 1.0 | 0.0 | 0.0 | 0.0 | 0.0 | 0.0 |
| 17 | Political | 0.0 | 1.0 | 0.0 | 0.0 | 2.0 | 0.0 | 0.0 |
| 18 | Psychology | 0.0 | 0.0 | 0.0 | 0.0 | 2.0 | 0.0 | 0.0 |
| 19 | Sociology | 0.0 | 0.0 | 0.0 | 0.0 | 1.0 | 0.0 | 0.0 |
| 20 | Theatre | 0.0 | 0.0 | 0.0 | 0.0 | 2.0 | 0.0 | 0.0 |

Undo    OK    Cancel

**Figure E1.3e**

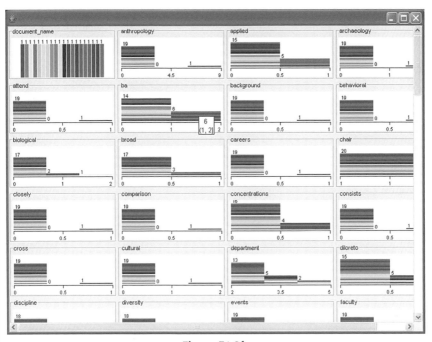

**Figure E1.3f**

"Departments-book-binary.arff" and "Departments-book-TFIDF.arff" (also available from the book Web site). Why are the Weka and the book versions slightly different? (See what is behind the "More" button of the StringToWordVector parameter setting window.)

5. Collect web documents from other domains (use the WebSPHINX crawler or web search) and follow the preceding steps to create ARFF data files for the term-count, Boolean, and TFIDF representations. Then load the files into Weka and analyze the document collections by examining the document–term table or the term distribution diagrams.

6. Find proper sets of keywords and evaluate the precision and recall provided by Google when searching documents in the CCSU A&S collection.

   a. Use the keywords *computer* and *program* with advanced search limited within the server domain. The query will be

   ```
   computer program site:www.artsci.ccsu.edu
   ```

   b. Using the query results, create a table similar to Table 1.6. Then compute the interpolated precision for different recall levels and create charts similar to those in Figure 1.5.

   c. Compare the charts based on the results from Google search with those based on cosine similarity (Figure 1.5).

   d. Use fewer or more terms and create the corresponding charts. Try terms with different IDF scores (use Figure 1.6). Compute the average precision. Analyze the results.

   e. Use terms that occur in all 20 documents (e.g., *department*, *phone*, *chair*). Explain why these documents are not always among the top 20 in the result list. Which documents occur in the top?

   f. Search for specific web pages (e.g., department Web sites) in wider domains (e.g., www.ccsu.edu) or in the entire Web. Use a different number of keywords and compute the precision and recall. Analyze the results.

# HYPERLINK-BASED RANKING

INTRODUCTION

SOCIAL NETWORKS ANALYSIS

PAGERANK

AUTHORITIES AND HUBS

LINK-BASED SIMILARITY SEARCH

ENHANCED TECHNIQUES FOR PAGE RANKING

## INTRODUCTION

So far we have focused on the textual content of web documents. We have also used the web hyperlink structure to add more textual content to documents by using the anchor text in backlinks. The hyperlinks play another, more important role for web documents, however; they provide an independent evaluation of web page popularity or authority. The role of web page links is similar to the role of citations in scientific literature, for example. Popular articles are often cited. Many hyperlinks pointing to a page draw the attention of web users just as citations to an article do for academics. In fact, the Web is an example of a *social network*, a network of entities such as individuals or organizations that connect (or interact with) each other in various ways. The notions of *popularity*, *authority*, and *prestige* are central to social networks. There is an approach called *bibliometrics*, which is used in library and information science to analyze the merit of scientific publications. Citation indices are examples of the bibliometrics approach. For example, the *impact factor* (number of citations in the preceding two years) uses the in-degree of the nodes in the network of scientific journals to evaluate the merit of a publication.

The measures of popularity, authority, and prestige can be used for ranking web pages retrieved by a search engine. The idea is to assign to each page on the Web a rank based on the hyperlink structure. This ranking can be done off-line (e.g., when pages are indexed) because it is independent of any query and web page textual

*Data Mining the Web: Uncovering Patterns in Web Content, Structure, and Usage*
By Zdravko Markov and Daniel T. Larose    Copyright © 2007 John Wiley & Sons, Inc.

content and is then used to rank the pages returned by the keyword search query. Combinations of relevance ranking and hyperlink-based ranking are also possible. Later in the chapter we discuss the notion of prestige in social networks and two important web page ranking algorithms, PageRank and HITS, which further develop that notion and combine it with a content-based web search.

## SOCIAL NETWORKS ANALYSIS

A social network can be represented formally as a directed graph with weights assigned to its edges. Without loss of generality we may assume that the nodes represent documents and the edges represent citations from one document to other documents. In this setting the notion of *prestige* can be associated with the number of input edges to a node (in-degree). An obvious assumption in any social network is that prestige depends on the authority (or again, the prestige) of citations. In other words, prestige has a *recursive* nature. Thus, the prestige score of a node is not simply equal to its in-degree but has to be defined recursively using the prestige scores of the nodes that cite it. We do this using some notions from *linear algebra*.

Consider the adjacency matrix $A$ of the document citation graph defined as follows: $A(u, v) = 1$ if document $u$ cites document $v$ and $A(u, v) = 0$ otherwise. Each node $u$ has a *prestige score* $p(u)$, which is defined as a sum of the prestige scores of the nodes that cite $u$; that is,

$$p(u) = \sum_{v} A(v, u)\, p(v)$$

Using matrix notation, the prestige scores $p(u)$ of all documents $u$ can be written as a column vector $P$. Then given some initial prestige vector $P$, the new prestige vector $P'$ is

$$P' = A^{\mathrm{T}} P$$

where $A^{\mathrm{T}}$ is the transpose of $A$. Plugging $P'$ for $P$ and recomputing the prestige vector a number of times leads to a *fixpoint* for $P$, which is the solution to the equation

$$\lambda P = A^{\mathrm{T}} P$$

Finding the solution to this equation is known in linear algebra as *eigen-decomposition* of a matrix. Generally, for a matrix of size $n \times n$ there are $n$ such vectors, called *eigenvectors*, each with an associated value for the scalar $\lambda$, called an *eigenvalue*. Among all eigenvectors of a matrix, we are interested in the *dominant* (or *principal*) *eigenvector*, the eigenvector associated with the largest eigenvalue.

Let us illustrate the computation of prestige with a simple graph of three documents, $a$, $b$, and $c$, shown in Figure 2.1. The adjacency matrix of this graph $A$ and its transpose $A^{\mathrm{T}}$ are

$$A = \begin{pmatrix} 0 & 1 & 1 \\ 0 & 0 & 1 \\ 1 & 0 & 0 \end{pmatrix} \qquad A^{\mathrm{T}} = \begin{pmatrix} 0 & 0 & 1 \\ 1 & 0 & 0 \\ 1 & 1 & 0 \end{pmatrix}$$

The prestige scores of the documents are shown in the nodes. They are computed by solving the vector equation $\lambda P = A^{\mathrm{T}} P$. The solution with the largest eigenvalue, $\lambda = 1.325$, is $P = (0.548 \ 0.414 \ 0.726)^{\mathrm{T}}$. Plugging these values back in the equation gives

$$1.325 \begin{pmatrix} 0.548 \\ 0.414 \\ 0.726 \end{pmatrix} = \begin{pmatrix} 0 & 0 & 1 \\ 1 & 0 & 0 \\ 1 & 1 & 0 \end{pmatrix} \begin{pmatrix} 0.548 \\ 0.414 \\ 0.726 \end{pmatrix}$$

The scores of the documents illustrate well the intuition behind the recursive definition of prestige. Document $c$ gets the highest score because it has two citations. Documents $a$ and $b$ get lower scores because each has one citation only, but $a$ gets a higher score than $b$ because $a$ is cited by a document with a higher prestige score ($c$).

One method to compute eigenvectors is first to find the eigenvalues by solving the characteristic equation $|A - \lambda I| = 0$ ($|M|$ is the determinant of matrix $M$ and $I$ is the identity matrix). Then for each of its $n$ (possibly, nondistinct) roots, a system of linear equations is solved to find the associated eigenvector. For our purposes, however, we do not need all eigenvectors. Therefore, a simpler algorithm can be used. It is based on the *power iteration method* and computes the dominant eigenvector as follows:

- $P \leftarrow P_0$
- loop:
  - $Q \leftarrow P$
  - $P \leftarrow A^{\mathrm{T}} Q$
  - $P \leftarrow \frac{1}{\|P\|} P$ (normalize $P$)
- while $\|P - Q\| > \varepsilon$

$P_0$ can be any nonzero vector and $\varepsilon$ is a parameter that controls the accuracy. The algorithm converges to the eigenvector associated with the largest eigenvalue. The eigenvector is normalized to unit length (i.e., $\|P\| = 1$) and the eigenvalue is $\lambda = \|A^{\mathrm{T}} P\|$. For example, with $P_0 = (1 \ 1 \ 1)^{\mathrm{T}}$ and $\varepsilon = 0.00016$, it takes 20 iterations to compute the prestige vector for the example shown in Figure 2.1.

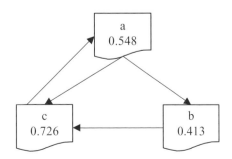

**Figure 2.1**   A Document network with prestige scores for the nodes.

## PAGERANK

The hyperlinks are not only ways to propagate the prestige score of a page to pages to which it links, they are also paths along which web users travel from one web page to another. In this respect, the popularity (or prestige) of a web page can be measured in terms of how often an average web user visits it. To estimate this we may use the metaphor of the "random web surfer," who clicks on hyperlinks at random with uniform probability and thus implements the *random walk* on the web graph. Assume that page $u$ links to $N_u$ web pages and page $v$ is one of them. Then once the web surfer is at page $u$, the probability of visiting page $v$ will be $1/N_u$. This intuition suggests a more sophisticated scheme of propagation of prestige through the web links also involving the out-degree of the nodes. The idea is that the amount of prestige that page $v$ receives from page $u$ is $1/N_u$ of the prestige of $u$. This idea is illustrated in Figure 2.2. This is also the idea behind the web page ranking algorithm PageRank [1], which was originally used in the search engine Google and contributed substantially to its success.

Let us first describe the simplified ranking scheme illustrated in Figure 2.2. Consider the web graph defined with its adjacency matrix $A$. To each page $u$ we assign a rank score $R(u)$ defined as

$$R(u) = \lambda \sum_v \frac{A(v, u)R(v)}{N_v}$$

where $N_v$ is the out-degree of node $v$ [the number of outlinks from $v$, i.e., $N_v = \sum_w A(v, w)$]. An example of rank calculation with three documents is shown in Figure 2.3. This is, in fact, the social network that we have used for computing prestige, now with weights on the edges and PageRank scores for the nodes. The solution of the rank equation is for $\lambda = 1$.

To use the matrix notation, we first need to redefine the adjacency matrix. Instead of using the adjacency information only (0's and 1's), we have to include edge weights that are equal to $1/N_u$, where $N_u$ is the out-degree of node $u$. This can be done easily by using the original adjacency matrix and replacing each 1 with 1 over the row total. Thus, for the network in Figure 2.3, we get the following

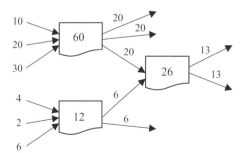

**Figure 2.2** Propagation of page rank.

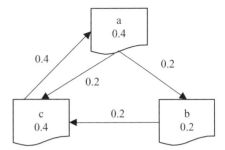

**Figure 2.3**  Document network with page-Rank scores.

matrix:

$$A = \begin{pmatrix} 0 & 0.5 & 0.5 \\ 0 & 0 & 1 \\ 1 & 0 & 0 \end{pmatrix}$$

The rank equation is the same as the one for prestige (i.e., $\lambda P = A^T P$) and its solution is the eigenvector of $A^T$ for $\lambda = 1$; that is,

$$\begin{pmatrix} 0.4 \\ 0.2 \\ 0.4 \end{pmatrix} = \begin{pmatrix} 0 & 0 & 1 \\ 0.5 & 0 & 0 \\ 0.5 & 1 & 0 \end{pmatrix} \begin{pmatrix} 0.4 \\ 0.2 \\ 0.4 \end{pmatrix}$$

This is also the solution, which is computed by power iteration with norm $L_1$ ($\|X\|_1 = x_1 + x_2 + \cdots + x_n$). The solution for norm $L_2$ ($\|X\|_2 = \sqrt{x_1^2 + x_2^2 + \cdots + x_n^2}$) is $P^T = (0.666 \quad 0.333 \quad 0.666)$, and the solution with integers only is $P^T = (2 \quad 1 \quad 2)$. Any of these solutions works for ranking because the scores are used only for ordering pages.

Clearly, the web graph includes loops. The simplified PageRank algorithm generally works with loops; however, there is a special configuration of nodes that the algorithm cannot deal with properly. Consider, for example, two pages that point to each other but do not point to other pages. Such an isolated loop is called a *rank sink*. If pointed to from an outside page, it accumulates rank but never distributes it to other nodes. To deal with the rank sink situation, we return to the random surfer model. As we have already noted, computing page rank is based on the idea of a random walk on the web graph, but the random surfer may get trapped into a rank sink. To avoid this situation we try to model the behavior of a real web surfer who gets bored running into a loop and jumps to some other web page outside the rank sink. For this purpose we introduce a *rank source E*, a vector over all web pages, which defines the probability distribution of jumping to a web page at random. Thus, the modified PageRank equation becomes

$$R(u) = \lambda \left[ \sum_v \frac{A(v, u)R(v)}{N_v} + E(u) \right]$$

The PageRank equation can be solved by using the eigenvector approach. Below we present an iterative algorithm, which basically implements the power iteration method for computing the dominant eigenvector with a small modification of the way the normalization is done.

- $R \leftarrow R_0$
- loop:
  - $Q \leftarrow R$
  - $R \leftarrow A^T Q$
  - $d \leftarrow \|Q\|_1 - \|R\|_1$
  - $R \leftarrow R + dE$
- while $\|R - Q\|_1 > \varepsilon$

The initial rank vector $R_0$ can be any vector over the web pages, $A^T$ is the transpose of the adjacency matrix with weights $1/N_u$, and $E$ is the rank source vector. The parameter $d$ implements the normalization step and also affects the rate of convergence positively. The alternative approach would be just to add $E$ to $R$ and then normalize ($R \leftarrow R/\|R\|_1$). As defined, the PageRank algorithm implements the random surfer model, where:

- The rank vector $R$ defines the probability distribution of a random walk on the graph of the Web.
- With some low probability the surfer jumps to a random page chosen according to the distribution $E$.

The source of rank $E$ is usually chosen as a uniform vector with a small norm (e.g., $\|E\|_1 = 0.15$). The way it affects the model of the random surfer is that the jumps to a random page happen more often if the norm of $E$ is larger. In terms of PageRank score, a larger $E$ means less contribution of the link structure to the final score (i.e., the rank distribution in $R$ gets closer to $E$).

The use of rank source solves the problem with the rank sink and allows the algorithm to work with a web graph with disconnected parts (which is the case in the real web). It also allows page rank to be adjusted for specific situations such as *manipulation by commercial interests* and *customized ranking*. For example, a web page score may be increased by including a link from an important page or a large number of links from nonimportant pages. Navigation links, copyright notices, and similar nonauthoritative links also create highly interconnected pages, which may get large page ranks. A proper choice of $E$ could minimize these undesired effects. One option is to include in $E$ the root pages of all web servers. This would distribute the rank sources evenly over the Web and make commercial manipulation more difficult.

Another option is to use just one web page (i.e., only one nonzero coordinate) for $E$. In this way the page chosen would get the highest rank, followed by its links. Such a page might be a trusted web directory, for example. This option would also allow implementing a *personalized web page ranking*. Suppose that the page chosen is somebody's home page. Then PageRank will assign the highest score to that page and its links, followed by related pages. In this way, ranking can be done from the perspective of a specific web user or in a particular context defined by a group of pages linked together. Page et al. [1] report such experiments with an early version of

Google. The page chosen was the home page of the famous computer scientist John McCarthy.

Other applications of PageRank include *estimating web traffic, optimal crawling*, and *web page navigation*. The random surfer model actually estimates the number of visits to a web page. Thus, the rank score of a web page may be used to estimate web traffic and the load of the hosting server. In this way, PageRank may be seen as a useful tool to measure and study the Web by complementing web usage data or filling gaps where such data are not available.

Web pages with high PageRank score are important because they are cited by many other pages and are also visited more often by web users. Therefore, it is desirable that such pages be fetched and indexed first by the web crawler. This can be achieved by using PageRank as an evaluation function in an informed graph search algorithm that the web crawler implements. As an independent indicator of web page importance, PageRank can enhance page navigation. One option is to show the page score on the link before the user clicks on it. Another option (currently used by Google) is to order web pages in a web directory by their PageRank score, thus providing both topical and authoritative criteria for selection of web pages.

## AUTHORITIES AND HUBS

Although it is widely acknowledged that link-based ranking and especially PageRank is fundamental to web search, there are problems using only the in-degree-based authority for this purpose. Often, links (e.g., navigational links) have nothing to do with authority. On the other hand, the most popular and authoritative pages are not necessarily the most relevant to a particular query. In other words, neither relevance nor popularity can do the job alone; there must be a good balance between the two. In this section we discuss an approach called HITS (hyperlink induced topic search), proposed by Kleinberg [2], which combines content-based relevance with link-based authority ranking. The basic idea is to focus on the relevant pages first and then compute authority. The approach also takes into account the *hub pages* (pages that point to multiple relevant authoritative pages).

In contrast to PageRank, the HITS algorithm works with the much smaller and, most important, query-dependent part of the web graph. It starts with keyword search and then analyzes the link structure of the relevant web pages obtained. The entire process is called *topic distillation*. Given a query $q$, the following steps are performed:

1. By using a standard IR system, a small set of relevant web pages called a *root set $R_q$* is found.

2. The root set is expanded by adding pages that point to and are pointed to by pages from the root set. This larger set is called a *base set $S_q$*.

3. The hyperlink structure of the base set $S_q$ is analyzed to find *authorities* and *hubs* as described below.

4. Let $E$ be the adjacency matrix of the web graph of $S_q$, where $E(u, v) = 1$ if page $u$ points to page $v$, and $E(u, v) = 0$ otherwise (both $u$ and $v$ belong to $S_q$).

**5.** Let $X = (x_1 x_2 \cdots x_n)$ be the authority vector and $Y = (y_1 y_2 \cdots y_n)$ be the hub vector, both over all pages in $S_q$. They can be computed by power iteration as follows ($k$ is a tuned parameter):

- $X \leftarrow (11 \ldots 1)$
- $Y \leftarrow (11 \ldots 1)$
- loop $k$ times
  - $\circ$ $x_u \leftarrow \displaystyle\sum_{\{v,E(v,u)=1\}} y_v$, for $u = 1, 2, \ldots, n$
  - $\circ$ $y_u \leftarrow \displaystyle\sum_{\{v,E(u,v)=1\}} x_v$, for $u = 1, 2, \ldots, n$
  - $\circ$ normalize $X$ and $Y$ by the $L_2$ norm
- end loop

Using the computed authority and hub vectors, the algorithm reports the pages that correspond to the highest coordinates in these vectors.

A disadvantage of HITS is that the hub and authority scores cannot be precomputed because they depend on the hyperlink structure of the web subgraph selected by the query. This slows down the response time, as the scores have to be computed online after documents relevant to the query are retrieved. At the same time, this is an advantage of HITS over PageRank, because hyperlink-based scores are computed using a relevant part of the web graph, thus avoiding situations where pages with low content-based relevance get high scores because they collect a lot of inlinks. An example of such a situation is the query "music program," which a user may want to use to search for documents in the area of radio, performance, or educational programs. Submitted to Google (based on PageRank), this query returns mostly documents related to computer music and music software, simply because the pages where the term *program* occurs along with *computer* and *software* are much more popular (collect more inlinks) than those where *program* occurs along with *music* only.

An important difference between HITS and PageRank is the way that page scores are propagated in the web graph. In HITS the hub collects its score from pages to which it points. In this way the propagation of authority and hub scores is bidirectional. The specific way that authority and hub scores are computed (taking turns at each step in the power iteration) allows even sibling pages to influence each other's score. The simple graph shown in Figure 2.4 illustrates this. At each step, page $u_1$ collects its hub score $h(u_1)$ as a sum of the authority scores of the pages to which

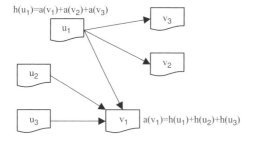

**Figure 2.4**   Computing hub ($h$) and authority ($a$) scores.

it points ($v_1$, $v_2$, and $v_3$). At the next step, page $v_1$ collects its authority score $a(v_1)$ as a sum of the hub scores of the pages that point to it. This process continues until all scores reach some fixpoint. If at some step $v_2$ gets a high authority score, then in the later steps it will be transferred to its siblings, $v_1$ and $v_3$. In this way the authority and hub vectors $X$ and $Y$ are computed, and each page $u_i$ get its authority score $x_i = a(u_i)$ and hub score $y_i = h(u_i)$. Computing hub scores is an advantage of HITS because the hub pages are important sources of information on the Web. PageRank does not compute hub scores, but practically, this is not a big disadvantage, because good hub pages quickly accumulate inlinks and thus also get high authority.

As defined, the HITS algorithm always follows the links (from and to pages in the base set) and therefore may be trapped in some irrelevant part of the web subgraph. This may happen when the base set contains a disconnected subgraph due to an ambiguous query. For example, the query "star" may retrieve several sets of possibly disconnected pages: from the area of movie stars, astronomy, newspapers with that popular name, and so on. Then only the pages in the largest subgraph will be ranked as authorities and hubs. The reason for this is that HITS actually finds the *dominant* eigenvectors (the eigenvectors associated with the largest eigenvalue) of $EE^{\mathrm{T}}$ (the hub vector) and $E^{\mathrm{T}}E$ (the authority vector), where $E$ is the adjacency matrix of the base set and dominant eigenvectors correspond to the largest subgraph. A solution to this problem is to compute not only the dominant eigenvector, but also others that correspond to smaller subgraphs.

Another solution to the problem with disconnected subgraphs is based on the *random walk model*. Similarly to PageRank, the HITS algorithm can be extended with a parameter that controls the random surfer. Let this be a value $d \in [0,\ 1]$. Then:

- With probability $d$, the surfer jumps to a random page in the base set.
- With probability $1 - d$, the surfer takes a random outlink from the current page or goes to a random page that points to the current one.

With $d = 0$, the algorithm works similar to that of the original HITS. The stability of the algorithm improves as $d$ increases, which means that pages tend to get more uniform hub and authority scores independent of the web subgraph structure. In the extreme case of $d = 1$, all pages get the same rank (i.e., there is no ranking).

## LINK-BASED SIMILARITY SEARCH

The HITS approach combines content-based search with link-based ranking. It also makes the basic assumption that if the pages from the root set are close to the query topic, the pages belonging to the base set (one link farther) are, by their content, similar to the query. This assumption is supported by experimental evidence showing that pages at a distance of one link usually belong to the same topic. (Observations also show that the topic usually changes after more than two links.) This idea can be used to implement a *link-based approach* to compute *similar pages*. This is an alternative to the content-based similarity discussed earlier and uses the HITS approach for computing hubs and authorities. The difference is that the root set is computed differently; instead of keyword search, links are used for this purpose. Given a page $u$ and a parameter $k$, the algorithm proceeds as follows:

1. Find $k$ pages pointing to page $u$ and use them to form the root set $R_u$.
2. Use $R_u$ to find the base set $S_u$.
3. Compute authorities and hubs in $S_u$.
4. Report the highest-ranking authorities and hubs as pages similar to $u$.

The intuition behind thus-defined link-based similarity search is that the pages in a close neighborhood (at most two links away) of a given page are similar to it. Then assuming that links are indicators of the same or a similar topic, the authorities and hubs in this neighborhood must be the most representative similar pages because they collect the most links. An advantage of the link-based approach to similarity is that it has no problems with pages that have very little text (consequently, very little overlap and low content similarity) and pages with nontextual content, such as images and programs.

## ENHANCED TECHNIQUES FOR PAGE RANKING

Both PageRank and HITS, along with their improvements that we have discussed, so far rely on the basic assumption that linked pages belong to a similar or the same topic. However, as we mentioned earlier, the topic changes quickly as the number of links between the pages increases. Thus, assuming that a set of pages are from the same topic, expansion of this set by one or more links may include pages from other topics. This process is called *topic generalization*. Topic generalization by a single link is used in HITS to form the base set and is the maximum that is feasible. Expansion by more than one link usually brings many unrelated pages and has to be avoided.

Another undesired situation is when a page from a single topic set of pages points to a large set of pages from another topic. Then expanding the former set would include in it pages from the larger set, thus changing the original topic. This process, called *topic drift*, poses problems to both HITS and PageRank. In HITS the top-ranked hubs and authorities may appear unrelated to the query, and PageRank may assign high scores to pages with low relevance. This effect may be used intentionally to bring up the rank of a page linked to a large, densely connected web subgraph.

Problems with topic generalization and drift are due basically to a single ranking system based dominantly on the web graph structure. A general solution to these and other problems is to use many ranking systems and to weight their scores when computing the final page rank. We have already discussed two: the content-based relevance that uses the vector space metric and the link-based ranking of PageRank and HITS. It is important to note that successful web search engines (e.g., Google) use these and other ranking schemes and sophisticated weighting techniques to combine them.

Other problems with link-based ranking include *nepotism* and *outliers*. Densely linked pages located on a single server cause problems with purely link-based ranking. Such links are called *nepotistic links* because they increase the page rank, but indicate hardly any authority and may also be used for commercial manipulation. Two-party and multiparty nepotisms are also possible, due basically to navigation links or links between different sites belonging to the same business. For example, Google has more than 20 sites all linked together: `http://froogle.google.com/`, `http://groups.google.com/`, `http://images.google.com/`, and others. Such sites may be completely unrelated with respect to page content. One simple approach to avoid nepotism is to assign weights of $1/k$ to the inlinks from pages belonging to a site with $k$ pages.

*Outliers* are web pages that are retrieved by keyword search and thus are relevant to the query but are somehow far from the central topic of the query. Such pages may be linked to outside the topic web subgraphs and thus may increase the probability of topic drift when the root set is expanded. Therefore, *outlier elimination* can stabilize the ranking algorithm and avoid undesired topic generalizations and drifts. Outliers can be detected by clustering because they are far from the cluster centroids. Following are the basic steps of a simple approach that uses the idea of centroids and is designed to stabilize the HITS algorithm.

1. Create vector space representation for the pages from the root set.
2. Find the centroid of the root set. This is the page that minimizes the sum (or the average) of its cosine similarity to all pages in the set.
3. When expanding the root set, discard pages (from the base set) that are too far from the centroid page (their cosine similarity to the centroid is below a given threshold).

There are also other approaches to enhance page ranking that are based on the structure of the web graph as well as on the HTML structure of web documents. Chakrabarti [3] provides an in-depth discussion of all these methods, including the basic PageRank and HITS algorithms and their improvements.

## REFERENCES

1. Lawrence Page, Sergey Brin, Rajeev Motwani, and Terry Winograd, *The PageRank Citation Ranking: Bringing Order to the Web*, Stanford Digital Library Technology Project, Stanford, University, Stanford, CA, 1998, `http://dbpubs.stanford.edu/pub/1999-66`.
2. Jon M. Kleinberg, Authoritative sources in a hyperlinked environment, *J. ACM*, 46(5): 604–632, 1999, `http://www.cs.cornell.edu/home/kleinber/auth.ps`.
3. Soumen Chakrabarti, *Mining the Web: Discovering Knowledge from Hypertext Data*, Morgan Kaufmann, San Francisco, CA, 2003.

## EXERCISES

1. Use the WebSPHINX crawler (`http://www.cs.cmu.edu/~rcm/websphinx/`, also available from the book series Web site `www.dataminingconsultant.com`), to create a document citation matrix for a small set of web pages. For example, use the domain `http://www.artsci.ccsu.edu/`.

**a.** To limit the web domain, crawl the server pages only (set Crawl: the server). As only the immediate citations are needed, the depth of crawling should be set to 1 hop.

**b.** Create a square matrix for the URLs collected from the pages crawled. For this purpose, crawl the server using each of these pages as a starting URL (again with a depth of 1 hop). The results of each crawl will include the pages cited by the page used as a starting URL, and thus will provide the information needed to fill the corresponding row of the adjacency matrix with 0's or 1's.

**c.** (Advanced project)   The entire process of creating the citation matrix may be automated by writing a program that uses the source code of the WebSPHINX crawler, the W3C Protocol Library (`http://www.w3.org/Library/`), or another package providing tools to manipulate web page links.

2. Compute the prestige score of the pages in the collection by finding the eigenvector associated with the largest eigenvalue of the citation matrix. Use a math package, such as MATLAB and MathWorks, or implement the power iteration algorithm described in this chapter.

3. Include weights in the adjacency matrix as explained in the section "PageRank." For this purpose, use the citation matrix created in Exercise 1. Analyze the structure of the web graph described with this matrix and determine whether or not it contains rank sinks. Use the eigenvector approach to compute the PageRank score of the web pages (see Exercise 2).

4. Investigate how a rank sink may affect page scores based on the simplified PageRank algorithm (without rank source). If the pages collected do not include a rank sink, modify the matrix to create one.

5. Implement the power iteration method for computing PageRank. Investigate how it deals with the rank sink situation. Use a uniform rank source with a small norm. Also experiment with different rank source vectors.

6. Find statistics for web page visits and try to match the PageRank scores with the frequency of visits for each page. How good is the PageRank estimate of web traffic? Change the rank source vector (e.g., use the pages visited most often) or extend the web subgraph (include more pages) and see how this changes the PageRank scores.

7. Rewrite the PageRank equation with the rank source in matrix notation.

PART *II*

# WEB CONTENT MINING

**The information** retrieval approaches discussed in Chapters 1 and 2 provide content-based access to the Web, while machine learning and data mining approaches organize the Web by content and thus respond directly to the major challenge of *turning the web data into web knowledge*. Combined, information retrieval, machine learning, and data mining provide a general framework for mining the web structure and content. In this part of the book we look into the machine learning and data mining components of the framework by focusing on two approaches to organizing the Web: clustering and classification (categorization). In clustering, web documents are grouped or organized hierarchically by similarity; that is, clustering is concerned with automatic structuring of the web content. Web document classification is based primarily on prediction methods, where documents are labeled by topic, preference, or usage, given sets of documents already labeled. Concept learning methods can also be used to generate explicit descriptions of sets of web documents, which can then be applied to categorization of new documents or to better understand the document area or topic.

# *CLUSTERING*

## INTRODUCTION

The most popular approach to learning is by example. Given a set of objects, each labeled with a class (category), the learning system builds a mapping between objects and classes which can then be used for classifying new (unlabeled) objects. As the labeling (categorization) of the initial (training) set of objects is done by an agent external to the system (teacher), this setting is called *supervised learning*. Clustering is another setting for learning, which does not use labeled objects and therefore is *unsupervised*. The objective of clustering is finding common patterns, grouping similar objects, or organizing them in hierarchies. In the context of the Web, the objects manipulated by the learning system are web documents, and the class labels are usually topics or user preferences. Thus, a supervised web learning system would build a mapping between documents and topics, while a clustering system would group web documents or organize them in hierarchies according to their topics.

A clustering system can be useful in web search for grouping search results into closely related sets of documents. Clustering can improve similarity search by focusing on sets of relevant documents. Hierarchical clustering methods can be used to create topic directories automatically, directories that can then be labeled manually. On the other hand, manually created topic directories can be matched against clustering hierarchies and thus the accuracy of the topic directories can be evaluated. Clustering is also a valuable technique for analyzing the Web. Matching the

*Data Mining the Web: Uncovering Patterns in Web Content, Structure, and Usage*
By Zdravko Markov and Daniel T. Larose    Copyright © 2007 John Wiley & Sons, Inc.

content-based clustering and the hyperlink structure can reveal patterns, duplications, and other interesting structures on the Web.

There exist various types of clustering, depending on the way that clusters are represented, the cluster properties, and the types of algorithms used for clustering. Thus, there are four dimensions along which clustering techniques can be categorized:

1. *Model-based (conceptual) versus partitioning.* Conceptual clustering creates models (explicit representations) of clusters, whereas partitioning simply enumerates the members of each cluster.

2. *Deterministic versus probabilistic.* Cluster membership may be defined as a Boolean value (in deterministic clustering) or as a probability (in probabilistic clustering).

3. *Hierarchical versus flat.* Flat clustering splits the set of objects into subsets, whereas hierarchical clustering creates tree structures of clusters.

4. *Incremental versus batch.* Batch algorithms use the entire set of objects to create the clustering, whereas incremental algorithms take one object at a time and update the current clustering to accommodate it.

Clustering can be applied to any set of objects as long as a suitable representation of these objects exists. The most common representation, which also works for other machine learning and data mining methods (such as classification), is the *attribute–value* (or *feature–value*) *representation*. In this representation a number of attributes (features) are identified for the entire population, and each object is represented by a set of attribute–value pairs. Alternatively, if the order of the features is fixed, a vector of values (data points) can be used instead. The document *vector space model* is exactly the same type of representation, where the features are terms.

Another approach to clustering considers documents as outcomes of random processes and tries to identify the parameters of these processes. In our classification this is a *probabilistic model-based approach* where each cluster is described by the probability distribution that is most likely to have generated the documents within it. In this *generative document modeling* framework, documents are random *events* represented by the terms they contain. However, in contrast to the vector space model, the terms here are not features (dimensions in the vector space); rather, they are considered as *elementary (atomic) random events.* Another difference with the vector space approach is that the generative models do not use similarity measures or distances between documents or clusters.

By using the standard vector space representation, all clustering approaches known from machine learning and data mining can be applied to document clustering. However, for various reasons (such as quality of results and efficiency) there are several algorithms that are particularly important in this area. These are *hierarchical agglomerative clustering* and *k-means clustering.* In the remainder of this chapter we describe these algorithms briefly and focus on their use for document clustering (for more information on the algorithms, see Larose [1]). We also describe the generative document modeling framework and a particular probabilistic clustering algorithm called *expectation maximization* (EM). We conclude the chapter with a short discussion on collaborative filtering (recommender systems), which is an area that uses clustering and involves not only documents but Web users, too. Approaches to evaluation of the clustering quality and clustering models are discussed in Chapter 4.

## Hierarchical Agglomerative Clustering

Hierarchical agglomerative clustering is a *hierarchical partitioning* approach to clustering. It produces a nested sequence of partitions of the set of data points which can be displayed as a tree with a single cluster, including all points at the root and singleton clusters (individual points) at the leaves. The visualization of a hierarchical partitioning tree is called a *dendrogram*. The dendrogram shown in Figure 3.1 displays the hierarchical partitioning of the set of numbers $\{1,2,4,5,8,10\}$. The height of the lines connecting clusters indicates the similarity between clusters at this level. The actual value of similarity can be seen on the vertical axis on the left. The similarity measure used in this example is computed as $(10 - d)/10$, where $d$ is the distance between data points or cluster centers.

There are two approaches to generating a hierarchical partitioning, the first called *agglomerative*. The algorithm starts with the data points and at each step merges the two closest (most similar) points (or clusters at later steps) until a single cluster remains. The second approach to hierarchical partitioning, called *divisible*, starts with the original set of points and at each step splits a cluster until only individual points remain. To implement this approach, we need to decide which cluster to split and how to perform the split.

The *agglomerative hierarchical clustering* approach is more popular, as it requires only the definition of a distance or similarity function on clusters or points. For data points in the Euclidean space, the *Euclidean distance* is the best choice. For documents represented as TFIDF vectors, the preferred measure is the *cosine similarity* defined as

$$\text{sim}\,(d_1, d_2) = \frac{d_1 \cdot d_2}{\|d_1\|\ \|d_2\|}$$

where $d_1$ and $d_2$ are the document vectors, $\cdot$ denotes the dot product, and $\|d_1\|$ and $\|d_2\|$ are the lengths of the vectors ($L_2$ norms). If the vectors are normalized to unit length, the similarity is just the dot product.

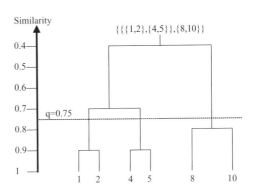

**Figure 3.1** Hierarchical partitioning of the set $\{1,2,4,5,8,10\}$.

What remains to be done is generalizing the similarity measure so that it also applies to clusters. There are several options for this. Assume that $S_1$ and $S_2$ are two sets (clusters) of documents. Then the similarity $sim(S_1, S_2)$ can be defined in one of the following ways:

- *Similarity between cluster centroids*: that is, $sim(S_1, S_2) = sim(c_1, c_2)$, where the centroid of cluster $S$ is $c = (1/|S|)\sum_{d \in S} d$.

- The *maximum similarity* between documents from each cluster: that is, $sim(S_1, S_2) = \max_{d_1 \in S_1, d_2 \in S_2} sim(d_1, d_2)$. The algorithm that uses this measure is called *nearest-neighbor clustering*.

- The *minimum similarity* between documents from each cluster: that is, $sim(S_1, S_2) = \min_{d_1 \in S_1, d_2 \in S_2} sim(d_1, d_2)$. The algorithm that uses this measure is called *farthest-neighbor clustering*.

- The *average similarity* between documents from each cluster: that is, $sim(S_1, S_2) = (1/|S_1||S_2|)\sum_{d_1 \in S_1, d_2 \in S_2} sim(d_1, d_2)$.

Note that as defined above, the similarity between clusters also works for individual documents, because each document $d$ can be represented as a singleton cluster $\{d\}$.

One of the objectives of clustering is to *maximize the similarity between documents within clusters (intracluster similarity)*. The similarity between clusters that are merged decreases with climbing up the hierarchy and reaches its lowest value at the top (see the dendrogram in Figure 3.1). Therefore, to obtain a better overall quality of clustering we may want to stop the process of merging clusters at some level of the hierarchy before reaching the top. To implement this idea, *control parameters* can be introduced. There two options for such parameters: to stop merging when a desired number of clusters is reached or when the similarity between the clusters to be merged becomes less than a specified threshold. The *agglomerative clustering algorithm* defined below uses two control parameters ($k$ and $q$) that account for both options:

1. $G \leftarrow \{\{d\} | d \in S\}$ (initialize $G$ with singleton clusters, each containing a document from $S$).

2. If $|G| \leq k$, then exit (stop if the desired number of clusters is reached).

3. Find $S_i, S_j \in G$ such that $(i, j) = \arg\max_{(i,j)} sim(S_i, S_j)$ (find the two closest clusters).

4. If $sim(S_i, S_j) < q$, exit (stop if the similarity of the closest clusters is less than $q$).

5. Remove $S_i$ and $S_j$ from $G$.

6. $G = G \cup \{S_i, S_j\}$ (merge $S_i$ and $S_j$, and add the new cluster to the hierarchy).

7. Go to step 2.

$S$ is the initial set of documents. The algorithm terminates in step 2 or 4 when the stopping conditions are satisfied and returns the clustering in $G$. If $k = 1$ and $q = 0$, $G$ is the complete clustering tree, including its root. When $k > 1$ there are $k$ top-level clusters. For example, with $k = 3$ or $q = 0.75$ the hierarchy in Figure 3.1 is cut off, so that the top-level clustering includes three clusters: $\{1,2\}$, $\{4,5\}$, and $\{8,10\}$.

To implement agglomerative clustering efficiently we need to compute the similarity between all pairs of document vectors once and for all and to store the results in an interdocument similarity table. Thus, for $n$ documents the *space complexity* of this is $O(n^2)$. It can be shown that the *time complexity* of the algorithm is also $O(n^2)$.

Let us now see how hierarchical agglomerative clustering can help organize a set of web documents. Consider our collection of web pages describing the departments in the CCSU school of Arts and Sciences that we used in Chapter 1 to illustrate web search approaches. We already have the TFIDF vector representation of the documents in this collection. For the agglomerative clustering experiments we shall use all 671 terms as features. Let us first see how the parameter $q$ affects clustering. Table 3.1 shows two horizontal trees representing clusterings obtained with $q = 0$ (left) and $q = 0.04$ (right), both from the nearest-neighbor algorithm ($k$ is set to 0). The documents appear as leaves in the tree. Nodes are numbered sequentially (the root is marked as 1), and next to each node number the similarity between the clusters that are merged into that node is shown in brackets. The level of the hierarchy is indicated by the left indention. Thus, the smaller the indention, the higher the tree level (the root has no indent). The nodes aligned at the same indention are siblings.

With $q = 0$ the algorithm always merges the closest clusters until the root is reached, no matter how low the similarity between them is. By setting $q = 0.04$, we avoid merging clusters with similarity below 0.04. These are clusters (on the left tree) 4 and 6 (that merge in 3) and 3 and 9 (that merge in 2). Thus, we get a hierarchy with four clusters at the highest level (shown on the right tree): 2, 11, 13, and 16. The similarity value at the root is not shown because it applies to two clusters only.

The similarity values suggest that the documents grouped together in clusters at the bottom of the tree are those that are most similar. These clusters are also quite intuitive. For example, Biology and Mathematics (cluster 10, right), grouped with Psychology (cluster 9) and then with Physics (cluster 8), form a nice cluster of similar science disciplines. Another nice grouping is the humanities cluster (4): History, Philosophy, English, and Languages. The advantage of having a hierarchy is that it also works as a flat clustering and at the same time shows the internal structure of the clusters. Thus, the immediate successors of any single node (including the root) represent a flat clustering of the documents at the leaves of the tree rooted at that node.

The hierarchy represents a *generality/specificity relation* between documents based on the terms they contain. For example, each of the History–Philosophy pair (cluster 5), and English–Languages pair (cluster 6) has some overlap of terms representing a common topic, while their parent cluster (4) has an overlap with all documents included, thus representing a more general topic that includes the two subtopics. These observations suggest that hierarchical clustering can be used to create *topic directories*. For example, the cluster of humanities can be seen as a starting point in the process of creating a directory of documents related to humanitarian sciences. The next steps would be to add more documents to the subclusters, which can be done manually or by using the classification approaches discussed later.

It is interesting to see how the type of cluster similarity function affects the clustering results. Table 3.2 shows two clusterings obtained with different cluster

**TABLE 3.1 Hierarchical Agglomerative Clusterings Produced by the Nearest-Neighbor Algorithm[a]**

| $q = 0$ | $q = 0.04$ |
|---|---|
| 1 [0.0224143] | 1 [] |
|  2 [0.0308927] |  2 [0.0554991] |
|   3 [0.0368782] |   3 [0.0662345] |
|    4 [0.0556825] |    4 [0.0864619] |
|     5 [0.129523] |     5 [0.177997] |
|     Art |     History |
|     Theatre |     Philosophy |
|    Geography |    6 [0.186299] |
|   6 [0.0858613] |     English |
|    7 [0.148599] |     Languages |
|     Chemistry |    7 [0.122659] |
|     Music |     Anthropology |
|    8 [0.23571] |     Sociology |
|     Computer |    8 [0.0952722] |
|     Political |     9 [0.163493] |
|  9 [0.0937594] |      10 [0.245171] |
|   10 [0.176625] |      Biology |
|    Communication |      Mathematics |
|    Economics |     Psychology |
|   Justice |    Physics |
| 11 [0.0554991] | 11 [0.0556825] |
|  12 [0.0662345] |  12 [0.129523] |
|   13 [0.0864619] |   Art |
|    14 [0.177997] |   Theatre |
|    History |  Geography |
|    Philosophy | 13 [0.0858613] |
|     15 [0.186299] |  14 [0.148599] |
|    English |   Chemistry |
|    Languages |   Music |
|     16 [0.122659] |   15 [0.23571] |
|    Anthropology |   Computer |
|    Sociology |   Political |
| 17 [0.0952722] |  16 [0.0937594] |
|  18 [0.163493] |   17 [0.176625] |
|   19 [0.245171] |    Communication |
|   Biology |    Economics |
|   Mathematics |   Justice |
|  Psychology | |
| Physics | |
| Average intracluster similarity $= 0.4257$ | Average intracluster similarity $= 0.4516$ |

[a] $q$ is the cluster similarity cut off parameter.

**TABLE 3.2   Hierarchical Agglomerative Clusterings Obtained Using Different Cluster Similarity Functions**

| Farthest Neighbor:<br>$\text{sim}(S_1, S_2) = \max\limits_{d_1 \in S_1, d_2 \in S_2} \text{sim}(d_1, d_2)$ | Intracluster Similarity:<br>$\text{sim}(S) = \frac{1}{|S|^2} \sum\limits_{d_i, d_j \in S} \text{sim}(d_i, d_j)$ |
|---|---|
| 1 [0.098857] | 1 [0.138338] |
|   2 [0.108415] |   2 [0.175903] |
|     3 [0.126011] |     3 [0.237572] |
|       4 [0.129523] |       4 [0.342219] |
|         5 [0.142059] |         5 [0.57103] |
|           6 [0.148069] |           Art |
|             7 [0.148331] |           Psychology |
|               8 [0.148599] |         6 [0.588313] |
|                 9 [0.169039] |           Communication |
|                   10 [0.17462] |           Economics |
|                     11 [0.176625] |       7 [0.39463] |
|                       12 [0.201999] |         8 [0.617855] |
|                         13 [0.202129] |           Computer |
|                           14 [0.223392] |           Political |
|                             15 [0.226308] |         9 [0.622585] |
|                               16 [0.23571] |           Biology |
|                               Computer |           Mathematics |
|                               Political |     10 [0.292074] |
|                         Economics |       11 [0.519653] |
|                         Chemistry |         Justice |
|                         Anthropology |         Theatre |
|                       17 [0.245171] |       12 [0.541863] |
|                         Biology |         Geography |
|                         Mathematics |         Physics |
|                         Communication |     13 [0.209028] |
|                     Physics |       14 [0.323349] |
|                     Psychology |         15 [0.56133] |
|                   Music |           Anthropology |
|               18 [0.177997] |           Sociology |
|                 History |       16 [0.5743] |
|                 Philosophy |         Chemistry |
|             19 [0.186299] |         Music |
|               English |     17 [0.357257] |
|               Languages |       18 [0.588999] |
|         Art |         History |
|       Theatre |         Philosophy |
|     Sociology |     19 [0.59315] |
|   Geography |       English |
| Justice |       Languages |
| Average intracluster similarity $= 0.304475$ | Average intracluster similarity $= 0.434181$ |

similarity functions. The *farthest-neighbor clustering* shows an interesting pattern. Although History and Philosophy, and English and Languages, are paired again (confirming their strong similarity), the rest of the tree is build by repeatedly grouping a cluster with a single document. This is quite typical for this approach when applied to a set of documents with relatively uniform similarity distribution (not too great variations in document-to-document similarity over the entire collection). The explanation is in the way that similarity between clusters is computed. Assume, for example, that the current clustering of four numbers is $\{\{1,2\}, \{3,4\},5\}$. The farthest neighbor will put together $\{3,4\}$ and 5, because the distance between them ($5 - 3 = 2$) is smaller (similarity is bigger) than the distance between $\{1,2\}$ and $\{3,4\}$ ($4 - 1 = 3$), whereas for the nearest-neighbor approach, $\{1,2\}$ and $\{3,4\}$ are at the same distance ($3 - 2 = 1$) as $\{3,4\}$ and 5 ($5 - 4 = 1$).

Generally, the farthest-neighbor algorithm works well when clusters are compact and roughly equal in size, whereas the nearest-neighbor algorithm can deal with irregular cluster sizes but is sensitive to outliers. For example, a small cluster or point between two large and well-separated clusters may serve as a bridge between the latter and thus produce strange results (this is known as the *chain effect*). In fact, the nearest-neighbor and farthest-neighbor algorithms use two extreme approaches to the computation of cluster similarity: the maximum and minimum measures. As in many other cases involving minima and maxima, they tend to be overly sensitive to some irregularities, such as outliers. A solution to these problems is the use of averaging. Two of the similarity functions that we listed earlier use averaging: similarity between centroids and average similarity. Interestingly, both functions provide insights with respect to the *quality of clustering*.

In step 3 of the agglomerative clustering algorithm we find the two most similar clusters, and in step 6 we merge them. When using average similarity, we take pairs of documents from each cluster and compute the average similarity over all such pairs. If, instead, we first merge the clusters and then compute the average pairwise similarity between all documents in the merger, we get a comparable measure of how close the two original clusters were. Most important, this measure also accounts for the compactness of the cluster or the *intracluster similarity*, defined as follows:

$$\text{sim}(S) = \frac{1}{|S|^2} \sum_{d_i, d_j \in S} \text{sim}(d_i, d_j)$$

The intracluster similarity may easily be computed once we have the cluster centroid. Assuming that the document vectors are normalized to unit length and substituting for $\text{sim}(d_i, d_j)$ in the formula above, we can see that the intracluster similarity is the square length of the cluster centroid.

$$\text{sim}(S) = \frac{1}{|S|^2} \sum_{d_i, d_j \in S} d_i \cdot d_j = \left( \frac{1}{|S|} \sum_{d_i \in S} d_i \right) \cdot \left( \frac{1}{|S|} \sum_{d_j \in S} d_j \right) = c \cdot c = \|c\|^2$$

The right clustering tree shown in Figure 3.3 is produced by the intracluster similarity function. The structure of the hierarchy is quite regular (no merges between clusters and single documents) and shows a close range of intracluster similarities for each level of clusters. This reveals a rather uniform distribution of our document vectors in the TFIDF vector space.

Along with several other measures, intracluster similarity is widely used for evaluating clustering quality. To evaluate the overall quality of a clustering hierarchy, we take the *average of intracluster similarity* over all clusters. These measures are shown in the last row of Tables 3.1 and 3.2. They show that the average similarity measure produces the best clustering and that cutting off the hierarchy improves the quality of clustering. In Chapter 4 we discuss other measures for evaluating clustering quality (also called *criterion functions for clustering*).

## *k*-MEANS CLUSTERING

Assume that we know in advance the number of clusters that the algorithm should produce. Then a divisible partitioning strategy would be more appropriate to use because the only decision that needs to be made is how to split clusters. This would also make the method more efficient than agglomerative clustering, where all possible candidates for merging should be evaluated. The best known approach that is based on this idea is *k-means clustering*, a simple and efficient algorithm used by statisticians for decades. The idea is to represent the cluster by the centroid of the documents that belong to that cluster (the centroid of cluster $S$ is defined as $c = (1/|S|) \sum_{d \in S} d$). The cluster membership is determined by finding the most similar cluster centroid for each document.

The algorithm takes a set of documents $S$ and a parameter $k$ representing the desired number of clusters and performs the following steps:

1. Select $k$ documents from $S$ to be used as cluster centroids. This is usually done at random.

2. Assign documents to clusters according to their similarity to the cluster centroids (i.e., for each document, find the most similar centroid and assign that document to the corresponding cluster).

3. For each cluster, recompute the cluster centroid using the newly computed cluster members.

4. Go to step 2 until the process converges (i.e., the same documents are assigned to each cluster in two consecutive iterations or the cluster centroids remain the same).

The key point in the algorithm is step 2. In this step documents are moved between clusters to maximize the intracluster similarity. The criterion function for clustering is based on cluster centroids and is analogous to the *sum of squared errors* in distance-based clustering, which uses the mean. Instead, we use centroids and similarity here. Thus, the function is

$$J = \sum_{i=1}^{k} \sum_{d_l \in D_i} \text{sim}(c_i, d_l)$$

where $c_i$ is the centroid of cluster $D_i$ and sim $(c_i, d_j)$ is the cosine similarity between $c_i$ and $d_j$. Clustering that *maximizes* this function is called *minimum variance clustering* (to avoid confusion, variance is defined with distance and maximizing similarity is equivalent to minimizing distance).

The $k$-means algorithm produces minimum variance clustering but does not guarantee that it always finds the global maximum of the criterion function. After each iteration the value of $J$ increases, but it may converge to a local maximum. Thus, the result depends greatly on the initial choice of cluster centroids. Because this choice is usually made at random, the clusterings obtained may vary from run to run. A simple approach to dealing with this problem is to run the algorithm several times with different random number seeds and then select the clustering that maximizes the criterion function.

Let us illustrate the $k$-means clustering algorithm using our department collection. Running the algorithm on the documents represented with all 671 features gives interesting results. In almost all runs the algorithm converges after only two iterations (for all $k$). This means that the initial choice of centroids in most cases fully determines the clustering; that is, after the first assignment of documents to clusters (step 2), the next assignment based on the newly computed centroids does not change the cluster membership, and thus the algorithm terminates. This behavior of $k$-means is typical for data without well-formed clusters. No wonder this happens with our document collection: The experiments with agglomerative clustering showed that with respect to their similarity, the documents are quite uniformly distributed in the 671-dimensional space.

To make things more interesting, we select six terms which best represent our documents: *history*, *science*, *research*, *offers*, *students*, and *hall*. This selection is made by using an *entropy-based technique* that we discuss in Chapter 5 along with other feature selection methods. For now we need only a representation that separates well the data points in vector space and thus may reveal clusters in the document collection. Table 3.3 shows TFIDF vectors described in this way. Note the difference with the sparsely populated Table 1.5 that we used in Chapter 1.

Let us set $k = 2$; that is, we want to find two clusters in this collection of documents. The algorithm first selects two documents at random as cluster centroids and then iterates assigning and reassigning documents to clusters. Let us, however, select the initial centroids manually so that we see two interesting situations. The first is when we use the two most similar documents for this purpose: Computer Science and Chemistry. Their similarity (simply the dot product, because the vectors are normalized to unit length) is 0.995461. Note that there are many very similar documents, so there is a good chance for this also to happen at random. Table 3.4 shows how clusters and the criterion function change through the iterations.

Initially, the documents selected appear in different clusters (as originally specified), but very soon Chemistry and similar documents are moved to cluster A. Meanwhile, the quality of clustering (the values of the criterion function) increases. The final clustering is unbalanced, however, and only cluster A seems to be compact with respect to document similarity. Cluster B is large and quite sparse; it includes vectors that are orthogonal, such as Criminal Justice and Economics (and many others, too) as well as very close documents, such as English and Modern Languages (similarity

**TABLE 3.3 TFDF Representation of the Department Document Collection with Six Attributes**

|  | *history* | *science* | *research* | *offers* | *students* | *hall* |
|---|---|---|---|---|---|---|
| Anthropology | 0 | 0.537 | 0.477 | 0 | 0.673 | 0.177 |
| Art | 0 | 0 | 0 | 0.961 | 0.195 | 0.196 |
| Biology | 0 | 0.347 | 0.924 | 0 | 0.111 | 0.112 |
| Chemistry | 0 | 0.975 | 0 | 0 | 0.155 | 0.158 |
| Communication | 0 | 0 | 0 | 0.780 | 0.626 | 0 |
| Computer Science | 0 | 0.989 | 0 | 0 | 0.130 | 0.067 |
| Criminal Justice | 0 | 0 | 0 | 0 | 1 | 0 |
| Economics | 0 | 0 | 1 | 0 | 0 | 0 |
| English | 0 | 0 | 0 | 0.980 | 0 | 0.199 |
| Geography | 0 | 0.849 | 0 | 0 | 0.528 | 0 |
| History | 0.991 | 0 | 0 | 0.135 | 0 | 0 |
| Mathematics | 0 | 0.616 | 0.549 | 0.490 | 0.198 | 0.201 |
| Modern Languages | 0 | 0 | 0 | 0.928 | 0 | 0.373 |
| Music | 0.970 | 0 | 0 | 0 | 0.170 | 0.172 |
| Philosophy | 0.741 | 0 | 0 | 0.658 | 0 | 0.136 |
| Physics | 0 | 0 | 0.894 | 0 | 0.315 | 0.318 |
| Political Science | 0 | 0.933 | 0.348 | 0 | 0.062 | 0.063 |
| Psychology | 0 | 0 | 0.852 | 0.387 | 0.313 | 0.162 |
| Sociology | 0 | 0 | 0.639 | 0.570 | 0.459 | 0.237 |
| Theatre | 0 | 0 | 0 | 0 | 0.967 | 0.254 |

**TABLE 3.4 *k*-Means Clustering with a Bad Choice of Initial Cluster Centroids**

| Iteration | Cluster *A* | Cluster *B* | Criterion Function J |
|---|---|---|---|
| 1 | {Computer Science, Political Science} | {Anthropology, Art, Biology, Chemistry, Communication, Criminal Justice, Economics, English, Geography, History, Mathematics, Modern Languages, Music, Philosophy, Physics, Psychology, Sociology, Theatre} | 1.93554 (cluster *A*) + 4.54975 (cluster *B*) = 6.48529 |
| 2 | {Chemistry, Computer Science, Geography, Political Science} | {Anthropology, Art, Biology, Communication, Criminal Justice, Economics, English, History, Mathematics, Modern Languages, Music, Philosophy, Physics, Psychology, Sociology, Theatre} | 3.82736 (cluster *A*) + 10.073 (cluster *B*) = 13.9003 |
| 3 | {Anthropology, Chemistry, Computer Science, Geography, Political Science} | {Art, Biology, Communication, Criminal Justice, Economics, English, History, Mathematics, Modern Languages, Music, Philosophy, Physics, Psychology, Sociology, Theatre} | 4.60125 (cluster *A*) + 9.51446 (cluster *B*) = 14.1157 |

**TABLE 3.5** *k*-Means Clustering with a Good Choice of Initial Cluster Centroids

| Iteration | Cluster *A* | Cluster *B* | Criterion Function J |
|---|---|---|---|
| 1 | {Anthropology, Biology, Economics, Mathematics, Physics, Political Science, Psychology} | {Art, Chemistry, Communication, Computer Science, Criminal Justice, English, Geography, History, Modern Languages, Music, Philosophy, Sociology, Theatre} | 5.04527 (cluster *A*) + 5.99025 (cluster *B*) = 11.0355 |
| 2 | {Anthropology, Biology, Computer Science, Economics, Mathematics, Physics, Political Science, Psychology, Sociology} | {Art, Chemistry, Communication, Criminal Justice, English, Geography, History, Modern Languages, Music, Philosophy, Theatre} | 7.23827 (cluster *A*) + 6.70864 (cluster *B*) = 13.9469 |
| 3 | {Anthropology, Biology, Chemistry, Computer Science, Economics, Geography, Mathematics, Physics, Political Science, Psychology, Sociology} | {Art, Communication, Criminal Justice, English, History, Modern Languages, Music, Philosophy, Theatre} | 8.53381 (cluster *A*) + 6.12743 (cluster *B*) = 14.6612 |

0.98353). This is obviously a bad choice of initial cluster centroids, which in turn illustrates well how sensitive the *k*-means algorithm is to any irregularities in data (something that is true for all search algorithms that use local criterion functions).

For the second run we choose two least similar documents: Economics and Art. Their similarity is 0, because they are orthogonal (in fact, there are more orthogonal vectors in our data; see Table 3.3). Table 3.5 shows how the clusters are built around these two documents in three iterations. Obviously, this choice of cluster centroids is better because the clusters are compact and well balanced by size and content. Cluster A collects all natural science–like documents, whereas cluster B collects the artlike documents. Obviously, the choice of cluster centroids is quite good; the initial value of the *J* function is high and does not change much through the iterations. The better quality of this clustering is also indicated by the bigger final value of the criterion function compared with the previous run. So it seems that this split of our department collection makes sense, and we shall be using it in the next chapters for document labeling and supervised learning.

Thinking of our primary goal in this chapter, organizing the web content, the clustering experiment shown in Table 3.5 can be seen as an example of *creating a web directory*. Assume that we know the topics of a small set of documents in a large collection. Then we can use documents from this set as cluster centroids and run *k*-means on the entire collection to obtain subsets according to the given topics. A similar approach based on similarity but with labeled documents (nearest-neighbor classification) is discussed in the context of supervised learning in Chapter 5. The $k$-means clustering algorithm is very popular because it is simple, efficient, and works well in practice, especially when the clusters are big, balanced, and well separated. By applying the algorithm recursively to the clusters obtained, $k$-means can easily be extended to produce hierarchical clustering.

Although we have described agglomerative and $k$-means clustering as based on *cosine similarity* between TFIDF vectors, these algorithms also work with other similarity functions. Two additional similarity measures based on document content have been discussed in Chapter 1: *Jaccard similarity* and *document resemblance*. The latter is especially useful for clustering large portions of the Web, because it scales up well and allows document resemblance to be computed efficiently using document *sketches*.

Similarity can also be defined by using the link structure of web pages. In Chapter 2 we outlined an approach to find similar pages based on the HITS algorithm for computing hubs and authorities. Link-based similarity can be defined in other ways, too. If $d_1$ and $d_2$ are nodes (documents) in the web graph, the similarity between them can be defined to be:

- The length of the shortest path between $d_1$ and $d_2$
- The number of common ancestors of (pages with links to both) $d_1$ and $d_2$
- Number of common successors of (pages that are pointed by links in both) $d_1$ and $d_2$

One common approach to computing the overall similarity is to take the maximum of the content similarity (cosine, Jaccard, or resemblance) and a weighted sum of the link-based similarities mentioned above.

## PROBABILTY-BASED CLUSTERING

In probability-based clustering, a document is considered as a random event that occurs according to different probability distributions depending on the cluster (or class[1]) to which the document belongs. The parameters involved in this setting are:

- The document class labels (may be known or unknown)
- The parameters of the probability distribution for each cluster
- The way that terms are used in the document representation

The last two parameters are related because the terms are considered as random variables, and the type of the latter determines the type of the probability distributions used to model documents. Generally, there are three ways that a term can be used in this model:

---

[1] Here we use the terms *class* and *cluster* interchangeably depending on the context. Both terms mean "topic" (or "category"), but if the labels are determined by using the group to which the document belongs, we use *cluster*, otherwise we use *class*.

1. As a *binary variable*, taking value 0 or 1 depending on whether or not the term occurs in the document. This is the *multivariate binary model*, where documents are binary vectors following a *multivariate binary distribution*.

2. As a *natural number*, indicating the number of occurrences (frequency) of the term in the document. In this representation a document is a *vector of natural numbers* and its probability is computed according to the *multinominal distribution*.

3. A normally distributed *continuous variable* taking TFIDF values. The documents in this representation are TFIDF vectors (described in the section "Vector Space Model" in Chapter 1) following a *multivariate normal distribution*.

The binary and multinominal distributions use the underlying document models directly: *set-of-words*, and *bag-of-words*, respectively. Both ignore *ordering* between terms but do not use much preprocessing, which may cause further loss of information or misrepresentation. Therefore, they are considered more natural than the TFIDF representation. It is also assumed that the probabilistic models take into account the importance of the terms (which the IDF measure accounts for) and can even capture the notion of stopwords.

All three models are commonly used for both probabilistic clustering and classification. Hereafter we illustrate the probabilistic clustering with the TFIDF model. The binary and multinominal models are discussed in Chapter 5 in the context of classification. The reason for this choice is the popularity of the normal distribution and the fact that it works not only for documents but in many other domains, too. It also has a nice visual representation that makes the approach easy to understand.

To start with, let us pick a term and represent each of our documents with a single value, the TFIDF component in the document vector that corresponds to that term. Because this value may describe documents of different classes (clusters), it may have different distributions. Thus, in a collection of documents from different classes we have a mixture of different distributions. In statistics this is called a *finite mixture model* (finite, because we assume a finite number of distributions). An example of a single-attribute two-class mixture is shown in Figure 3.2.

The data include the list of values of the term *offers* taken from our department collection (see Table 3.3). The label (*A* or *B*) corresponds to the cluster, where the document with that value of *offers* belongs to according to the *k*-means clustering shown in Table 3.5. Thus, we have a mixture of two *normal (Gaussian) distributions*. The graphs shown next to the data in Figure 3.2 are plots of the *probability density functions (bell-shaped curves)* for these distributions. The distributions are defined by their *mean* and *standard deviations*. The mixture model also includes the *probability of sampling* for each class (the probability that a random value belongs to a particular class). All these parameters are also shown in Figure 3.2. Using the mixture model, we can define three problems: a *finite mixture problem*, a *classification problem*, and a *clustering problem*.

## Finite Mixture Problem

Given a *labeled data set* (i.e., we know the class for each attribute value) the problem is to find the mean, standard deviation, and the probability of sampling for each

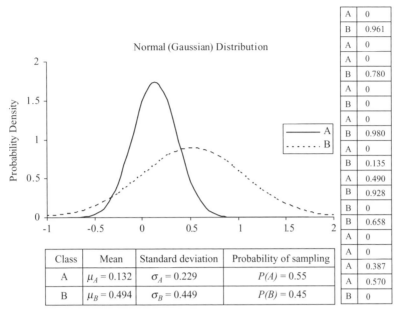

Normal (Gaussian) Distribution

| | |
|---|---|
| A | 0 |
| B | 0.961 |
| A | 0 |
| A | 0 |
| B | 0.780 |
| A | 0 |
| B | 0 |
| A | 0 |
| B | 0.980 |
| A | 0 |
| B | 0.135 |
| A | 0.490 |
| B | 0.928 |
| B | 0 |
| B | 0.658 |
| A | 0 |
| A | 0 |
| A | 0.387 |
| A | 0.570 |
| B | 0 |

| Class | Mean | Standard deviation | Probability of sampling |
|---|---|---|---|
| A | $\mu_A = 0.132$ | $\sigma_A = 0.229$ | $P(A) = 0.55$ |
| B | $\mu_B = 0.494$ | $\sigma_B = 0.449$ | $P(B) = 0.45$ |

**Figure 3.2**   Two-class mixture model for the term *offers*.

cluster. The solution to this problem is a straightforward application of the formulas. The *mean* $\mu_C$ for each class $C$ is the average value of the attribute (variable $x$) for documents belonging to that class:

$$\mu_C = \frac{1}{|C|} \sum_{x \in C} x$$

For our department data set we take all values with label $A$ (Figure 3.2) and compute

$$\mu_A = \tfrac{1}{11}(0 + 0 + 0 + 0 + 0 + 0 + 0.49 + 0 + 0 + 0.387 + 0.57) = 0.132$$

Similarly, for documents labeled $B$, we have

$$\mu_B = \tfrac{1}{9}(0.961 + 0.780 + 0 + 0.980 + 0.135 + 0.928 + 0 + 0.658 + 0) = 0.494$$

The *standard deviation* formula is

$$\sigma_C = \sqrt{\frac{1}{|C|} \sum_{x \in C} (x - \mu_C)^2}$$

In practice, however, the square root of the bias-corrected variance is used (the only difference being that the denominator is $|C| - 1$). Thus, for our data set we have $\sigma_A = 0.229$ and $\sigma_B = 0.449$.

   *The probability of sampling* $P(C)$ is computed as the proportion of instances in class $C$ to the size of the entire data set. That is,

$$P(A) = \tfrac{11}{20} = 0.55 \qquad P(B) = \tfrac{9}{20} = 0.45$$

The set of parameters we computed above actually describes our data set. In terms of clustering, each tuple $\langle \mu_C, \sigma_C, P(C) \rangle$ is a *generative document model* of cluster $C$.

## Classification Problem

Assume that we have already computed the mixture model for the attribute *offers*. That is, the three parameters $\mu_C$, $\sigma_C$, and $P(C)$ are known for each class $C$. The problem now is to find the *classification of a document* which has a given value $x$ for the attribute *offers*. To solve the problem we need to decide from which distribution the value $x$ comes, cluster $A$ or $B$, which in turn will allow us to classify the document accordingly. The idea is to compute the *conditional probabilities* $P(A \mid x)$ and $P(B \mid x)$. Then the distribution that has the biggest probability is the one that $x$ comes from.

If $x$ comes from a *discrete distribution* (such as the binary distribution we discussed earlier), we may easily compute $P(C \mid x)$ by applying *Bayes' rule*:

$$P(C \mid x) = \frac{P(x \mid C) P(C)}{P(x)}$$

where $P(C)$ is known from the mixture model and $P(x \mid C)$ is the probability of $x$ according to the document distribution in cluster $C$. Then the probability $P(x \mid C)$ would simply be the number of occurrences of $x$ in cluster $C$ divided by the total number of documents in $C$. We use this approach later for classification. In the current situation, however, $x$ is the value of a *continuous random variable*. Then, strictly speaking, the probability of a continuous random variable being *exactly equal* to any particular real value is zero. A practical solution to this problem is to use the value of the probability *density function* instead. That is,

$$f_C(x) = \frac{1}{\sqrt{2\pi}\,\sigma_C} e^{-(x-\mu_C)^2/2\sigma_C^2}$$

Of course, this is not exactly the probability we need, but it appears that it works for our purposes. The reason is that in practice we never know the exact value of a variable. Moreover, in computer arithmetic we always have some degree of approximation. Then instead of $P(x \mid C)$, we may use $P(x - \varepsilon \leq x \leq x + \varepsilon \mid C)$, where $\varepsilon$ is the accuracy of computation. To compute the latter, we may now use the *density function* for class $C$. This is the area under the bell-shaped curve between the points $x - \varepsilon$ and $x + \varepsilon$, which for small $\varepsilon$ is $2\varepsilon f_C(x)$. However, as we don't know the accuracy $\varepsilon$ (and also because it is the same for all classes), we may simply ignore it and use the value of the density function $f_C(x)$ instead, as an estimate of the *likelihood* that $x$ comes from distribution $C$. Thus, we arrive at a formula that works for the continuous case (note that we use the symbol $\approx$ instead of $=$):

$$P(C \mid x) \approx \frac{f_C(x) P(C)}{P(x)}$$

One may think that computing $P(x)$ causes similar problems; however, we don't need this probability because it appears in the expressions for all classes. We may calculate only the numerators and thus compare likelihoods instead of probabilities. Further, because the probabilities sum up to 1 $[P(A \mid x) + P(B \mid x) = 1]$, we may normalize the likelihoods by their sum. Then we will have the correct probabilities.

Let us illustrate the classification problem with a simple example. Assume that we don't know the class label of Communication. The value of the *offers* attribute for this document is 0.78 (the fifth row in the data table in Figure 3.2). Thus, the problem is to compute $P(A \mid 0.78)$ and $P(B \mid 0.78)$, and whichever is bigger will determine the class label of Communication. Plugging 0.78 and the corresponding values for $\mu_A$, $\sigma_A$ and $\mu_B$, $\sigma_B$ (from Figure 3.2) in the formula for $f_C(x)$, we get $f_A(0.78) = 0.032$ and $f_B(0.78) = 0.725$. Then

$$P(A|0.78) \approx f_A(0.78)P(A) = (0.032)(0.55) = 0.018$$

$$P(B|0.78) \approx f_B(0.78)P(B) = (0.725)(0.45) = 0.326$$

These likelihoods clearly indicate that the value 0.78 comes from the distribution of cluster $B$ (i.e., the Communication document belongs to class B). Further, we can easily get the actual probabilities by normalization:

$$P(A \mid 0.78) = \frac{0.018}{0.018 + 0.326} = 0.05$$

$$P(B \mid 0.78) = \frac{0.326}{0.018 + 0.326} = 0.95$$

In fact, this classification is quite clear if we look at the plot of the densities in Figure 3.2; the value of 0.78 is well under the "bell" of distribution $B$.

Let us, however, try another value, which may not be that conclusive for the classification problem. Looking at the data table in Figure 3.2, we see that a value of 0 clearly cannot distinguish between the two classes. There are eight 0's labeled with $A$ and three 0's labeled with $B$. Doing the actual calculations results in $P(A \mid 0) = 0.788$ and $P(B \mid 0) = 0.212$. Thus, all documents will be classified as $A$, which means three wrongly classified documents: Criminal Justice, Music, and Theatre (originally labeled as $B$). Obviously, one attribute is not enough to make a correct classification.

The mixture model can easily be extended to more than one attribute provided that the *independence assumption* is made. It states that the joint probability of all attributes in a vector is calculated as a product of the probabilities of the individual attributes; that is,

$$P(x_1, x_2, ..., x_n \mid C) = \prod_{i=1}^{n} P(x_i \mid C)$$

In terms of *probability theory* this means that the events of different attributes having particular values are *independent*. For example, knowing the value of *science* in the Music document should not tell us anything about the values of the other attributes in that document. This may not be true, however. In the particular example, if *science* is 0, we may expect that *research* is also 0 (because they often go together). In fact, the independence assumption rarely holds (or it is difficult to prove, as this would require a large amount of data), but despite that, the formula above works well in practice. This is the reason that the independence assumption is also called *naive Bayes assumption*. It plays a key role in the *naive Bayes classification algorithm*, which we just described. We shall revisit this algorithm in Chapter 5 and illustrate its use with different distributions, as we mentioned earlier.

Using the same idea as in the one-dimensional case, we may estimate the likelihood of the vector using the density functions for its components:

$$P(C \mid (x_1, x_2, ..., x_n)) \approx \prod_{i=1}^{n} f_C^i(x_i) \frac{P(C)}{P((x_1, x_2, ..., x_n))}$$

Let us now illustrate how to use the naive Bayes assumption to classify the Theatre document by using more attributes. The six-dimensional vector for Theatre is $(0,0,0,0,0.967,0.254)$. Then the problem is to compute the probabilities $P(A \mid (0, 0, 0, 0, 0.976, 0254))$ and $P(B \mid (0, 0, 0, 0, 0.976, 0254))$. For estimating the probabilities with likelihoods, we use the density functions for six attributes: *history*, *science*, *research*, *offers*, *students*, and *hall*. Thus, we have

$$P(A \mid (0, 0, 0, 0, 0.976, 0.254) \approx \frac{f_A^1(0)f_A^2(0)f_A^3(0)f_A^4(0)f_A^5(0.976)f_A^6(0.254)P(A)}{P((0, 0, 0, 0, 0.976, 0254))}$$

where $f_A^1$ through $f_A^6$ are the density functions of the attributes in the order in which they are listed above. To compute these functions we need to compute the means and the standard deviations for each of these attributes within cluster $A$. However, when computing $f_A^1(0)$, we run into a little problem. The density function is undefined for *history*, because its standard deviation is 0 (all values in cluster $A$ are the same). There are different approaches to solving this problem. The simplest is to assume a prespecified minimum value, say 0.05, which results in $f_A^1(0) = 7.979$. After completing the calculations, we have

$$P(A \mid (0, 0, 0, 0, 0.976, 0.254))$$
$$\approx (7.979)(0.5)(0.423)(1.478)(0.007)(1.978)(0.55) = 0.019$$

Similarly, by using the parameters for cluster $B$ (using the same fix for the zero deviations of *science* and *research*), we compute the likelihood of class B.

$$P(B \mid (0, 0, 0, 0, 0.976, 0.254))$$
$$\approx (0.705)(7.979)(7.979)(0.486)(0.698)(1.604)(0.45) = 10.99$$

After normalization we have the following probabilities:

$$P(B \mid (0, 0, 0, 0, 0.976, 0.254)) = \frac{0.019}{0.019 + 10.99} = 0.002$$

$$P(B \mid (0, 0, 0, 0, 0.976, 0.254)) = \frac{10.99}{0.019 + 10.99} = 0.998$$

Clearly, the Theatre document belongs to class B, which is now the correct classification because this is its original cluster.

## Clustering Problem

So far we have discussed two tasks associated with our probabilistic setting: *learning* (creating models given labeled data) and *classification* (predicting labels using models). Recall, however, that the cluster labels were created automatically by $k$-means clustering. So a natural question is whether we can also get these labels automatically within a probabilistic setting.

*Expectation maximization* (EM) is a popular algorithm used for clustering in the context of mixture models. EM was originally proposed by Demster et al. [2] for the purposes of estimating missing parameters of probabilistic models. Generally, this is an *optimization approach*, which given some initial approximation of the cluster parameters, *iteratively* performs two steps: first, the expectation step computes the values expected for the cluster probabilities, and second, the maximization step computes the distribution parameters and their likelihood given the data. It iterates until the parameters being optimized reach a fixpoint or until the *log-likelihood function*, which measures the quality of clustering, reaches its (local) maximum.

To simplify the discussion we first describe the one-dimensional case (i.e., the data collection is a set of values $x_1$, $x_2$, ..., $x_n$ of a normally distributed random variable). The algorithm takes a parameter $k$ (predefined number of clusters, as in $k$-means) and starts with selecting (usually at random) a set of initial cluster parameters $\mu_C$, $\sigma_C$, and $P(C)$ for each cluster $C$. It can also start by assigning labels to the data points (again, at random), which will determine the cluster parameters (as was done earlier for the mixture problem). Then the algorithm iterates through the following steps:

1. For each $x_i$ and for each cluster $C$, the probability $w_i = P(C \mid x_i)$ that $x_i$ belongs to cluster $C$ is computed. For this purpose the likelihood of this event is obtained using the approach described in the preceding section; that is, $w_i \approx f_C(x_i)P(C)$, where $f_C(x_i)$ is the density function. As the members of each cluster are not known explicitly, $P(C)$ is computed as the sum of the weights $w_i$ (from the preceding step) for cluster $C$ normalized across all clusters. Likelihoods $w_i$ are also normalized across clusters in order to get the correct probabilities.

2. The standard formulas for mean and standard deviation are adjusted to use the cluster membership probabilities $w_i$ as weights. Thus, the following *weighted mean* and *standard deviation* are computed:

$$\mu_C = \frac{\sum_{i=1}^{n} w_i\, x_i}{\sum_{i=1}^{n} w_i}$$

$$\sigma_C^2 = \frac{\sum_{i=1}^{n} w_i\, (x_i - \mu_C)^2}{\sum_{i=1}^{n} w_i}$$

Note that the sums go for all values, not only for those belonging to the corresponding cluster. Thus, given a sample size $n$, we have an $n$-component weight vector for each cluster.

The iterative process is similar to that of $k$-means; the data points are redistributed among clusters repeatedly until the process reaches a fixpoint. The $k$-means algorithm stops when the cluster membership does not change from one iteration to the next. $k$-Means uses "hard"[2] cluster assignment, however, whereas the EM uses

---

[2] In fact, there exist versions of $k$-means with soft assignment, which are special cases of EM.

"soft" assignment—probability of membership. Consequently, EM may not be able to reach the actual fixpoint; although it converges to it, the probabilities may keep changing forever. Another indication that the algorithm is close to the fixpoint is when the *criterion function* that measures the quality of clustering reaches a maximum. For our probabilistic setting, this is the overall likelihood that the data come from distributions defined with the parameters given. The overall likelihood is computed as a product of the probabilities of all individual data points $x_i$. As this product may include thousands of terms, we usually take a log to smooth its value and avoid possible underflow. Thus, we get the *log-likelihood criterion function*:

$$L = \sum_{i=1}^{n} \log \sum_{A} P(x_i \mid A) P(A)$$

Practically, each log is taken from the sum of the $w_i$ values for the corresponding cluster, but before normalization (otherwise, the sum will be 1 and the log will be 0).

After each iteration the value of $L$ increases, and when the difference between two successive values becomes negligible, the algorithm stops. It is guaranteed that the algorithm converges to a maximum of the log-likelihood function. This may be a local maximum, however. To find the global maximum we may use the same technique that was suggested for $k$-means—run the algorithm several times with different initial parameters and choose the clustering that maximizes the log-likelihoods from each run.

To illustrate the approach discussed so far, let us run the EM algorithm on a sample from our department data with one attribute: *students*. Thus, we have a vector $(x_1, x_2, \ldots, x_{20})$ with values taken from the row *students* in Table 3.3. Let us also choose $k = 2$; that is, we want to find two clusters $A$ and $B$ defined probabilistically with their sets of parameters $\{\mu_A, \sigma_A, P(A)\}$ and $\{\mu_B, \sigma_B, P(B)\}$. First, we need to choose the initial cluster parameters. Let us use the labeling approach for this purpose. For each value $x_i$ we toss a coin, and if it is a head, we assign label $A$; otherwise, we assign label $B$. In other words, we initialize the weight vectors for clusters $A$ and $B$ with 1's and 0's, thus determining the probabilities of cluster membership for each $x_i$. Using the initial weight vectors, the algorithm computes the cluster parameters, the weighted versions of $\mu_A, \sigma_A, P(A)$ and $\mu_B, \sigma_B, P(B)$. In the next step these parameters are used to recompute the weight vectors, which further, will determine the new cluster parameters, and so on. At each step the log-likelihood function is computed so that the iterations stop when its maximum is reached. The entire process with the values of all parameters involved is shown in Table 3.6.

The first column shows the data vector $(x_1, x_2, \ldots, x_{20})$. The next column (iteration 0) shows the initial setting with the random choice of values for the weight vectors of clusters $A$ and $B$ and the corresponding cluster parameters (in the lower four rows): sum of weights, cluster probabilities (computed by normalizing the sum of weights), weighted mean, and standard deviation. These parameters are used to compute the weight vectors for iteration 1. The latter determine the cluster parameters for iteration 1, which in turn are used to compute the weights for iteration 2, and so on. In these terms the expectation step of the algorithm is the computation of the weight

**TABLE 3.6 EM Iterations on One-Attribute Data (Attribute *students*)**

| Iteration: | | 0 | | 1 | | 2 | | 3 | | 4 | | 5 | | 6 | |
| Data: | | $w_i$ | | $w_i$ | | $w_i$ | | $w_i$ | | $w_i$ | | $w_i$ | | $w_i$ | |
| $i$ | $x_i$ | A | B | A | B | A | B | A | B | A | B | A | B | A | B |
|---|---|---|---|---|---|---|---|---|---|---|---|---|---|---|---|
| 1 | 0.67 | **1** | 0 | **0.99** | 0.01 | **1** | 0 | **1** | 0 | **1** | 0 | **1** | 0 | **1** | 0 |
| 2 | 0.19 | **1** | 0 | 0.4 | **0.6** | 0.35 | **0.65** | 0.29 | **0.71** | 0.26 | **0.74** | 0.23 | **0.77** | 0.21 | **0.79** |
| 3 | 0.11 | 0 | **1** | 0.41 | **0.59** | 0.29 | **0.71** | 0.19 | **0.81** | 0.13 | **0.87** | 0.1 | **0.9** | 0.09 | **0.91** |
| 4 | 0.15 | 0 | **1** | 0.39 | **0.61** | 0.31 | **0.69** | 0.23 | **0.77** | 0.18 | **0.82** | 0.15 | **0.85** | 0.13 | **0.87** |
| 5 | 0.63 | **1** | 0 | **0.99** | 0.01 | **1** | 0 | **1** | 0 | **1** | 0 | **1** | 0 | **1** | 0 |
| 6 | 0.13 | 0 | **1** | 0.4 | **0.6** | 0.3 | **0.7** | 0.2 | **0.8** | 0.15 | **0.85** | 0.12 | **0.88** | 0.1 | **0.9** |
| 7 | 1 | **1** | 0 | **1** | 0 | **1** | 0 | **1** | 0 | **1** | 0 | **1** | 0 | **1** | 0 |
| 8 | 0 | 0 | **1** | **0.53** | 0.47 | 0.35 | **0.65** | 0.22 | **0.78** | 0.14 | **0.86** | 0.1 | **0.9** | 0.08 | **0.92** |
| 9 | 0 | **1** | 0 | **0.53** | 0.47 | 0.35 | **0.65** | 0.22 | **0.78** | 0.14 | **0.86** | 0.1 | **0.9** | 0.08 | **0.92** |
| 10 | 0.53 | **1** | 0 | **0.92** | 0.08 | **0.99** | 0.01 | **1** | 0 | **1** | 0 | **1** | 0 | **1** | 0 |
| 11 | 0 | **1** | 0 | **0.53** | 0.47 | 0.35 | **0.65** | 0.22 | **0.78** | 0.14 | **0.86** | 0.1 | **0.9** | 0.08 | **0.92** |
| 12 | 0.2 | **1** | 0 | 0.4 | **0.6** | 0.35 | **0.65** | 0.3 | **0.7** | 0.26 | **0.74** | 0.24 | **0.76** | 0.22 | **0.78** |
| 13 | 0 | **1** | 0 | **0.53** | 0.47 | 0.35 | **0.65** | 0.22 | **0.78** | 0.14 | **0.86** | 0.1 | **0.9** | 0.08 | **0.92** |
| 14 | 0.17 | 0 | **1** | 0.39 | **0.61** | 0.32 | **0.68** | 0.25 | **0.75** | 0.2 | **0.8** | 0.17 | **0.83** | 0.15 | **0.85** |
| 15 | 0 | **1** | 0 | **0.53** | 0.47 | 0.35 | **0.65** | 0.22 | **0.78** | 0.14 | **0.86** | 0.1 | **0.9** | 0.08 | **0.92** |
| 16 | 0.31 | **1** | 0 | **0.52** | 0.48 | **0.61** | 0.39 | **0.72** | 0.28 | **0.8** | 0.2 | **0.83** | 0.17 | **0.84** | 0.16 |
| 17 | 0.06 | **1** | 0 | 0.45 | **0.55** | 0.3 | **0.7** | 0.18 | **0.82** | 0.12 | **0.88** | 0.09 | **0.91** | 0.07 | **0.93** |
| 18 | 0.31 | 0 | **1** | **0.51** | 0.49 | **0.61** | 0.39 | **0.71** | 0.29 | **0.79** | 0.21 | **0.82** | 0.18 | **0.84** | 0.16 |
| 19 | 0.46 | 0 | **1** | **0.82** | 0.18 | **0.95** | 0.05 | **0.99** | 0.01 | **1** | 0 | **1** | 0 | **1** | 0 |
| 20 | 0.97 | **1** | 0 | **1** | 0 | **1** | 0 | **1** | 0 | **1** | 0 | **1** | 0 | **1** | 0 |
| $\sum w_i$ | | 13 | 7 | 12.2 | 7.8 | 11.1 | 8.9 | 10.2 | 9.8 | 9.6 | 10.4 | 9.2 | 10.8 | 9.1 | 10.9 |
| Cluster probability | | 0.65 | 0.35 | 0.61 | 0.39 | 0.56 | 0.44 | 0.51 | 0.49 | 0.48 | 0.52 | 0.46 | 0.54 | 0.45 | 0.55 |
| Weighted $\lambda$ | | 0.35 | 0.19 | 0.40 | 0.14 | 0.44 | 0.11 | 0.49 | 0.10 | 0.52 | 0.09 | 0.54 | 0.09 | 0.55 | 0.09 |
| Weighted $\sigma$ | | 0.35 | 0.14 | 0.34 | 0.12 | 0.33 | 0.10 | 0.32 | 0.09 | 0.31 | 0.09 | 0.30 | 0.09 | 0.29 | 0.09 |
| Log-likelihood | | -2.92201 | | -1.29017 | | -0.099039 | | 0.47888 | | 0.697056 | | 0.769124 | | 0.792324 | |

81

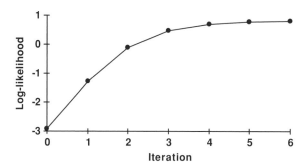

**Figure 3.3**  Log-likelihood graph for the example in Table 3.6.

vectors (including the initial vector, which is determined as a random expectation), while the maximization step is the computation of cluster parameters, which is based on the probabilities expected (the weights) and is aimed at maximizing them.

The last row in Table 3.6 shows the values of the log-likelihood function, which measures the overall clustering quality and is also used as a stopping condition. A graph of the function is shown in Figure 3.3. We see a sharp increase over the first few iterations and then a slower increase in the later iterations, which is an indication that the function reaches its (local) maximum. By setting a threshold of 0.03 for the difference between two successive values of the log-likelihood, we can make the algorithm stop at iteration 6.

The cluster parameters and weights show similar behavior: big changes over the first few iterations and quick convergence in the later steps. This is also the most commonly observed behavior of the EM algorithm in practice; generally, it converges to a fixpoint very quickly, but unfortunately, the fixpoint may be a local maximum. As we have already mentioned, the fix is to restart the algorithm several times with different initial choice for the weights, and then choose the clustering that maximizes the log-likelihood function.

So far we have examined probabilities only, but we can also see the actual partitioning of documents into clusters. By determining the bigger one of the two weights (i.e., probabilities) we can obtain the cluster membership of each $x_i$: cluster $A$ or cluster $B$ (the maximal $w_i$ in each pair is printed in boldface in Table 3.6). For example, $x_8 = 0$ belongs to cluster $B$ in iteration 0 (with probability 1) and to cluster $A$ in iteration 1 (with probability 0.53). By looking back at the document vectors to which these values belong, we obtain the document clusters. Thus, the initial (random) clustering is

$A = \{$Anthropology, Art, Communication, Justice, English, Geography, History, Mathematics, Languages, Philosophy, Physics, Political, Theatre$\}$

$B = \{$Biology, Chemistry, Computer, Economics, Music, Psychology, Sociology$\}$

and the final one (after iteration 6) is

$A = \{$Anthropology, Communication, Justice, Geography, Physics,
        Psychology, Sociology, Theatre$\}$

$B = \{$Art, Biology, Chemistry, Computer, Economics, English, History,
        Mathematics, Music, Languages, Philosophy, Political$\}$

However, keeping in mind our general objective, organizing documents by topic, the final clustering looks far from the natural document grouping that we may have expected to see (e.g., the one obtained from $k$-means, shown in Table 3.5). And the obvious reason for this is that we have used only one attribute to describe our documents: the term *students*. Fortunately, the EM algorithm can also easily handle multiple attributes. A simple way of doing this is to use the independence (naive Bayes) assumption. We saw earlier how to compute the joint probability of multiple attributes as a product of the individual probabilities. Thus, by making the following changes, the algorithm can easily be generalized to cover *multivariate normal distributions*:

1. Maintain independently the weighted mean and standard deviation for each attribute. Use the same formulas for their calculation.

2. When computing the weight $w_i$ (probability of $x_i$), use the product of the density functions of all attributes.

The computation of cluster probabilities (as normalized sums of weights) and the overall loop of the algorithm remain unchanged.

Table 3.7 shows the results of two runs (with random choice of initial distributions) of the *multivariate* EM algorithm on our department data with the six attributes that we selected earlier for our clustering experiments. The weights indicate the cluster membership of each document (shown in boldface), and above the weight columns we see the log-likelihood for each run. The table includes the labels obtained by the $k$-means experiment (Table 3.5). This is also the labeling that we have assumed to be the natural grouping of our documents according to their topic: natural sciences and arts and humanities.

The result from the first run (EM1) is close to that obtained from $k$-means: only three documents are labeled differently (Physics, Psychology, and Sociology). The second run (EM2) shows six differences with the $k$-means clustering; however, the log-likelihood is substantially higher. So we see here a situation in which the criterion function is not in agreement with the natural topic-based grouping of our documents. In fact, similar to $k$-means experiments, here we have chosen two clusterings, one good and one bad, out of many others that can be obtained from EM with different initial settings. It is important to note that especially in the multiple-attribute case, the landscape of the log-likelihood function is very complex, which means that the EM algorithm could possibly find many local maxima and consequently, many different clusterings.

Another important observation is that in some cases our intuitive notion of document topics may differ from that suggested by the criterion function for clustering. This is contrary to what we have seen in experiments with $k$-means clustering (Tables 3.4 and 3.5), where the criterion function was in agreement with the document

TABLE 3.7 Document Clustering with Multivariate EM Using Six Attributes

| Document | $k$-Means Labels | EM1: Log-Likelihood = 0.1334 | | EM2: Log-Likelihood = 4.8131 | |
|---|---|---|---|---|---|
| | | $w_i$(Cluster A) | $w_i$(Cluster B) | $w_i$(Cluster A) | $w_i$(Cluster B) |
| Anthropology | A | **1** | 0 | **0.99999** | 0.00001 |
| Art | B | 0 | **1** | **0.9066** | 0.0934 |
| Biology | A | **0.99995** | 0.00005 | **1** | 0 |
| Chemistry | A | **1** | 0 | **1** | 0 |
| Communication | B | 0 | **1** | **0.96278** | 0.03722 |
| Computer Science | A | **1** | 0 | **1** | 0 |
| Criminal Justice | B | 0.0118 | **0.9882** | **0.98363** | 0.01637 |
| Economics | A | **0.70988** | 0.29012 | **0.99999** | 0.00001 |
| English | B | 0 | **1** | **0.81042** | 0.18958 |
| Geography | A | **1** | 0 | **0.99999** | 0.00001 |
| History | B | 0.01348 | **0.98652** | 0 | **1** |
| Mathematics | A | **1** | 0 | **0.99999** | 0.00001 |
| Modern Languages | B | 0 | **1** | **0.71241** | 0.28759 |
| Music | B | 0.01381 | **0.98619** | 0 | **1** |
| Philosophy | B | 0 | **1** | 0 | **1** |
| Physics | A | 0.06692 | **0.93308** | **0.99999** | 0.00001 |
| Political Science | A | **1** | 0 | **1** | 0 |
| Psychology | A | 0.0368 | **0.9632** | **0.99999** | 0.00001 |
| Sociology | A | 0.00016 | **0.99984** | **0.99982** | 0.00018 |
| Theatre | B | 0.0023 | **0.9977** | **0.98818** | 0.01182 |

topic structure. A possible explanation for this is that the intracluster similarity criterion may suit our topic structure better than the probabilistically defined log-likelihood function.

# COLLABORATIVE FILTERING (RECOMMENDER SYSTEMS)

So far we have discussed approaches to content-based retrieval and clustering of documents, where the basic relation that is used in the document description is "document contains term." At some point we looked into the role of web users as a source of feedback to improve the document ranking. However, we may consider web users as entities in a relation such as the document–term relation. This may, for example, be "web user likes web page." Then we can build a user–document matrix and use documents to describe users in terms of web pages they like. A more general approach would be to consider persons and items again connected by the relation "person likes item." This is the approach taken in the area of *collaborative filtering* (also called *recommender systems*) [3].

Assume that we have $m$ persons and $n$ items (e.g., books, songs, movies, web pages). We arrange them in a $m \times n$ matrix $M$, where each row is a person, each column is an item, and the cells represent the binary relation "likes." Thus, if person $i$

likes item $j$, then $M(i, j) = 1$; otherwise, $M(i, j) = 0$. The problem is that many cells are empty (i.e., we don't know whether or not a person likes an item). The task of a collaborative filtering system is to predict the missing values by using the rest of the information in the matrix.

On-line shopping sites usually keep records of who purchased what. A person who has purchased a couple of items identifies a vector in the person × item matrix, which the collaborative filtering system fills in with predicted values. Thus, the system may recommend to that person other items that he or she also may want to buy ("customers who bought this also bought …").

A straightforward approach to solve the collaborative filtering task is to use clustering. The items are used as features to represent persons as vectors (rows in the person × item matrix). Then person vectors are clustered by using any clustering algorithm that we have discussed so far (e.g., $k$-means or EM). Finally, the missing values are taken from the cluster representation, where each person belongs. A problem in applying this approach involves the highly sparse data: In each person vector there are many missing values. The probabilistic algorithms can easily handle missing values; they are simply omitted from the computation of probabilities and the algorithm proceeds as usual. In similarity-based clustering such as $k$-means, a little adjustment is made for the missing feature values. They are assumed as least similar or at maximal distance. However, there is still another problem: As people usually have multiple interests, persons often appear in multiple clusters.

The clustering approach to collaborative filtering uses only the similarity between persons. However, the items may also be considered as vectors defined by persons. Or more generally, persons and item may be considered as symmetric. The basic idea is to cluster both persons and items at the same time. An EM-like algorithm for this purpose can be sketched as follows:

1. Assign random cluster labels to persons and items.
2. Take a person and an item at random; then
   a. Compute the probabilty that the person belongs to the person clusters.
   b. Compute the probabilty that the item belongs to the item clusters.
   c. Compute the probabilty that the person likes the item.
3. Esimate the maximum likelihood values of the foregoing probabilities.
4. If the parameter estimation is satisfactory, terminate; else, go to step 2.

Collaborative filtering is related to *user profiling* and *web personalization*. In collaborative filtering, similarity between users is defined by items they like or dislike. Thus, in the context of web, collaborative filtering is concerned basically with *web usage*, whereas in user profiling and web personalization, users are modeled by using the *content* of the web pages they like or dislike. For the latter, web documents are represented by using the standard *content-based approaches*, such as those we have used for clustering, and documents are labeled by user preferences. Then supervised learning methods are applied to create models of the users, which in turn may be used for personalized web services. We discuss supervised learning approaches in Chapter 5.

# REFERENCES

1. Daniel Larose, *Discovering Knowledge in Data: An Introduction to Data Mining*, Wiley, Hoboken, NJ, 2005.
2. A. P. Dempster, N. M. Laird, and D. B. Rubin, Maximum likelihood from incomplete data via the EM algorithm, *J. R. Stat. Soci. Ser. B*, 39(1):1–38, 1977.
3. J. Breese, D. Heckerman, and C. Kadie, Empirical analysis of predictive algorithms for collaborative filtering, *in Uncertainty in Artificial Intelligence: Proceedings of the 14th Conference*, Morgan Kaufmann, San Francisco, CA, 1998, pp. 43–52.

# EXERCISES

1. Collect a number of web pages by browsing a web directory, crawling a web domain, or by web search. Use their topic categories (if available) or classify them (manually) into two or more categories. Create a Weka data file to represent the collection. Follow the steps below.

    **a.** Make sure that in each category there are between 20 and 50 pages. Choose pages with more text and less graphics.

    **b.** After collecting each web page, convert it into plain text. For example, load the web page in Internet Explorer and use the "Save As . . . " option with "Save as type: Text File (*.txt)" (or "Plain Text" in MS Word). Make sure that the size of the text file is more than 1k and less than 10k.

    **c.** Create a single text file in the Weka ARFF format (with attributes of type string) that includes all text files extracted from the web pages (see the description of the ARFF format at `http://www.cs.waikato.ac.nz/~ml/weka/`). The content of each text file should appear on a single line (remove all CR and LF characters) and must be enclosed in quotation marks ("_"). Add the page title at the beginning of the line and the page category at the end. Then create a file header as follows:

    ```
    @relation web_pages_in_string_format
    @attribute web_page_name string
    @attribute web_page_content string
    @attribute web_page_class string
    @data
    "Internet Archive", "internet archive web moving...", info
    ...
    ```

    The data section (the lines after `@data`) includes the actual web page text: one (long) line per page.

    A Weka data file created as explained above is available from the book series Web site `www.dataminingconsultant.com`. The file name is "Top-100-websites.arff" and contains 100 top-ranked web pages returned by Google search "web" on April 18, 2006. The class is assigned (manually) as "prof" for web pages intended for IT professionals, and "info" for web pages that provide various types of information or direct web services.

2. Load the data set created in Exercise 1 (or "Top-100-websites.arff") in Weka, convert it into binary, term-count, and TFIDF formats, and store each representation in a separate ARFF file. Use the StringToWordVector filter and follow the steps explained

in Exercises 3 and 4 of Chapter 1. The conversions of "Top-100-websites.arff" into binary, term-count, and TFIDF formats are also available from the book series Web site www.dataminingconsultant.com as "Top-100-websites-binary.arff," "Top-100-websites-counts.arff," and "Top-100-websites-TFIDF.arff" correspondingly.

3. Load the binary data set and analyze the attributes by examining their visualization in Weka's preprocess mode.

   a. What is the most frequent pattern observed in the attribute visualization window? What does a pattern with a high 0-bar and low 1-bar tell about the sparsity of data? How about the reverse pattern?

   b. What do the class colors tell about the importance of an attribute for clustering? How about the frequency distribution?

   c. What would be the best pattern for the purposes of well-balanced clustering?

   d. Compare the following attributes (from the data set "Top-100-websites-binary.arff"): *input, accounting, internet, web, support, software,* and *design*. Analyze their bar diagrams along the lines of previous questions.

4. Analyze the visualizations of the term counts and TFIDF attributes (using the corresponding data sets created in Exercise 2). What changes with the representation? Why? Which attributes would now be better for clustering, with thicker or thinner bars?

5. Perform clustering[3] experiments using "Top-100-websites-binary.arff" with $k$-means and two clusters (numClusters = 2). Ignore the class attribute.

   a. Use different random number seeds (i.e., different initial cluster centroids) and see how the results change. Explain why the algorithm is so sensitive to changes in the initial settings.

   b. Find the most balanced clustering and save the cluster assignments in a new data file. Right-click on the result line in the result list window and choose "Visualize cluster assignments." Then use the "Save" button in the "Clusterer visualize" window; a new attribute is added (as last) with values corresponding to the cluster membership of each instance.

   c. Load the file with the clustering results and visualize the original class attribute using the new cluster attribute as color. Analyze the results (this explains how Weka performs the classes-to-clusters evaluation discussed in Chapter 4).

6. Perform the experiments from Exercise 5, but with the term-counts ("Top-100-websites-counts.arff") and TFIDF ("Top-100-websites-TFIDF.arff") representations of the data set. Compare the results.

7. Remove all attributes except the following: website_title, developers, support, partners, developer, solutions, html, software, gov, national, design, and website_class. Also ignore the class attribute. Run the $k$-means and EM algorithms with two clusters using the three data sets binary, term-counts, and TFIDF.

   a. For $k$-means, examine the effect of changing the seed. Compare the behavior of the algorithm with that on the full data set. Explain the difference.

   b. Compare $k$-means and EM on the tree data sets. Analyze the class distribution over clusters (see Exercise 5b and c). Which algorithm performs better on which data

---

[3] Note that Weka requires a lot of memory to run with large data files, so make sure that all available memory is used by setting the "–Xmx" command line parameter properly.

sets? Explain why. Note that the Weka implementation of $k$-means uses Euclidean distance (not cosine similarity) and EM assumes normal distribution.

**c.** For EM, examine the log-likelihood evaluation reported by Weka and compare it with the accuracy-based evaluation obtained from visualization of cluster assignments (class distribution over clusters).

**d.** For EM, examine how the log-likelihood changes with the number of iterations. Try max-iterations $= 1, 2, 3, \ldots$ and observe the values of the log likelihood. Create a graph such as the one shown in Figure 3.3. Experiment with different number of attributes (say, 1, 2, 3, 5, 10) and vary the random number seed. Comment on the results.

**8.** Remove all attributes except the website_title, website_class, and any other 10 attributes different from those used in Exercise 7. Ignore the class attribute and run the $k$-means and EM algorithms with two clusters using the three data sets binary, term-counts, and TFIDF.

    **a.** Perform the experiments, do the analysis, and answer the questions as described in Exercise 7a–d.

    **b.** Compare the results with those obtained in Exercise 7 and explain the differences (examine the visualizations of the different sets of attributes used).

**9.** Using the TFIDF data sets, pick one attribute from those used in Exercise 7 and one from those used in Exercise 8, and create a normal mixture model for each.

    **a.** Apply the unsupervised instance filter RemoveWithValues to obtain the set of instances from each class and then use the mean and standard deviation shown by Weka.

    **b.** For each attribute, create graphs of the probability density functions within each class (similar to that shown in Figure 3.2). This can be done in Microsoft Excel, for example.

    **c.** By inspecting the normal density curves, determine which attribute is more relevant for the classification task.

# *EVALUATING CLUSTERING*

## APPROACHES TO EVALUATING CLUSTERING

Clustering algorithms group documents by similarity or create statistical models based solely on the document representation, which in turn reflects document content. Then the criterion functions evaluate these models *objectively* (i.e., using only the document content). In contrast, when we label documents by topic we use additional knowledge, which is generally not explicitly available in document content and representation. Labeled documents are used primarily in *supervised learning* (*classification*) to create a mapping between the document representation and the external notion (concept, category, class) provided by the teacher through labeling. Preclassified documents can also be used for selecting attributes (terms) that best represent the class (we discuss this issue in Chapter 5). However, labeled documents can also be useful in unsupervised setting. By matching manual labeling and automatic clustering, we can achieve two goals:

1. If we know that our labeling is correct and reflects closely the content (representation) of documents, we can evaluate the quality of clustering. For example, considering the example from Table 3.7, we may decide that clustering EM1 is better than EM2 because the former has 15% errors and the latter has 30% errors with respect to manual classification (labeling).

*Data Mining the Web: Uncovering Patterns in Web Content, Structure, and Usage*
By Zdravko Markov and Daniel T. Larose    Copyright © 2007 John Wiley & Sons, Inc.

**2.** On the other hand, we may know that our algorithm works well and the representation reflects accurately the content of documents. Then we can judge the quality of manual labeling by comparing it to the clustering. For example, a manually created topic directory can be evaluated and then extended or modified accordingly by clustering.

The basic idea of clustering—grouping similar documents—also suggests criteria for clustering quality. Any function that evaluates the degree of similarity between documents within clusters can be used for this purpose. In some cases we would also like to evaluate dissimilarity of objects placed in different clusters. One may argue that probabilistic approaches use a different criterion for clustering. However, it is again based implicitly on similarity. If documents have a high probability of belonging to the same cluster, this is because they have features with close values: for example, attribute values close to the mean for the cluster. The difference is that some similarity approaches rely on pairwise similarity, or similarity of cluster members to the cluster center, which is a kind of *local* measure. Probability approaches, on the other hand, are always *global*; they take into account statistical properties, which are computed on the entire sample of documents. We have already mentioned two similarity-based functions, *intracluster similarity* and *sum of squared errors*, and one probability-based function, *log-likelihood*. Hereafter we summarize the properties of these functions and discuss further another probability-based criterion and a criterion function based on classified data, called *classes-to-clusters evaluation*.

## SIMILARITY-BASED CRITERION FUNCTIONS

One of the most popular criterion functions for clustering is the *sum of squared errors*. Originally, it uses *Euclidean distance* and evaluates clustering, where each cluster is represented by its *center* (*centroid* or *mean* in the case of numerical data). Such clustering can be produced, for example, by the *k-means* algorithm. The idea of this evaluation function is that the mean $m_i$ best represents cluster $D_i$ if it minimizes the sum of the lengths of the "error" vectors $x - m_i$ for all $x \in D_i$. Thus, the overall evaluation of a clustering is the sum of these "intracluster errors" over all $k$ clusters:

$$J_e = \sum_{i=1}^{k} \sum_{x \in D_i} \|x - m_i\|^2$$

where $m_i$ is the mean of $D_i$; that is,

$$m_i = \frac{1}{|D_i|} \sum_{x \in D_i} x$$

By simple algebraic manipulation the mean can be eliminated from the expression for $J_e$, thus obtaining an equivalent form of the evaluation function based on *pairwise distance* between cluster members:

$$J_e = \frac{1}{2} \sum_{i=1}^{k} \frac{1}{|D_i|} \sum_{x_j, x_l \in D_i} \|x_j - x_l\|^2$$

For document clustering the *cosine similarity* is used instead of distance, and the best clustering should *maximize* the *sum of centroid similarity* function:

$$J_s = \sum_{i=1}^{k} \sum_{d_j \in D_i} \text{sim}(c_i, d_j)$$

where $\text{sim}(c_i, d_j)$ is the cosine similarity between the cluster centroid $c_i$ of cluster $D_i$ and the vector $d_j$, defined by the cosine of the angle between the two vectors in the TFIDF vector space. That is,

$$\text{sim}(c_i, d_j) = \frac{c_i \cdot d_j}{\|c_i\| \, \|d_j\|}$$

The cluster centroid $c_i$ is the average vector in cluster $D_i$:

$$c_i = \frac{1}{|D_i|} \sum_{d_j \in D_i} d_j$$

The equivalent form of this function based on pairwise similarity is then

$$J_s = \frac{1}{2} \sum_{i=1}^{k} \frac{1}{|D_i|} \sum_{d_j, d_l \in D_i} \text{sim}(d_j, d_l)$$

Another simple transformation shows that this function actually uses *intracluster similarity*—one of the evaluation functions that control merging of clusters in hierarchical agglomerative clustering:

$$J_s = \frac{1}{2} \sum_{i=1}^{k} \frac{1}{|D_i|} \sum_{d_j, d_l \in D_i} \text{sim}(d_j, d_l) = \frac{1}{2} \sum_{i=1}^{k} |D_i| \, \text{sim}(D_i)$$

where $\text{sim}(D_i)$ is the average pairwise similarity between members of cluster $D_i$.

In summary, the *similarity-based criterion function* has two equivalent forms: *centroid* and *pairwise similarity*, depending on the clustering approach in which it is used. As we mentioned earlier, clustering that maximizes this function is called *minimum variance clustering*. Therefore, the functions from this family are called *minimum variance criterion functions*.

Another issue related to evaluating the quality of clustering is comparing clusterings with a different number of partitions or different hierarchical structures. In partitioning, the criterion function grows with the number of clusters, reaching its maximum at the extreme case of single-element clusters, whereas in hierarchical clustering it decreases with climbing the hierarchy, reaching its smallest value at the root (a single cluster for the entire sample). We illustrate the behavior of the minimum variance criterion with four examples of clustering in our department domain. Table 4.1 shows four horizontal trees, corresponding to different clusterings of our 20 documents obtained with the agglomerative approach (average similarity criterion for merging clusters) and $k$-means with $k = 2$, 3, and 4.

The value of the sum of centroid similarity function is shown in brackets after the node number. Note that this value corresponds to the cluster that includes all leaves of the subtree rooted at the node. For example, node 3 from the agglomerative tree

**TABLE 4.1  Sum of Centroid Similarity Evaluation of Four Clusterings**

| Agglomerative | k-means  (k = 2) | k-means  (k = 3) | k-means  (k = 4) |
|---|---|---|---|
| 1 [12.0253] | 1 [12.0253] | 1 [12.0253] | 1 [12.0253] |
| 2 [9.43932] | 2 [8.53381] | 2 [2.83806] | 2 [3.81771] |
| 3 [5.64819] |   Anthropology |   History |   Art |
| 4 [4.6522] |   Biology |   Music |   Communication |
| 5 [3.8742] |   Chemistry |   Philosophy |   English |
| 6 [2.95322] |   Computer Science | 3 [6.09107] |   Modern Languages |
| 7 [1.99773] |   Economics |   Anthropology | 3 [5.44416] |
|   Chemistry |   Geography |   Biology |   Biology |
|   Computer Science |   Mathematics |   Chemistry |   Economics |
|   Political Science |   Physics |   Computer Science |   Mathematics |
|   Geography |   Political Science |   Geography |   Physics |
|   Anthropology |   Psychology |   Mathematics |   Psychology |
|   Psychology |   Sociology |   Political Science |   Sociology |
| 8 [1.98347] | 3 [6.12743] | 4 [7.12119] | 4 [2.83806] |
|   Criminal Justice |   Art |   Art |   History |
|   Theatre |   Communication |   Communication |   Music |
| 9 [5.44416] |   Criminal Justice |   Criminal Justice |   Philosophy |
| 10 [2.81679] |   English |   Economics | 5 [5.64819] |
| 11 [1.97333] |   History |   English |   Anthropology |
|   Psychology |   Modern Languages |   Modern Languages |   Chemistry |
|   Sociology |   Music |   Physics |   Computer Science |
|   Mathemetics | | | |

12 [2.90383]
13 [1.96187]
  Biology
  Economics
    Physics
14 [5.40061]
15 [2.83806]
16 [1.98066]
  History
  Music
Philosophy
17 [3.81771]
18 [2.97634]
19 [1.99175]
  English
  Modern Languages
  Art
  Communication

**14.83993 (clusters 2 + 14)**

Philosophy
Theatre

Psychology
Sociology
Theatre

Criminal Justice
Geography
Political Science
Theatre

14.6612                16.05032                17.74812

**TABLE 4.2**

| Partitioning | Sum of Centroid Similarity |
|---|---|
| {2,14} | 14.8399 |
| {3,9,14} | 16.493 |
| {2,15,17} | 16.0951 |
| {4,8,9,14} | 17.4804 |
| {3,9,15,17} | 17.7481 |
| {4,8,9,15,17} | 18.7356 |
| {3,10,12,15,17} | 18.0246 |
| {4,8,10,12,14} | 17.7569 |
| {4,8,10,12,15,17} | 19.0121 |

represents the cluster {Chemistry, Computer Science, Political Science, Geography, Anthropology, Criminal Justice, Theatre} with the value of the sum of centroid similarity 5.64819. Therefore, the value at the node is *not* equal to the sum of values at the constituent clusters. This is also the reason that the value at the root (12.0253) is the same for all clusterings. The idea of this representation is to show an evaluation of each cluster *individually*. Then if we want to see the quality of a particular partitioning, we simply sum up the evaluations of the constituent clusters. These sums for top-level partitioning (the immediate successors of the root) are shown in the bottom row of the table.

When analyzing the agglomerative clustering we first identify six clusters at the lowest level that jointly cover the entire sample: 4, 8, 10, 12, 15, and 17. There are also even smaller clusters; however, we do not consider them as the lowest-level samples, because otherwise there would be individual documents at the same level, such as cluster 7 and the document Political Science. Then we look at various combinations of those basic clusters and see how the quality of the resulting partitioning changes. All such combinations are shown in Table 4.2 along with the values of the centroid similarity criterion function (the sum of those functions for the constituent clusters). The table shows clearly that the criterion function increases with the number of partitions. We have different combinations with the same number of partitions (three, four and five). From those we can choose those with the highest value of similarity. Intuitively, we want to create bigger clusters. However, when merging clusters, the quality of clustering decreases. Therefore, we need a good balance between quality and size. One way to ensure this is to look at the topics (if they are known). According to its topic, cluster 8 belongs to cluster 14; however, the tree structure does not allow merging it with the latter. So we can keep cluster 8 for top-level partitioning and merge the other branches of the tree, thus obtaining the clustering {4,8,9,14}. If we don't know the topic structure, a better choice would be clusters at the same level of the hierarchy (starting from the six lowest-level nontrivial clusters, because that is the way the hierarchy was created). Such clusters are usually well balanced in size and quality, too. A good choice according to this criterion is {3,9,14}.

For $k$-means clustering we use a different strategy to find the number of clusters. We first run the algorithm with $k = 5$, 6, and 7 to get three additional data points and

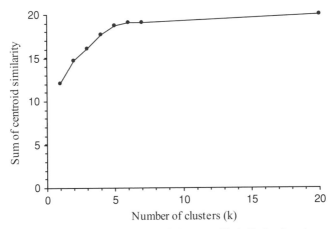

**Figure 4.1**  Graph of the sum of the centroid similarity function.

then plot the criterion function for $k$ values from 1 to 20 (see Figure 4.1). The value for $k = 20$ is clearly 20 because each document is a cluster with centroid similarity 1. The plot shows a sharp increase in the criterion function with the first several values of $k$, after which the curve goes almost flat. This is typical behavior of the criterion function and suggests a way of choosing $k$. The general objective here is to maximize the criterion function. However, this comes at the price of too many clusters. In such situations a good balance is usually found at a point where the curve sharply changes its slope. In our case this is the area around $k = 5$. Another candidate is $k = 2$, where for the first time the increase in quality starts to slow down with $k$. Of course, these considerations hold only in situation where we know very little about our data and want to determine the best number of partitions. For the particular example of the department documents, we have already assumed that the documents belong to two topics. Therefore, the more reasonable choice is $k = 2$.

## PROBABILISTIC CRITERION FUNCTIONS

In probabilistic clustering, a document is considered a *random event*. Then the criterion functions use the probability or likelihood of documents combined in various ways. The most commonly used expressions in this framework are:

- Probability of document:

$$P(d) = \sum_A P(d \mid A)P(A)$$

- Probability of sample (assuming that documents are independent events):

$$P(d_1, d_2, \ldots, d_n) = \prod_{i=1}^{n} \sum_A P(d_i \mid A)P(A)$$

- Log-likelihood (log of probability of sample):

$$L = \sum_{i=1}^{n} \log \sum_{A} P(d_i \mid A) P(A)$$

In practice, probabilities are replaced with likelihoods. The reason is that the criterion functions are used for comparing different clusterings, and therefore the correct probabilities are not needed. The log is taken mainly for practical reasons: it turns the product into a sum, thus making the function less sensitive to sharp changes of its arguments, and second, this helps avoid possible underflow. There is also a conceptual reason to take a log of probability; according to Shannon's information theory, this is a quantitative measure of information. We look into this aspect of criterion functions later in the chapter.

Another probabilistic approach looks into the probabilities of attributes having particular values within clusters and across clusters. The idea proposed by Gluck and Corter [1] is inspired by psychological experiments with the categorization of objects. They suggest a function called *category utility* (CU), which measures both the probability that two objects in the same category have attribute values in common and the probability that objects from different categories have different attribute values. Thus, according to the definition of clustering, maximizing CU means maximizing intracluster similarity and minimizing intercluster similarity. The category utility function was used in the incremental conceptual clustering system Cobweb [2] and in related projects. Hereafter we discuss category utility as a criterion function because it is useful intuitively for probabilistic clustering. The use of Cobweb for web document clustering is outside the scope of our discussion.

Category utility is originally defined for *nominal attributes* (*features*) $a_j$ with finite number of values $v_{ij}$. To better explain the intuition behind this criterion, we first consider the expression

$$\sum_{k} \sum_{i} \sum_{j} P(a_j = v_{ij} \mid C_k) \, P(C_k \mid a_j = v_{ij}) \, P(a_j = v_{ij})$$

where the sums are taken over all categories (clusters) $C_k$, attributes $a_j$, and values $v_{ij}$ in the clustering that is being evaluated. The terms involved in the expression have the following meaning:

- $P(a_j = v_{ij} \mid C_k)$ is the probability that an object has value $v_{ij}$ for its attribute $a_j$ given that it belongs to category $C_k$. The higher this probability, the more likely it is that two objects in a category share attribute values.
- $P(C_k \mid a_j = v_{ij})$ is the probability that an object belongs to category $C_k$ given that it has value $v_{ij}$ for its attribute $a_j$. The greater this probability, the less likely that objects from different categories have attribute values in common.
- $P(a_j = v_{ij})$ works as a weight, assuring that frequent attribute values have a stronger influence on the evaluation.

Applying Bayes' rule to $P(C_k \mid a_j = v_{ij})$ and substituting in the expression, we get

$$\sum_k P(C_k) \sum_i \sum_j P(a_j = v_{ij} \mid C_k)^2$$

Gluck and Corter have shown that the term $\sum_i \sum_j P(a_j = v_{ij} \mid C_k)^2$ represents the expected number of attribute values that one can correctly guess for an arbitrary member of cluster $C_k$ using a *probability matching strategy* (guesses match the probability of occurrence).

Assume now that we don't know the categories (clusters) in our sample. Then the number of correct guesses of attribute values expected will be $\sum_i \sum_j P(a_j = v_{ij})^2$. The basic idea of category utility is to measure the *increase* in the expected number of attribute values that can be guessed correctly, given a set of $n$ categories, over the expected number of correct guesses without such knowledge. Thus, the final expression for the function is

$$CU(C_1, C_2, \ldots, C_n) = \frac{1}{n} \sum_k P(C_k) \sum_i \sum_j \left[ P(a_j = v_{ij} \mid C_k)^2 - P(a_j = v_{ij})^2 \right]$$

The expression is divided by $n$ to allow comparison of clusterings with different numbers of clusters. In fact, this addition to the formula cannot be justified probabilistically because the information about the categories is already taken into account by including the sum over categories weighted with the probability $P(C_k)$. Rather, the reason is that without the denominator, the formula gives preference to clustering with more categories. In the extreme case of singleton clusters, the probability $P(a_j = v_{ij} \mid C_k)$ is 1 for the single member of cluster $C_k$ and 0 elsewhere, and thus the numerator reaches its maximum of $m - \sum_i \sum_j P(a_j = v_{ij})^2$, where $m$ is the number of features. Therefore, the additional factor in the CU formula can be seen as a heuristic for avoiding *overfitting*. This is essential for use of the function in the clustering algorithm Cobweb, because the latter does not use a predefined number of clusters. Cobweb is an *incremental* algorithm which takes an object at a time and decides whether it should be accommodated in an existing cluster or added to the hierarchy as a new cluster. This decision is made by computing the CU scores of the two alternatives. So without this additional factor, Cobweb will always create singleton clusters.

Let us now apply category utility to evaluate document clustering. As the function is originally defined for nominal attributes, we first use the Boolean representation of our document vectors. This will also illustrate the way that probabilities over discrete variables are computed. Next, we discuss briefly an extension that works for continuous normally distributed features and thus can be used for the TFIDF document representation. The Boolean document representation with the six terms that we have used so far for clustering is shown in Table 4.3. Given this data set, let us evaluate the three clusterings shown in Table 3.7. First, let us consider the intuitive topic-based labeling (also produced by k-means). The clusters are $A = \{1,3,4,6,8,10,12,16,17,18,19\}$ and $B = \{2,5,7,9,11,13,14,15,20\}$, where for brevity, row numbers are used instead of document names. To simplify the notation we also split the expression into subexpressions, which correspond to the category utility of

**TABLE 4.3 Six-Feature Boolean Representation of the Department Collection**

| Document | No. | history $a_1$ | science $a_2$ | research $a_3$ | offers $a_4$ | students $a_5$ | hall $a_6$ |
|---|---|---|---|---|---|---|---|
| Anthropology | 1 | 0 | 1 | 1 | 0 | 1 | 1 |
| Art | 2 | 0 | 0 | 0 | 1 | 1 | 1 |
| Biology | 3 | 0 | 1 | 1 | 0 | 1 | 1 |
| Chemistry | 4 | 0 | 1 | 0 | 0 | 1 | 1 |
| Communication | 5 | 0 | 0 | 0 | 1 | 1 | 0 |
| Computer Science | 6 | 0 | 1 | 0 | 0 | 1 | 1 |
| Criminal Justice | 7 | 0 | 0 | 0 | 0 | 1 | 0 |
| Economics | 8 | 0 | 0 | 1 | 0 | 0 | 0 |
| English | 9 | 0 | 0 | 0 | 1 | 0 | 1 |
| Geography | 10 | 0 | 1 | 0 | 0 | 1 | 0 |
| History | 11 | 1 | 0 | 0 | 1 | 0 | 0 |
| Mathematics | 12 | 0 | 1 | 1 | 1 | 1 | 1 |
| Modern Languages | 13 | 0 | 0 | 0 | 1 | 0 | 1 |
| Music | 14 | 1 | 0 | 0 | 0 | 1 | 1 |
| Philosophy | 15 | 1 | 0 | 0 | 1 | 0 | 1 |
| Physics | 16 | 0 | 0 | 1 | 0 | 1 | 1 |
| Political Science | 17 | 0 | 1 | 1 | 0 | 1 | 1 |
| Psychology | 18 | 0 | 0 | 1 | 1 | 1 | 1 |
| Sociology | 19 | 0 | 0 | 1 | 1 | 1 | 1 |
| Theatre | 20 | 0 | 0 | 0 | 0 | 1 | 1 |

individual clusters:

$$\mathrm{CU}(A, B) = \tfrac{1}{2}[\mathrm{CU}(A) + \mathrm{CU}(B)]$$

where

$$\mathrm{CU}(A) = P(A) \left\{ \sum_{j=1}^{6} \left[ P(a_j = 0 \,|\, A)^2 - P(a_j = 0)^2 \right] \right.$$

$$+ \left. \sum_{j=1}^{6} \left[ P(a_j = 1 \,|\, A)^2 - P(a_j = 1)^2 \right] \right\}$$

$$\mathrm{CU}(B) = P(B) \left\{ \sum_{j=1}^{6} \left[ P(a_j = 0 \,|\, B)^2 - P(a_j = 0)^2 \right] \right.$$

$$+ \left. \sum_{j=1}^{6} \left[ P(a_j = 1 \,|\, B)^2 - P(a_j = 1)^2 \right] \right\}$$

The category probabilities are $P(A) = 11/20 = 0.55$ and $P(B) = 9/20 = 0.45$. The probabilities of feature values are calculated as proportions of the value counts in the entire data set. For example, $P(a_1 = 0) = 17/20 = 0.85$ and $P(a_1 = 1) = 3/20 = 0.15$. The conditional probabilities are computed as proportion of value counts within clusters. For example, $P(a_1 = 0 \,|\, A) = 1$ because all values in column $a_1$ and the rows corresponding to the documents in cluster $A$ are 0; whereas $P(a_1 = 0 \mid B) = 6/9 = 0.667$, because in the rows of cluster $B$ there are six 0's out of a total of nine values. Computing all probabilities similarly and substituting in the formulas, we get $CU(A) = 4.87295$ and $CU(B) = 1.80028$. Then overall category utility is the average of the two:

$$CU(A, B) = \tfrac{1}{2}(4.87295 + 1.80028) = 3.3366$$

So far we can see that cluster $B$ looks better than cluster $A$, which is the opposite of what the centroid similarity function suggests (see Table 3.5, iteration 3). This comes as no surprise because the two functions rely on different aspects of clustering. We have already mentioned that the sum of the centroid similarity measure looks *locally* into the similarity within the cluster only, whereas CU has a *global* view on the similarity within the cluster and dissimilarity with the rest of the documents belonging to the other cluster. Note also that they use different representations: TFIDF and Boolean (although this does not affect the ranking of the two clusters).

Let us now compute the CU score of the other two clusterings (EM1 and EM2). For EM1 we obtain $CU(A) = 3.72$, $CU(B) = 2.5466$, and $CU(A, B) = 3.1333$. For EM2 the scores are $CU(A) = 4.7425$, $CU(B) = -0.3925$, and $CU(A, B) = 2.175$. Interestingly, these scores rank EM1 as better than EM2, which is contrary to the log-likelihood ranking (see Table 3.7). The explanation here is that the log-likelihood function only adds the likelihoods of all individual documents, whereas CU also takes intercluster similarities into account. A further explanation is that cluster $B$ in EM2 gets a negative CU score. According to the original meaning of CU, this is an indication that intercluster similarity exceeds intracluster similarity. The strange thing is that the cluster we are talking about, {History, Music, Philosophy}, looks good because it shows up in many different clusterings (see, e.g., Table 4.1: agglomerative and $k$-means with $k = 3$). The problem is, however, that this cluster, although including highly similar members, is very small, and consequently, the intercluster similarity of its three members to the much bigger cluster $A$ prevails. In fact, this is an advantage of the CU criterion function—it gives preference to more balanced clusterings.

The category utility function can easily be extended to continuous attributes by assuming normal distribution and replacing probabilities with densities (as we have done to solve the mixture problem). Then the sums over the probabilities of feature values correspond to integrals and the function is

$$CU(C_1, C_2, \ldots, C_n) = \frac{1}{n} \sum_{k=1}^{n} P(C_k) \sum_i \left[ \int f(v_{ik}) \, dv_{ik} - \int f(v_i) \, dv_i \right]$$

where $f(\cdot)$ is the probability density function for normal distribution (as defined in Chapter 3.) After solving the integrals, we obtain

$$CU(C_1, C_2, \ldots, C_n) = \frac{1}{n} \sum_{k=1}^{n} P(C_k) \frac{1}{2\sqrt{\pi}} \sum_i \left( \frac{1}{\sigma_{ik}} - \frac{1}{\sigma_i} \right)$$

where $\sigma_{ik}$ and $\sigma_i$ are the standard deviations of attribute $a_i$ within cluster $C_k$ and in the entire sample correspondingly. The zero standard deviation causes the same problem as in the mixture problem—it produces an infinite value of CU. The solution here is also the same as the one suggested for the mixture models: using a predefined minimum value for the standard deviation.

## MDL-BASED MODEL AND FEATURE EVALUATION

So far we have been discussing various approaches to creating and evaluating clusterings. Let us now look at this task from another perspective: *finding regularities in data*, which is also regarded within the unsupervised setting for learning, to which clustering belongs. Consider a cluster with a high category utility score. This means that its members have a goodly number of attributes that share values. In other words, there is a *pattern* that repeats within this cluster so the cluster can be described by this pattern. Such a description may include the attribute values that are the same for all members of the cluster and omit those that have different values. This type of description, common for concept learning, is called *generalization* by *dropping conditions*. For example, the natural topic-based clustering of our department documents (the labeling shown in Table 3.7) can be described by four pairs of values (in the Boolean case) for the attributes *science* and *research*: (0,1), (1,0), (1,1), (0,0). These patterns can be written as classification *rules* as follows:

$$H_1 = \begin{cases} R_1\text{: IF } (science = 0) \text{ AND } (research = 1) \text{ THEN class} = \text{A} \\ R_2\text{: IF } (science = 1) \text{ AND } (research = 0) \text{ THEN class} = \text{A} \\ R_3\text{: IF } (science = 1) \text{ AND } (research = 1) \text{ THEN class} = \text{A} \\ R_4\text{: IF } (science = 0) \text{ AND } (research = 0) \text{ THEN class} = \text{B} \end{cases}$$

We say that a rule *covers* a set of documents if the attribute values on the left-hand side of the rule occur in those documents. Thus rule $R_1$ *covers* documents 8, 16, 18, and 19. The coverage of $R_2$ is the set $\{4,6,10\}$, the coverage of $R_3$ is $\{1,3,12,17\}$, and the coverage of $R_4$ is $\{2,5,7,9,11,13,14,15,20\}$. All four rules cover all documents jointly and each is produced by *generalizing* the corresponding subset of documents. The generalization is performed by dropping from that subset attributes that have different values in the documents.

The set of rules above actually represents a *mapping* between documents and classes (clusters). In other words, these rules are a *hypothesis* (*model*) that describes (explains) the data. Let us denote the foregoing hypotheses as $H_1$ and look for other clustering hypotheses. If we pick an attribute, it can naturally split the set of documents into two subsets (in the Boolean case), each including documents that share the same value of that attribute. Thus, we can create simple hypotheses, such as

$$H_2 = \begin{cases} R_1\text{: IF } offers = 0 \text{ THEN class} = \text{A} \\ R_2\text{: IF } offers = 1 \text{ THEN class} = \text{B} \end{cases}$$

This hypothesis partitions the data into two clusters:

$$A = \{1,3,4,6,7,8,10,14,16,17,20\}$$
$$B = \{2,5,9,11,12,13,15,18,19\}$$

Note that $H_2$ looks *simpler* than $H_1$ in terms of *description length*. The idea is that dropping more conditions produces simpler and more general hypotheses. In this respect we have two extreme cases. One is when we put all documents in one cluster. Then we have the simplest hypothesis of all with the empty set of conditions. This is also the most general hypothesis. The other extreme is a set of 20 singleton clusters, for which we need 20 rules with six conditions each: obviously the most complex hypothesis, which is equivalent to the original data set. This hypothesis is the least general and obviously *overfits* the data. Both situations are undesirable in learning because neither the most general nor the least general hypothesis provides a meaningful description of the data that can be used for explanation or classification.

## Minimum Description Length Principle

After all these considerations a natural question comes in mind: Is there any connection between the simplicity of the hypothesis and the quality of the clustering it describes? Interestingly, there is a natural answer to this question, known as *Occam's razor*. In the fourteenth century William of Occam formulated a very general principle stating that "Entities are not to be multiplied beyond necessity." In other words, among several alternatives, the simplest is usually the best choice. Occam's razor has proven its validity in many areas; however, its application to formal decision making such as clustering and classification requires a formal definition of simplicity. The *minimum description length* (MDL) *principle* suggested by Rissanen [3] provides a formal framework for the application of Occam's razor. Hereafter we briefly describe the basic idea behind the MDL principle and illustrate its use for evaluation of clustering models and attribute selection.

Assume that we are given a data set $D$ (e.g., our document collection) and a set of hypotheses $H_1, H_2, \ldots, H_n$, each describing $D$. The problem is to find the one that best describes the data. Probabilistically thinking, we want to find the most likely hypothesis given the data; that is,

$$H_i = \arg\max_i P(H_i \mid D)$$

As direct estimation of the conditional probability $P(H_i \mid D)$ is difficult, we apply Bayes' rule first:

$$P(H_i \mid D) = \frac{P(H_i)P(D \mid H_i)}{P(D)}$$

Then we take a negative logarithm of both sides of this equation. The result is

$$-\log_2 P(H_i \mid D) = -\log_2 P(H_i) - \log_2 P(D \mid H_i) + \log_2 P(D)$$

If we consider hypotheses and data as messages, we will be able to apply Shannon's information theory, which defines the information in a message as a negative logarithm of its probability. As we use the log of base 2, this information is equal to the minimum number of bits needed to encode the message. Thus, we arrive at the analog of Bayes' rule, which uses code lengths:

$$L(H_i \mid D) = L(H_i) + L(D \mid H_i) - L(D)$$

Now, our original goal of choosing a hypothesis turns into the following minimization problem:

$$H_i = \arg\min_i \left[ L(H_i) + L(D \mid H_i) - L(D) \right]$$

The interpretation of $L(H_i)$ and $L(D)$ is the minimum number of bits needed to encode the hypothesis and the data, and $L(D|H_i)$ indicates the number of bits needed to encode $D$ if we know $H$. The latter term makes a great deal of sense if we think of $H$ as a pattern that repeats in $D$. Once we know the pattern, we don't have to encode all its occurrences; rather, we encode only the pattern itself and the differences that identify each item in $D$; thus, the more regular the data, the shorter the description length $L(D|H_i)$. Of course, we have to balance this term with the description length of $H$, because if $H$ describes the data *exactly* (as in the situation with 20 singleton clusters), $L(D|H_i)$ will be 0 but $L(H_i)$ will be large. Also, we can exclude $L(D)$ because it does not depend on the choice of hypotheses. Thus, we arrive at the *minimum description length* principle: *The best hypothesis should minimize the expression $L(H_i) + L(D|H_i)$.*

## MDL-Based Model Evaluation

Let us now apply MDL to hypotheses $H_1$ and $H_2$ discussed earlier. The key to applying MDL is to find some way of encoding the hypotheses and the data given the hypotheses. The encoding scheme (i.e., the measurement units) should be the same for both, because we are adding code lengths and want to keep the balance between them. It is important to note that we don't need the actual codes; only an estimate of the code length is needed. One simple scheme used for this purpose is based on the assumption that hypotheses and data are distributed uniformly and the probability of occurrence of an item in a total of $n$ alternatives is $1/n$. Thus, the minimum code length of the message informing us that a particular item has occurred is $-\log_2 1/n = \log_2 n$. So what is left to be done is given a *description language* (e.g., rules) to count all possible hypotheses and data items given each hypothesis. When doing so we omit the technicalities of encoding the description language and the actual format of the data and hypotheses, because it is assumed that both the sender and the recipient of the message know that.

Let us first compute the MDL of hypothesis $H_1$. In the Boolean representation the description language consists of six attributes, each with two possible values, for a total of 12 attribute–value pairs. Each rule of the hypothesis selects a subset of those which are used to determine the documents covered by that rule. For example, rule $R_1$ covers documents 8, 16, 18, and 19. Nine different attribute–value pairs occur in these documents: $\{history = 0\}$, $\{science = 0\}$, $\{research = 1\}$, $\{offers = 0\}$, $\{offers = 1\}$, $\{students = 0\}$, $\{students = 1\}$, $\{hall = 0\}$, and $\{hall = 1\}$. Specifying this rule is equivalent to selecting nine of 12 attribute–value pairs, which can be done in $\binom{12}{9}$ different ways. Thus, we need $\log_2 \binom{12}{9}$ bits to encode the right-hand side of rule $R_1$. In addition, we need one bit (a choice of one of two cluster labels—$A$ or $B$, which is

$\log_2 2 = 1$) to encode the class. In this way we have

$$L(R_1) = \log_2 \binom{12}{9} + 1 = \log_2 220 + 1 = 8.78136 \text{ bits}^1$$

Similarly, we compute the code lengths of $R_2$, $R_3$, and $R_4$ and obtain

$$L(R_2) = \log_2 \binom{12}{7} + 1 = \log_2 792 + 1 = 10.6294$$

$$L(R_3) = \log_2 \binom{12}{7} + 1 = \log_2 792 + 1 = 10.6294$$

$$L(R_4) = \log_2 \binom{12}{10} + 1 = \log_2 66 + 1 = 7.04439$$

Using the additivity of information to obtain the code length of $H_1$, we simply add the code lengths of its constituent rules, thus, $L(H_1) = 37.0845$.

To estimate the code size $L(D|H_1)$ we consider the message exchange setting, where the hypothesis $H_1$ has already been communicated. This means that the recipient of that message already knows the subset of attribute–value pairs selected by each rule. For example, rule $R_1$ selects nine pairs (which takes $L(R_1) = 8.78136$ bits to encode). Then to communicate each document of those covered by $R_1$, we need to choose six (the pairs occurring in each document) out of those nine pairs. This choice will take $\log_2\binom{9}{6}$ bits to encode. As $R_1$ covers four documents (8, 16, 18, 19), the code length needed for all four will be

$$L(\{8, 16, 18, 19\}|R_1) = 4 \times \log_2 \binom{9}{6} = 4 \times \log_2 84 = 25.5693$$

We compute similarly the code length of the subsets of documents covered by the other rules:

$$L(\{4,6,10\}|R_2) = 3 \times \log_2 \binom{7}{6} = 3 \times \log_2 7 = 8.4220$$

$$L(\{1,3,12,17\}|R_3) = 4 \times \log_2 \binom{7}{6} = 4 \times \log_2 7 = 11.2294$$

$$L(\{2,5,7,9,11,13,14,15,20\}|R_4) = 9 \times \log_2 \binom{10}{6} = 9 \times \log_2 210 = 69.4282$$

The code length needed to communicate all documents given hypothesis $H_1$ will be the sum of all these code lengths [i.e., $L(D|H_1) = 114.649$]. Adding this to the code length of the hypothesis, we obtain

$$MDL(H_1) = L(H_1) + L(D|H_1) = 37.0845 + 114.649 = 151.733$$

---

[1] The fractional value of bits is a theoretical minimum and works only for the purposes of evaluation. If it comes to actual encoding, the minimal code length will be the nearest larger integer.

Following the same steps, we compute the code lengths corresponding to hypothesis $H_2$. Thus,

$$\text{MDL}(H_2) = L(H_2) + L(D|H_2) = 9.16992 + 177.035 = 186.205$$

According to the MDL principle, hypothesis $H_1$ is better than hypothesis $H_2$, which in fact agrees with out intuitive understanding of the document sample. These figures also illustrate well how MDL keeps track of the balance between the description length of hypotheses and data. We have already seen that $H_1$ is more complex (has more rules and more conditions) than $H_2$. Now this is confirmed by their description lengths: $L(H_1) > L(H_2)$. However, what happens with the code lengths of the data? It is obvious (and quite intuitive) that if the hypothesis is simple, it takes more bits to encode the data, and vice versa. In this respect it will be interesting to see what the MDL principle says about the most general and most specific hypotheses that we mentioned at the beginning of our discussion. The most general hypothesis (the empty rule { }) does not restrict the choice of attribute–value pairs, so it selects 12 of 12 pairs, and thus its code length is

$$L(\{\ \}) = \log_2 \binom{12}{12} + 1 = 1$$

The code for the data given this hypothesis is just the prior code for the data without knowing any hypotheses.

$$L(D|\{\ \}) = L(D) = 20 \times \log_2 \binom{12}{6} = 20 \times \log_2 924 = 197.035$$

The most specific hypothesis (let us call it $S$) has 20 rules, one for each document. Each of these rules has on its right-hand side all attribute–value pairs of the single document that it covers. Thus, it selects six pairs out of 12. Thus, the code length of hypothesis $S$ is

$$L(S) = 20 \times \left(\log_2 \binom{12}{6} + 1\right) = 20 \times (\log_2 924 + 1) = 217.035$$

The code lengths of { } and $S$ are close, with $S$ having slightly greater length because of the need to encode the class label for each singleton cluster (document). The most general and most specific hypotheses represent two extreme cases, both undesirable in learning: *overgeneralization* and *overspecialization* (also called *overfitting*). The MDL approach gives a slight preference to overgeneralization.

Note that the MDL of both $H_1$ and $H_2$ is smaller than the description length of the data itself. This fact can be expressed in terms of *data* (or *information*) *compression*. The principle of compression states that a good hypothesis should compress the data; that is, the description length of the hypothesis plus the description length of the data given the hypothesis should be less than the description length of the data itself. Formally,

$$L(H) + L(D\,|\,H) < L(D)$$

In other words, the best hypothesis should maximize the data compression:

$$H_i = \arg\max_i [L(D) - L(H_i) - L(D|H_i)]$$

This may be seen as another way of expressing MDL; however, it also allows hypotheses to be evaluated on an absolute scale compared to data only (assuming the same encoding scheme for hypotheses and data). Another important aspect of the data compression principle is that compression allows us to *evaluate data* with respect to the degree of *regularity* (or inversely, *randomness*) that it exhibits. For example, if we are able to prove that no hypothesis can be found that provides a positive compression, this will be an indication that the data are completely random. Also, the greater the compression that can be achieved, the more regularity there is in data.

## Feature Selection

We have already mentioned the importance of using the correct terms to represent our documents. The TFIDF framework is designed especially for this purpose. Once terms have been selected by their IF and IDF scores, they become features (attributes) in the document representation. The problem is that there are still too many. Most learning methods are designed to work with data where the number of data items (documents) substantially exceeds the number of features. So we need to evaluate further and select the features with respect to the specific learning task. Hereafter we illustrate a simple MDL approach for *unsupervised feature evaluation*. Supervised methods are discussed in Chapter 5.

As mentioned at the beginning of our discussion on MDL, an attribute can naturally split a set of documents into subsets, each including documents that share the same value of that attribute. We can consider this split as a clustering and evaluate its MDL score. Doing this for each attribute will provide a ranking that can be used to select the best attributes. We have already evaluated the attribute *offers* from our six-attribute document sample. It was used to create hypothesis $H_2$, which splits the set of documents into two subsets. The MDL score of $H_2$ was computed as 186.205. The results of applying the same approach to the rest of the attributes are shown in Table 4.4.

The table also shows the split produced by each attribute. The attributes are ordered by their MDL score. The best attribute (with the lowest MDL) is *science*. Note that the second-best attribute is *research*, which was used along with *science* to create hypothesis $H_1$, with an even better MDL score of 151.733. Combining a predefined number of top-ranking attributes (with the lowest MDL score) is an approach common to attribute selection.

Attribute selection is important for reducing the computational cost of both clustering and classification. However, in terms of accuracy, it is more important to classification than to clustering. Clustering reveals regularities in data and therefore is not too sensitive to sparse vector spaces simply because sparsely populated attributes cannot contribute significantly to any strong pattern. Whereas in classification, attributes that are sparse or not representative for the data can be wrongly associated with class labels because classification may disagree with the natural regularities in data.

**TABLE 4.4   MDL Attribute Evaluation**

| | Split | | |
|---|---|---|---|
| Attribute | Value = 0 | Value = 1 | MDL |
| *science* | 2, 5, 7, 8, 9, 11, 13, 14, 15, 16, 18, 19, 20 | 1, 3, 4, 6, 10, 12, 17 | 173.185 |
| *research* | 2, 4, 5, 6, 7, 9, 10, 11, 13, 14, 15, 20 | 1, 3, 8, 12, 16, 17, 18, 19 | 179.564 |
| *students* | 8, 9, 11, 13, 15 | 1, 2, 3, 4, 5, 6, 7, 10, 12, 14, 16, 17, 18, 19, 20 | 182.977 |
| *history* | 1, 2, 3, 4, 5, 6, 7, 8, 9, 10, 12, 13, 16, 17, 18, 19, 20 | 11, 14, 15 | 183.023 |
| *offers* | 1, 3, 4, 6, 7, 8, 10, 14, 16, 17, 20 | 2, 5, 9, 11, 12, 13, 15, 18, 19 | 186.205 |
| *hall* | 5, 7, 8, 10, 11 | 1, 2, 3, 4, 6, 9, 12, 13, 14, 15, 16, 17, 18, 19, 20 | 186.205 |

MDL is an important tool for evaluating hypotheses and data and finds many applications in data/web mining and machine learning. There are various forms of MDL, depending on the encoding schemes. It is also used differently for supervised and unsupervised learning. The approach we described here is designed for unsupervised learning. In supervised learning the classification made by the hypothesis may disagree with the predefined data labels. The task is, however, to communicate the data along with their predefined labels. This is achieved by first sending the hypothesis (encoded by using the technique that we discussed earlier) and then communicating the exceptions (i.e., the data items that have been misclassified by the hypothesis). Other approaches use entropy: an information theory measure that estimates the purity of data samples with respect to class labels. We discuss entropy-based hypothesis evaluation in Chapter 5.

# CLASSES-TO-CLUSTERS EVALUATION

Assume that the classification of the documents in a sample is known (i.e., each document has a class label). Then any clustering of these documents can be evaluated with respect to this predefined classification. It is important to note that the class labels are not used in the process of clustering, but only for the purpose of evaluation of the clustering results. This process is called *classes-to-clusters evaluation* and proceeds as follows. Each cluster is assigned with the class label of the majority of documents in it. Then the *error* is computed as the proportion of documents with different class and cluster labels. Inversely, the *accuracy* is the proportion of documents with the same class and cluster label.

Let us illustrate the classes-to-clusters evaluation approach with department documents, each labeled as belonging to either class A or class B, according to its topic. Table 4.5 shows the *accuracy evaluation* of six different clusterings obtained by

**TABLE 4.5   Classes-to-Clusters Evaluation**

| history 14/20 | | science 16/20 | | research 17/20 | | offers 14/20 | | students 14/20 | | hall 12/20 | |
|---|---|---|---|---|---|---|---|---|---|---|---|
| A (11/17) | B (3/3) | B (9/13) | A (7/7) | B (9/12) | A (8/8) | A (8/11) | B (6/9) | B (4/5) | A (10/15) | B (3/5) | A (9/15) |
| 1-A | 11-B | 2-B | 1-A | 2-B | 1-A | 1-A | 2-B | 8-A | 1-A | 5-B | 1-A |
| 2-B | 14-B | 5-B | 3-A | 4-A | 3-A | 3-A | 5-B | 9-B | 2-B | 7-B | 2-B |
| 3-A | 15-B | 7-B | 4-A | 5-B | 8-A | 4-A | 9-B | 11-B | 3-A | 8-A | 3-A |
| 4-A | | 8-A | 6-A | 6-A | 12-A | 6-A | 11-B | 13-B | 4-A | 10-A | 4-A |
| 5-B | | 9-B | 10-A | 7-B | 16-A | 7-B | 12-A | 15-B | 5-B | 11-B | 6-A |
| 6-A | | 11-B | 12-A | 9-B | 17-A | 8-A | 13-B | | 6-A | | 9-B |
| 7-B | | 13-B | 17-A | 10-A | 18-A | 10-A | 15-B | | 7-B | | 12-A |
| 8-A | | 14-B | | 11-B | 19-A | 14-B | 18-A | | 10-A | | 13-B |
| 9-B | | 15-B | | 13-B | | 16-A | 19-A | | 12-A | | 14-B |
| 10-A | | 16-A | | 14-B | | 17-A | | | 14-B | | 15-B |
| 12-A | | 18-A | | 15-B | | 20-B | | | 16-A | | 16-A |
| 13-B | | 19-A | | 20-B | | | | | 17-A | | 17-A |
| 16-A | | 20-B | | | | | | | 18-A | | 18-A |
| 17-A | | | | | | | | | 19-A | | 19-A |
| 18-A | | | | | | | | | 20-B | | 20-B |
| 19-A | | | | | | | | | | | |
| 20-B | | | | | | | | | | | |

splitting the set of documents using the values of single attributes (as shown in Table 4.4). For each attribute the two clusters are shown with their members as document number–class label pairs. The cell on top of each cluster shows the cluster label (the majority of class labels among its members) and the cluster accuracy as the proportion of the documents with the majority label. In the row above we see the overall accuracy for each clustering. The best clustering is produced by the attribute *research*, with 17 correctly classified documents out of 20, which makes 85% accuracy. The second best clustering is produced by the *science* attribute (80% accuracy).

This example also illustrates an approach to *error-based attribute evaluation*.[2] According to this approach, attributes are ranked by the classes-to-clusters accuracies (or errors) of the splits based on their values. Note, however, that this is a *supervised* method for attribute evaluation because it uses labeled data. Interestingly, the two best attributes selected by error-based evaluation are the same as those preferred by the unsupervised MDL evaluation approach. This is an indication that the classification

---

[2] This approach to attribute evaluation is used in a simple but efficient algorithm for supervised learning called OneR. It selects just one attribute and creates a set of classification rules based on the values of that attribute. In our case, OneR will create the rules: IF *research* = 0, THEN class = B; IF *research* = 1, THEN class = A.

of the documents done manually agrees with similarity-based clustering produced by single attributes.

## PRECISION, RECALL, AND *F*-MEASURE

The overall error of clustering is computed by adding all differences between class and cluster labels. However in some cases we need to look into the type of these differences, because they may have different importance to the learning task. In machine learning this issue is usually called *error cost*. For example, in an e-mail filtering system the cost of classifying nonspam e-mails as spam is higher than classifying spam as nonspam, because one would allow for some spam e-mails but could not afford to miss important e-mails.

For a two-cluster problem there are two types of errors: A document from class A is assigned to cluster *B* or a document from class B is assigned to cluster *A*.

Along with the two correct situations—both class and cluster labels are either A or B—we have four possibilities. As the most common clustering and classification problems involve two classes, they are usually called *positive* and *negative*. Also, the original class labels are referred to as *actual*, and those determined by the clustering (or classification) algorithm are called *predicted*. According to this terminology, the classes-to-cluster evaluation assigns to each document one of the following four labels:

- *True positive* (TP): actual positive and predicted as positive
- *False positive* (FP): actual negative but predicted as positive
- *True negative* (TN): actual negative and predicted as negative
- *False negative* (FN): actual positive but predicted as negative

The easiest way to see the structure of the error is to include the number of documents falling in each of the categories above in a matrix called a *confusion matrix* (also, *contingency table*) as follows:

|  | Predicted (Clusters) | |
| --- | --- | --- |
| Actual (Classes) | Positive | Negative |
| Positive | TP | FN |
| Negative | FP | TN |

In these terms the overall classes to clusters error and accuracy are the following:

$$\text{error} = \frac{FP + FN}{TP + FP + TN + FN} \qquad \text{accuracy} = \frac{TP + TN}{TP + FP + TN + FN}$$

For example, the confusion matrices for the clusterings produced by the attributes *research* and *hall* follow:

|                    | *research* | | *hall* | |
|--------------------|-----------|-----------|-----------|-----------|
|                    | Predicted (Clusters) | | Predicted (Clusters) | |
| Actual (Classes)   | *A* | *B* | *A* | *B* |
| A                  | 8 | 3 | 9 | 2 |
| B                  | 0 | 9 | 6 | 3 |

Classes-to-clusters evaluation of a good clustering should produce a confusion matrix in which most of the documents fall in the main diagonal cells (A–A, B–B), such as the matrix for attribute *research*. The numbers outside the main diagonal indicate errors. Two additional measures account for these errors: *precision* and *recall*. In fact, these are the same measures that are used in *information retrieval* (see Chapter 1), where the actual labels correspond to relevant documents and the labels predicted correspond to documents retrieved. Formally, we define precision and recall as follows:

$$\text{precision} = \frac{\text{TP}}{\text{TP} + \text{FP}} \qquad \text{recall} = \frac{\text{TP}}{\text{TP} + \text{FN}}$$

For example, for clustering with the attribute *research*, the precision is 1.0 and the recall is 0.73. For the attribute *hall*, the precision is much lower, 0.6 but the recall is higher, 0.82. The interpretation of these figures depends on the application domain. For example, if we consider e-mail filtering, where the positive class means nonspam, the latter clustering may be considered as better, because it would allow more nonspam (82%), despite the fact that the overall accuracy of the former clustering is higher.

A confusion matrix can be built with more than two classes and clusters by using more rows (for the classes) and more columns (for the clusters). Thus, we can define a generalized confusion matrix for $m$ classes and $k$ clusters as shown in Table 4.6. The number $n_{ij}$ in each cell indicates the number of documents from cluster $j$ that belong to class $i$. Now we can define recall and precision with respect to class $i$ and cluster $j$

**TABLE 4.6**

| Classes | Clusters | | | | |
|---------|------|---------|------|---------|------|
|         | 1 | $\cdots$ | $j$ | $\cdots$ | $k$ |
| 1       | $n_{11}$ | $\cdots$ | $n_{1j}$ | $\cdots$ | $n_{1k}$ |
| $\vdots$ |   |          |          |          |          |
| $i$     | $n_{i1}$ | $\cdots$ | $n_{ij}$ | $\cdots$ | $n_{ik}$ |
| $\vdots$ |   |          |          |          |          |
| $m$     | $n_{m1}$ | $\cdots$ | $n_{mj}$ | $\cdots$ | $n_{mk}$ |

as follows:

$$P(i,j) = \frac{n_{ij}}{\sum_{i=1}^{m} n_{ij}} \qquad R(i,j) = \frac{n_{ij}}{\sum_{j=1}^{k} n_{ij}}$$

If we set $m = 2$ and $k = 2$, the terms $P(1,1)$ and $R(1,1)$ correspond to the precision and recall defined previously for a two-class clustering problem.

The problem of using precision and recall is the trade-off between them (see the section "Evaluating Search Quality" in Chapter 1). For specific domains where we know the error cost (e.g., e-mail filtering), this may not be a problem. However, to evaluate clustering in other domains, such as topic directories, we need a single criterion function such as the *F-measure*. This is a function that combines precision and recall and is especially popular for *evaluating text document clustering*. With respect to a specific pair of class and cluster $(i,j)$, it is defined to be

$$F(i,j) = \frac{2\,P(i,j)\,R(i,j)}{P(i,j) + R(i,j)}$$

To get rid of the indices we take the maximum of $F(i,j)$ over all clusters and then sum across classes. As classes generally include different numbers of documents, we weight their contribution to the sum with the proportion of documents in each. Thus, we obtain the $F$-measure for the entire clustering.

$$F = \sum_{i=1}^{m} \frac{n_i}{n} \max_{j=1,\ldots,k} F(i,j)$$

where $n_i = \sum_{j=1}^{k} n_{ij}$ (the number of documents belonging to class $i$, or row $i$ total) and $n = \sum_{i=1}^{m} \sum_{j=1}^{k} n_{ij}$ (the total number of documents in the sample).

As an illustration, let us see how the $F$-measure would evaluate two of the clusterings shown in Table 4.4, those for attributes *offers* and *students*, which have the same overall accuracy of $14/20 = 0.7$. We start with the confusion matrices:

| | offers | | students | |
|---|---|---|---|---|
| $n_{11} = 8$ | $n_{12} = 3$ | $n_{11} = 10$ | $n_{12} = 1$ |
| $n_{21} = 3$ | $n_{22} = 6$ | $n_{21} = 5$ | $n_{22} = 4$ |

Then we compute the precision and recall, the $F$-measure for each cell, and the overall $F$-measure for each clustering.

| offers | |
|---|---|
| $P(1,1) = 0.73,\ R(1,1) = 0.73$ | $P(1,2) = 0.33,\ R(1,2) = 0.27$ |
| $F(1,1) = 0.73$ | $F(1,2) = 0.30$ |
| $P(2,1) = 0.27,\ R(2,1) = 0.33$ | $P(2,2) = 0.67,\ R(2,2) = 0.67$ |
| $F(2,1) = 0.30$ | $F(2,2) = 0.67$ |
| $F = \frac{11}{20}0.73 + \frac{9}{20}0.67 = 0.70$ | |

| students |
| --- |

$$P(1, 1) = 0.67, \quad R(1, 1) = 0.91 \qquad P(1, 2) = 0.2, \quad R(1, 2) = 0.09$$
$$F(1, 1) = 0.77 \qquad\qquad F(1, 2) = 0.12$$
$$P(2, 1) = 0.33, \quad R(2, 1) = 0.56 \qquad P(2, 2) = 0.8, \quad R(2, 2) = 0.44$$
$$F(2, 1) = 0.42 \qquad\qquad F(2, 2) = 0.57$$
$$F = \tfrac{11}{20}0.77 + \tfrac{9}{20}0.57 = 0.68$$

The *F*-measure shows that the clustering produced by the attribute *offers* is slightly better than the clustering produced by the attribute *students* despite the fact that they both have the same overall accuracy. Obviously, the *F*-measure provides a more precise account for the error than does the overall accuracy. The explanation is that the *F*-measure is actually the *harmonic mean*[3] of precision and recall. The harmonic mean is used for averaging rates (ratios of two quantities specified in different units, such as distance/time and price/count). The precision and recall can be seen as rates, although not of the same kind, but it seems that the harmonic mean works well for averaging them.

## ENTROPY

Let us now take a probabilistic approach by considering the class label as a random event. This would allow us to evaluate its probability distribution in each cluster. The probability of class $i$ in cluster $j$ can be estimated by the proportion of occurrences of class label $i$ in cluster $j$. Using the notation of the confusion matrix, this is

$$p_{ij} = \frac{n_{ij}}{\sum_{i=1}^{m} n_{ij}}$$

In fact, this is exactly the precision $P(i, j)$. As for the precision, the ideal situation would be a one-to-one mapping between classes and clusters (i.e., $p_{ij} = 1$ for each cluster). However, this is rarely achieved, and therefore we try to minimize the *entropy* of the class distribution in each cluster. The entropy is an information-based measure of "impurity" and accounts for the average information of getting an arbitrary message about the class label. It can also be interpreted as a measure of *uncertainty* or *expected surprise* of the recipient of that message. Formally, the entropy in cluster $j$ is defined as

$$H_j = - \sum_{i=1}^{m} p_{ij} \log p_{ij}$$

A "pure" cluster, where all documents have a single class label, has an entropy of 0; the highest entropy is achieved when all class labels have the same probability

---

[3] The harmonic mean $H$ of $n$ positive numbers $x_1, x_2, \ldots, x_n$ is defined by $1/H = (1/n)\sum_{i=1}^{n} x_i$. For $n = 2$ it can be written as $H = 2x_1x_2/(x_1 + x_2)$.

(the situation with the highest uncertainty). For example, for a two-class problem the 50–50 situation has the highest entropy, $-0.5 \log 0.5 - 0.5 \log 0.5 = 1$. Similar to the $F$-measure for evaluating the entire clustering, we sum up the entropies of individual clusters weighted with the proportion of documents in each. That is,

$$H = \sum_{j=1}^{k} \frac{n_j}{n} \, H_j$$

where $n_j$ is the number of documents in cluster $j$ and $n$ is the total number of documents. For example, computing the entropies of the clusterings discussed previously for the attributes *offers* and *students*, we obtain the following results:

$$H(\textit{offers}) = \tfrac{11}{20} \left(-\tfrac{8}{11} \log \tfrac{8}{11} - \tfrac{3}{11} \log \tfrac{3}{11}\right) + \tfrac{9}{20} \left(-\tfrac{3}{9} \log \tfrac{3}{9} - \tfrac{6}{9} \log \tfrac{6}{9}\right)$$
$$= 0.878176$$

$$H(\textit{students}) = \tfrac{15}{20} \left(-\tfrac{10}{15} \log \tfrac{10}{15} - \tfrac{5}{15} \log \tfrac{5}{15}\right) + \tfrac{5}{20} \left(-\tfrac{1}{5} \log \tfrac{1}{5} - \tfrac{4}{5} \log \tfrac{4}{5}\right)$$
$$= 0.869204$$

Interestingly, the entropy of *students* is slightly lower, which means that this clustering is slightly better than the one obtained with the attribute *offers*. These results are the opposite of what the $F$-measure suggests. Which one of the two evaluations is more trustworthy? Obviously, the values of the evaluation functions are too close to be conclusive. The $F$-measure takes a weighted sum over classes, whereas the entropy does this over clusters. It seems that the big cluster with 15 documents and relatively low entropy makes the *students* clustering prevail.

Similar to the error-based approach, the entropy measure can be used for attribute evaluation. The *entropy-based attribute evaluation*, also known as *information gain* [4], is one of most popular supervised attribute selection mechanisms. It also plays a major role in a very popular algorithm for decision tree learning, ID3.

## REFERENCES

1. M. A. Gluck and J. E. Corter, Information, uncertainty and the utility of categories, in *Proceedings of the 7th Annual Conference of the Cognitive Science Society*, Lawrence Erlbaum Associates, Mahwah, NJ, 1985, p. 283–287.
2. D. H. Fisher, Knowledge acquisition via incremental conceptual clustering, *Mach. Learn.*, 2:139–172, 1987.
3. J. Rissanen, Modeling by shortest data description, *Automatica*, 14:465–471, 1978.
4. J. Ross Quinlan, Induction of decision trees, *Mach. Learn.*, 1(1):81–106, 1986.

## EXERCISES

1. Show that the sum of squared errors is equivalent to the average pairwise distance between cluster members. That is, derive

$$J_e = \frac{1}{2} \sum_{i=1}^{k} \frac{1}{|D_i|} \sum_{x_j, x_l \in D_i} \|x_j - x_l\|^2 \text{ from } J_e = \sum_{i=1}^{k} \sum_{x \in D_i} \|x - m_i\|^2 \text{ and } m_i = \frac{1}{|D_i|} \sum_{x \in D_i} x$$

**2.** Show that the centroid similarity is equivalent to the average pairwise similarity.

**3.** Run *k*-means with the binary and TFIDF data sets. Vary the random number seed and comment on the results. Note that Weka uses Euclidean distance (not cosine similarity).

    **a.** Observe the two parameters reported by Weka in the output window: number of iterations and within-cluster sum of squared errors. Do you find any correlation between them?

    **b.** Monitor the clustering result and correlate the balanced and unbalanced clusterings with the number of iterations and within a cluster sum of squared errors.

    **c.** Apply the "Normalize" unsupervised instance filter and rerun the same experiments. What changes? Comment on differences.

**4.** Use the six-attribute representation of the department data set (Table 4.3) and show all steps in computing the MDL score of the hypothesis:

$$H = \begin{cases} R_1\colon \text{IF } science = 0 \text{ THEN class} = A \\ R_2\colon \text{IF } science = 1 \text{ THEN class} = B \end{cases}$$

    **a.** Load the data set "Departments-binary.arff" and remove all attributes except those used in the MDL calculation.

    **b.** Use the Weka attribute statistics and visualization to determine the number of attribute–value pairs for each rule of the hypothesis. Select the attribute used in the hypothesis (*science*) and set each of the six attributes as class and examine the bar diagram. For example, the screenshot in Fig. E4.4b illustrates the process of determining the number of pairs with the attribute *history* in both clusters.

    The left bar corresponds to {*science* = 0}, and its mixed class colors mean that the instances in the corresponding cluster (*A*) include two different values of *history*. Thus, we have two pairs to count: {*history* = 0} and {*history* = 1}. The right bar corresponds

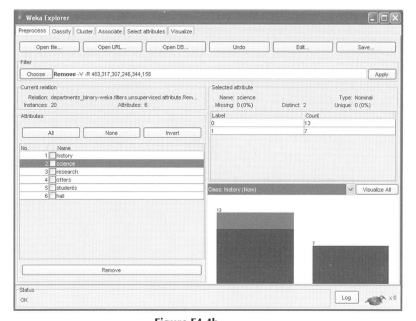

**Figure E4.4b**

to $\{science = 1\}$ and the single color (blue, representing 0) means that there is only one value for history in cluster $B$: $\{history = 0\}$. The counts in the statistics panel show the number of instances in each cluster: 13 in cluster $A$ and 7 in cluster $B$.

**c.** Do the MDL calculations as described in the section "MDL-Based Model and Feature Evaluation" and verify the result with that shown in Table 4.4.

5. Use the data set "Top-100-websites-binary.arff" and select a small subset of attributes (e.g., using a supervised selection method). Then compute the MDL score of the top three attributes using the method described in Exercise 4.

6. Use the data set "Top-100-websites-binary.arff" and evaluate the attributes *design*, *software*, and *support* individually and jointly using $k$-means ($k = 2$) with the classes-to-clusters method.

   **a.** Examine the clustering and its confusion matrix based on the values of each attribute. To create such a clustering, remove all attributes except the one being evaluated and run $k$-means with classes-to-clusters evaluation.

   **b.** Run $k$-means with classes-to-clusters evaluation on the data set with all three attributes and examine the clustering and confusion matrix.

   **c.** Compare the clusterings and their confusion matrices produced by each attribute individually and all three together. Note the cluster centroids. Rank attributes by the total error. Comment on the importance of each attribute for the clustering quality.

   **d.** Using the confusion matrices, compute the $F$-measure and the entropy for the same clusterings. Rank the attributes accordingly and compare results with error-based ranking (part c).

7. Rerun the experiments described in Exercise 6 but use the EM algorithm ($k = 2$). Note the cluster representation. Analyze the results.

8. Rerun the experiments described in Exercise 6 ($k$-means with $k = 2$), but using the data set "Top-100-websites-TFIDF.arff." Note the cluster representation. Analyze the results.

9. Rerun the experiments described in Exercise 6, but using the data set "Top-100-websites-TFIDF.arff" and the EM algorithm ($k = 2$). Note the cluster representation. Analyze the results.

10. Compare the result from the experiments for evaluating the attributes *design*, *software*, and *support* with the $k$-means and EM algorithms produced with the binary and TFIDF data sets (Exercises 6 to 9). Comment on the similarities and differences.

# CLASSIFICATION

GENERAL SETTING AND EVALUATION TECHNIQUES

NEAREST-NEIGHBOR ALGORITHM

FEATURE SELECTION

NAIVE BAYES ALGORITHM

NUMERICAL APPROACHES

RELATIONAL LEARNING

## GENERAL SETTING AND EVALUATION TECHNIQUES

In clustering we use the document class labels for evaluation purposes only. In classification they are, however, an essential part of the input to the learning system. The objective of the system is to create a mapping (also called a *model* or *hypothesis*) between a set of documents and a set of class labels. This mapping is then used to determine automatically the class of new (unlabeled) documents. In a narrow sense the latter process is called *classification*, while the general framework for classification includes the model creation phase and other steps. Therefore, the general framework is usually called *supervised learning* (also, *learning from examples, concept learning*) and includes the following steps:

- *Step 1: Data collection and preprocessing*. At this step, documents are collected, cleaned, and properly organized, the terms (features) identified, and a vector space representation created. We discussed this process in Chapter 1. The only difference here is that documents are labeled according to their topic, user preference, or any other criterion that may be used to organize documents in classes (categories). At this step the data may be divided into two subsets:
  - *Training set*. This part of the data will be used to create the model. In some cases this set is then split in two: the actual model construction subset and a *model validation subset* needed to tune the learner parameters.
  - *Test set*. This part of the data is used for testing the model.

*Data Mining the Web: Uncovering Patterns in Web Content, Structure, and Usage*
By Zdravko Markov and Daniel T. Larose    Copyright © 2007 John Wiley & Sons, Inc.

- *Step 2: Building the model.* This is the actual learning (also called *training*) step, which includes the use of the learning algorithm. It is usually an iterative and interactive process that may include other steps and may be repeated several times so that the best model is created:
  - ○ Feature selection
  - ○ Applying the learning algorithm
  - ○ Validating the model (using the validation subset to tune some parameters of the learning algorithm)
- *Step 3: Testing and evaluating the model.* At this step the model is applied to the documents from the test set and their actual class labels are compared to the labels predicted. Note that at this step the document labels are used for evaluation only (similar to the classes-to-cluster evaluation), which is not the case at the earlier validation step, where the class labels are actually used by the learning algorithm.
- *Step 4: Using the model to classify new documents* (with unknown class labels).

This four-step supervised learning scenario applies not only to web documents but to any type of data instances. The web documents exhibit some specific properties, however, which may require some adjustment or use of proper learning algorithms. Here are the basic ones:

- Text and web documents include thousands of words. Even after the preprocessing step, the resulting features are still too many. The real problem is not the amount of data, but rather, the asymmetry between two basic parameters in learning: the number of features and the number of instances. The terms substantially outnumber the documents, which makes the document space sparsely populated.
- The document features inherit some of the properties of the natural language text from which they are derived. Many features are irrelevant to the classification task and they are often correlated. This violates two basic assumptions that many learning algorithms rely on: the equal importance of all attributes and their statistical independence.
- Documents are of different sizes and thus can best be represented by different numbers of features. However, the learning algorithms need uniform-size vectors, which in turn contributes further to the sparsity of the instance space.

All this increases the importance of *feature selection*, especially for similarity-based methods, which are more sensitive to the problems mentioned above. Also, this is the main reason for the popularity of probabilistic approaches to document classification, which generally cope with these problems more easily. Further, in this chapter we discuss one major similarity-based approach to classification, the nearest-neighbor algorithm, and will see how feature selection affects its performance. Then we present the most popular probabilistic approach to classification, the naive Bayes algorithm. First we discuss briefly basic methods to evaluate the performance of classification algorithms.

The main evaluation criterion for classifiers is the *accuracy* of classification. This is the main approach used in supervised learning, which we explore further in some detail. Other criteria include *computational efficiency* (time and space complexity and scalability), ease of *model interpretation*, and *simplicity* (Occam's razor, MDL). The *benchmark data* comprise an important component of any evaluation approach. For machine learning and data mining in general, two of the most popular repositories of benchmark data are the UCI Machine Learning Repository [1] and the UCI KDD Archive [2]. Although these repositories include text and web data, there also exist separate data collections of this type. The *Reuters data* (http://www.daviddlewis.com/resources/testcollections/reuters21578/) and the *TREC data* (http://trec.nist.gov/data.html) are often cited in this category.

There are two basic approaches to evaluating the accuracy of classification. They both use the idea of splitting the available data into training and test sets and differ in the way in which this split is made. In the *holdout approach* we reserve a certain amount of data (usually, one-third) for testing and use the remainder (two-thirds) for training. The major problem with this approach is that the samples may not be representative. For example, some classes may be represented by very few documents or even by no documents at all. The solution is called *stratification*: sampling for training and test set within classes. This ensures that each class is represented with approximately equal proportions in both subsets. A further improvement of the holdout method is the *repeated holdout*. Accuracy/error estimates can be made more reliable by repeating the process with different subsamples. This is achieved by random selection of the training and test sets, repeating the process several times, and then averaging the success/error rates.

In holdout, because of the random selection, different test sets may overlap or some documents may never be used for testing. *Cross-validation* (CV) is an evaluation method that provides a solution to this problem. In *k-fold cross-validation* we first split the data into *k* subsets of equal size (usually, by random sampling and possibly with stratification). Then each subset in turn is used for testing and the remainder for training. The error estimates are averaged to yield an overall error estimate.

*Stratified tenfold cross-validation* is a standard method for evaluation. Extensive experiments have shown that this is the best choice for geting an accurate estimate. Repeated stratified cross-validation is even better: Tenfold cross-validation is repeated 10 times and the results are averaged. A special case of cross-validation is *leave-one-out cross-validation* (LOO-CV). LOO-CV is an *n*-fold cross-validation, where *n* is the number of training documents. That is, *n* classifiers are built for all possible $(n-1)$-element subsets of the training set and then tested on the remaining single document. LOO-CV makes maximum use of the data and avoids random sampling. However, it is very computationally expensive and stratification is not possible. Actually, this method guarantees a nonstratified sample (there is only one instance in the test set).

Finally, we can include the cost of errors by computing *precision* and *recall* or by combining them into the *F-measure*. We discussed this approach in Chapter 4.

# NEAREST-NEIGHBOR ALGORITHM

The nearest-neighbor algorithm is a straightforward application of similarity (or distance) for the purposes of classification. It predicts the class of a new document using the class label of the closest document from the training set. Because it uses just one instance from the training set, this basic version of the algorithm is called *one-nearest neighbor* (1-NN). The closeness is measured by minimal distance or maximal similarity. The most common approach is to use the TFIDF framework to represent both the test and training documents and to compute the cosine similarity between the document vectors.

Let us again consider our department document collection, represented as TFIDF vectors with six attributes along with the class labels for each document, as shown in Table 5.1. Assume that the class of the Theatre document is unknown. To determine the class of this document, we compute the cosine similarity between the Theatre vector and all other vectors. The results of these calculations are shown in Table 5.2, which shows the documents sorted by their similarity to the document being classified. The 1-NN approach simply picks the most similar document (the first one from the top of the list), Criminal Justice, and uses its label B to predict the class of Theatre. Obviously, this is a correct prediction because it coincides with the actual class of the document. However, if we look at the nearest neighbor of Theatre (Criminal Justice) we see only one nonzero attribute, which in fact produced the prediction. This is just a tiny portion of our training data. Because of the sparsity

**TABLE 5.1 TFDF Representation of Department Documents with Class Labels**

|  | *history* | *science* | *research* | *offers* | *students* | *hall* | Class |
|---|---|---|---|---|---|---|---|
| Anthropology | 0 | 0.537 | 0.477 | 0 | 0.673 | 0.177 | A |
| Art | 0 | 0 | 0 | 0.961 | 0.195 | 0.196 | B |
| Biology | 0 | 0.347 | 0.924 | 0 | 0.111 | 0.112 | A |
| Chemistry | 0 | 0.975 | 0 | 0 | 0.155 | 0.158 | A |
| Communication | 0 | 0 | 0 | 0.780 | 0.626 | 0 | B |
| Computer Science | 0 | 0.989 | 0 | 0 | 0.130 | 0.067 | A |
| Criminal Justice | 0 | 0 | 0 | 0 | 1 | 0 | B |
| Economics | 0 | 0 | 1 | 0 | 0 | 0 | A |
| English | 0 | 0 | 0 | 0.980 | 0 | 0.199 | B |
| Geography | 0 | 0.849 | 0 | 0 | 0.528 | 0 | A |
| History | 0.991 | 0 | 0 | 0.135 | 0 | 0 | B |
| Mathematics | 0 | 0.616 | 0.549 | 0.490 | 0.198 | 0.201 | A |
| Modern Languages | 0 | 0 | 0 | 0.928 | 0 | 0.373 | B |
| Music | 0.970 | 0 | 0 | 0 | 0.170 | 0.172 | B |
| Philosophy | 0.741 | 0 | 0 | 0.658 | 0 | 0.136 | B |
| Physics | 0 | 0 | 0.894 | 0 | 0.315 | 0.318 | A |
| Political Science | 0 | 0.933 | 0.348 | 0 | 0.062 | 0.063 | A |
| Psychology | 0 | 0 | 0.852 | 0.387 | 0.313 | 0.162 | A |
| Sociology | 0 | 0 | 0.639 | 0.570 | 0.459 | 0.237 | A |
| Theatre | 0 | 0 | 0 | 0 | 0.967 | 0.254 | ? (B) |

TABLE 5.2   Documents Sorted by Similarity to Theatre

| Document | Class | Similarity to Theatre |
| --- | --- | --- |
| Criminal Justice | B | 0.967075 |
| Anthropology | A | 0.695979 |
| Communication | B | 0.605667 |
| Geography | A | 0.510589 |
| Sociology | A | 0.504672 |
| Physics | A | 0.385508 |
| Psychology | A | 0.343685 |
| Mathematics | A | 0.242155 |
| Art | B | 0.238108 |
| Music | B | 0.207746 |
| Chemistry | A | 0.189681 |
| Computer Science | A | 0.142313 |
| Biology | A | 0.136097 |
| Modern Languages | B | 0.0950206 |
| Political Science | A | 0.0762211 |
| English | B | 0.0507843 |
| Philosophy | B | 0.0345299 |
| History | B | 0 |
| Economics | A | 0 |

of the vector space, similar situations often occur in real web document collections with thousands of attributes and documents. In fact, no matter how large the training set is, the 1-NN algorithm makes the prediction using a single instance, often relying on few attributes. All this makes the algorithm extremely sensitive to noise (wrong values of some attributes) and irrelevant attributes. Therefore, when using 1-NN, two assumptions have to be made: There is *no noise*, and *all attributes are equally important* for the classification. The problem is that these assumptions are not realistic, especially for large text document collections. Of course, this is where feature selection may help (we discuss this in the next section). However, there also exist extensions of 1-NN that address this problem: *k-NN* and *distance-weighted k-NN*.

k-NN is a generalization of 1-NN, where the prediction is made by taking the majority vote over the $k$ nearest neighbors. The parameter $k$ is selected to be a small odd number (usually, 3 or 5). For example, 3-NN would again, classify Theatre as of class B, because this is the majority label in the top three documents (B,A,B). However, 5-NN will predict class A, because the set of labels of the top five documents is {B,A,B,A,A} (i.e., the majority label is A). Which prediction is more feasible? One may suggest continuing with $k = 7, 9 \ldots$. However, this is the wrong direction to go, because we are taking votes from documents being less and less similar to the document being classified. So the idea is to take votes only from close neighbors. But because all $k$ nearest neighbors are considered equally important with respect to the classification, the choice of $k$ is crucial. This is the reason that 1-NN is the most popular version of the nearest-neighbor algorithms.

The other extension, *distance-weighted k-NN*, actually builds on the problem with the choice of the parameter $k$ that we just mentioned. The basic idea is to weight votes with the similarity (or distance) of the documents from the training set to the document being classified. Instead of adding 1's for each label, we may use a term that is proportional to the similarity (or inversely proportional to the distance). The simplest option is just the similarity function $\text{sim}(X,Y)$. Other options are $1/[1 - \text{sim}(X,Y)]$ or $1/[(1 - \text{sim}(X,Y))]^2$. For example, the distance-weighted 3-NN with the simplest weighting scheme $[\text{sim}(X,Y)]$ will predict class B for the Theatre document because the weight for label B (documents Criminal Justice and Communication) is $B = 0.967075 + 0.605667 = 1.572742$, while the weight for Antropology is $A = 0.695979$, and thus $B > A$. With the weighting scheme it makes sense to use a larger $k$, even a $k$ equal to the number of documents in the training set. For example, for $k = 19$ (all documents excluding Theatre) the prediction for Theatre is A, because the weight for A is 3.2269 and the weight for B is 2.198931.

The distance-weighting approach actually allows the algorithm to use not just a single instance, but more or even all instances. In this respect it is interesting to evaluate and compare the performance of various versions of NN. We use LOO-CV for this purpose because it is the best choice for small data sets: Computational complexity is not a concern and stratification is not needed because the algorithm does not build a model. Table 5.3 summarizes the LOO-CV accuracy evaluation of 1-NN, 3-NN, 5-NN, and 19-NN with and without distance weighting on the document collection shown in Table 5.1. To investigate the effect of more and possibly irrelevant attributes, we run the same experiments with the complete set of 671 attributes. The results show clearly that a small set of relevant attributes works much better than all attributes. Another important observation is that distance weighting does not help much. With a set of relevant attributes, the algorithm works perfectly with $k = 1$ and $k = 3$, and thus there is not much left to be improved. Only for $k = 5$ do we see a little improvement. On the other hand, distance weighting makes no difference in experiments with all attributes. Because of the sparseness of the vector space, the range of similarity values is small (minimum $= 0.022$ and maximum $= 0.245$, whereas for the six-attribute case, minimum $= 0$ and maximum $= 0.995$), and thus weighted votes are not much different from nonweighted votes. Overall, 1-NN is a clear winner in all cases. In general, we may expect improvement with $k > 1$ and distance weighting only in situations with noise (obviously not present in out data) and not too many irrelevant attributes.

The nearest-neighbor algorithm has been used successfully by statisticians for more than 50 years. As a machine learning approach it falls in the category of

**TABLE 5.3  LOO-CV of the Nearest-Neighbor Algorithm**

| Attributes | No Distance Weighting | | | | Distance Weighting | | | |
| --- | --- | --- | --- | --- | --- | --- | --- | --- |
| | 1-NN | 3-NN | 5-NN | 19-NN | 1-NN | 3-NN | 5-NN | 19-NN |
| 6 | 1.00 | 1.00 | 0.90 | 0.55 | 1.00 | 1.00 | 1.00 | 0.85 |
| 671 | 0.85 | 0.85 | 0.75 | 0.55 | 0.85 | 0.85 | 0.75 | 0.55 |

*instance-based learning* [3] because the classification is based on a number of instances from the training data. It is also considered as *lazy learning*, because the model creation phase (step 2) does not involve any computation; rather, the instances are simply stored. All the computation takes place during the classification step, when similarity is calculated for each instance in the training set. This makes the algorithm *computationally expensive* (to improve efficiency for large document collections such as the Web, a smaller random sample called a *window* is used). In contrast, *eager learners* do most of the computation during the learning phase when the model is created. Then the use of the model for prediction is usually straightforward. Despite these drawbacks, the nearest-neighbor algorithm is the most popular similarity-based approach to text and web document classification.

## FEATURE SELECTION

The objective of feature selection is to find a subset of attributes that best describe a set of documents with respect to the classification task (i.e., the attributes with which the learning algorithm achieves maximal accuracy). This simple definition suggests a simple solution: to try all subsets and pick the one that maximizes accuracy. Unfortunately, this solution is impractical, due to the huge number of subsets that have to be investigated ($2^n$ for $n$ attributes). Therefore, we make a strong, but practical assumption that *attributes are independent*. Now we can evaluate attributes individually and assume that the set of the best attributes selected in such a way would best describe our documents collectively. This type of reasoning leads to an attribute selection approach called *ranking*. In ranking we evaluate each attribute individually and then sort the list of attributes according to their evaluation score (rank). Then we pick a predefined number of attributes from the top of the list. There are many attribute evaluation schemes and we have already mentioned two in the context of clustering: *error-based* and *information gain attribute evaluation*. In fact, these two schemes are used mostly in classification but can also work in clustering when labeled data are available. Hereafter we formally define information gain, describe a similarity-based approach, and illustrate the effect of feature selection with the performance of the nearest-neighbor algorithm.

First, we define *entropy*. Let $S$ be a set of document vectors from $k$ classes $C_1, C_2, \ldots, C_k$. Then the number of vectors in $S$ is $|S| = |S_1| + |S_2| + \cdots + |S_k|$, where $S_i$ is the set of vectors belonging to class $C_i$. The entropy is the *average information* needed to predict the class of an arbitrary vector in $S$. It is defined to be

$$H(S) = - \sum_{i=1}^{k} P(C_i) \log P(C_i)$$

where the probability of class $C_i$ is calculated as the proportion of instances in it [i.e., $P(C_i) = |S_i|/|S|$]. Assume now that attribute $A$ has $m$ values – $v_1, v_2, \ldots, v_m$. Then $A$ splits the set $S$ into $m$ subsets, $A_1, A_2, \ldots, A_m$, each including the documents that have value $v_i$ for $A$. The *entropy in the split* based on attribute $A$ is defined to be

$$H(A_1, A_2, \ldots, A_m) = \sum_{i=1}^{m} \frac{|A_i|}{|S|} H(A_i)$$

where $H(A_i)$ is the entropy of the class distribution in set $A_i$.

After splitting a set of documents the entropy in the split decreases. The best split (produced by the best attribute) will put in each $A_i$ documents from a single class, and thus its entropy will be 0. The *information gain* [5] measures the quality of a split (respectively an attribute) by the decrease of entropy: that is,

$$\text{gain}(A) = H(S) - H(A_1, A_2, \ldots, A_m)$$

In the section "Entropy" in Chapter 4 we illustrated computation of the entropy of splits produced by the attributes *offers* and *students* on the Boolean data. For numerical attributes (TFIDF) the information gain is computed after *discretization* [6]. The attribute values are divided into intervals, so that the gain is maximized.

Another feature selection technique, called *similarity-based* (or *instance-based*) *feature selection* [4], uses the idea of the nearest-neighbor algorithm. It assigns weights as follows to attributes that reflect their relevance to the classification:

- For each vector a certain number of nearest neighbors from the same and different classes called *near hits* and *near misses*, respectively, are found.
- If a near hit has a different value for a certain attribute, that attribute appears to be irrelevant and its weight should be decreased.
- For near misses, attributes with different values are relevant and their weights should be increased.

The algorithm for computing weights starts with equal weights for all attributes (say, 0) and adjusts them repeatedly (adding or subtracting small amounts) as explained above. The vectors used to find near hits and misses are usually picked at random. This allows ordering attributes by relevance. Let us use the nearest neighbors of the Theatre vector (assuming now that we know its class label) and adjust the relevance of some attributes. From Table 5.2 we determine that Criminal Justice is a near hit and Anthropology is a near miss. Now let us look at the values of the attributes in Table 5.4. The attributes *history* and *offers* have the same value in Theatre and in the near hit and near miss, so there is no change in their weights. The attributes *science* and *research* receive an increase, however, because they have different values in the near miss Anthropology. *Hall* receives a decrease, because its value is different in the near hit Criminal Justice.

**TABLE 5.4  Attribute Values**

|  | history | science | research | offers | students | hall | Class |
|---|---|---|---|---|---|---|---|
| Anthropology | 0 | 0.537 | 0.477 | 0 | 0.673 | 0.177 | A |
| Criminal Justice | 0 | 0 | 0 | 0 | 1 | 0 | B |
| Theatre | 0 | 0 | 0 | 0 | 0.967 | 0.254 | B |

**TABLE 5.5 Top 10 Ranking Attributes in the Department Collection Selected by Two Evaluation Measures**

| Rank | InfoGain | Similarity |
|------|----------|------------|
| 1 | *research* | *research* |
| 2 | *science* | *offers* |
| 3 | *hall* | *science* |
| 4 | *study* | *concentrations* |
| 5 | *civilization* | *courses* |
| 6 | *integral* | *study* |
| 7 | *expression* | *studies* |
| 8 | *oral* | *based* |
| 9 | *craine* | *theoretical* |
| 10 | *specific* | *diverse* |

Table 5.5 shows the top 10 attributes from the set of 671 attributes of the department documents collection ordered by info gain and by similarity-based evaluation. Not surprisingly, the attributes *research* and *science* get the highest scores in both rankings; we have already seen these attributes on top of the error-based and MDL rankings. However there are also differences in the ranking produced by the two schemes. In fact, except for the clear winners, *research* and *science*, only one other attribute (*study*) appears in both top tens. Obviously, this happens because these two attributes are very strongly correlated with the class.

The class distribution can be visualized by *histograms*. Because the attributes we discuss are numerical, they are first discretized by simple binning (the actual entropy and information gain are computed using a different type of discretization, mentioned earlier). Figure 5.1 shows the histograms of the top 10 attributes selected by InfoGain. The four best attributes show single class intervals (uniformaly colored bars) or intervals with a dominant class, which indicate low entropy. The rest of the attributes show one interval with 19 instances that follows closely the overall class distribution (it corresponds to the value of 0), and another single class interval but with just one instance (the only nonzero value of that attribute). The former one has high entropy, whereas the latter has an entropy of zero. However, this contributes too little to the overall information gain, because it is just one instance (the weight coefficient is $1/20$).

It is interesting to see how the nearest-neighbor algorithm works with these two sets of attributes. Also, we may try to investigate how adding more attributes with lower relevance affects performance. The experimental setting for this purpose is the following. We use 1-NN and start with the top-ranked attribute (*research*). Then at each later step we add the next attribute in the list and evaluate the classification accuracy by LOO-CV. The results are shown in Figure 5.2.

The InfoGain graph illustrates very well the typical behavior of NN when the number of attributes increases; adding attributes always lowers the accuracy unless they are all relevant. Once the curve reaches a maximum accuracy of 100% with two attributes (*research* and *science*), it stays at that level through a total of 50 attributes,

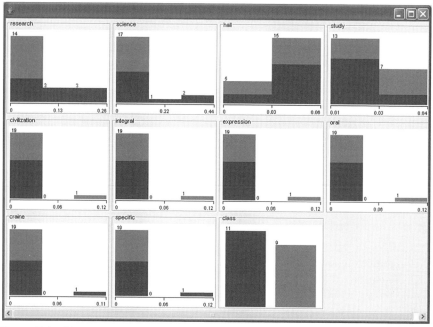

**Figure 5.1**   Class distribution histograms of the best 10 attributes selected by InfoGain produced by Weka (http://www.cs.waikato.ac.nz/ml/weka/, [9]).

which means that all attributes being added are relevant. After that the additional attributes generally lower the accuracy (with some fluctuations). The similarity curve is more unstable; it reaches its maximum at three attributes (which again include the two best, *research* and *science*) and then goes down quickly. This clearly shows that many irrelevant attributes occur among the top-ranked attributes, which is an indication that the ranking produced by this method is not as good as the one produced by InfoGain. The explanation is that the similarity approach uses the underlying mechanism of NN and thus suffers from the presence of irrelevant attributes, as the

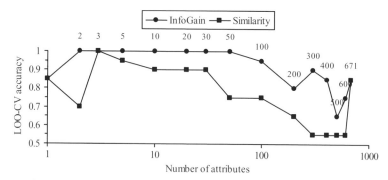

**Figure 5.2**   Accuracy of 1-NN with an increasing number of attributes.

original NN does. Their effect is not critical, however, because of random sampling and the large number of near hits and misses that are taken into account. Another observation supported by the peak in the end of both graphs is that using all attributes is a better choice than any subset that includes irrelevant attributes. The obvious reasoning here is that this guaranties the presence of all relevant attributes.

## NAIVE BAYES ALGORITHM

Let us now take the probabilistic approach and consider again the mixture modeling framework that we discussed in Chapter 3. Hereafter we discuss the classification problem, where the class labels are known and the objective is to create probabilistic models, which can then be used to classify new documents. In the section "Classification Problem" in Chapter 3 we assumed that the values of the TFIDF attributes have normal (Gaussian) distribution and showed how to classify new documents using the naive Bayes approach. However, the TFIDF values of the document attributes are computed using the information about *term occurrences* in documents, which are the actual random events that we are trying to model. In statistics, there are *discrete distributions* especially suitable for variables used for counting the number of occurrences of certain events, that is, taking values from the set of natural numbers $(0, 1, 2, \ldots)$. This is the *Poisson distribution* and the *multinominal distribution* (for the multivariate case). In the Boolean representation, the random event is the presence of a term in the document (ignoring the number of occurrences), which can be modeled by *discrete probabilities*. Hereafter we discuss two Bayesian classification approaches: one based on the Boolean document representation and another based on document representation by term counts.

Consider the set of Boolean document vectors shown in Table 5.6 and the task of classifying the Theatre document given the rest of documents with known class labels. The Bayesian approach determines the class of document $x$ as the one that maximizes the conditional probability $P(C \mid x)$. According to Bayes' rule,

$$P(C \mid x) = \frac{P(x \mid C)\, P(C)}{P(x)}$$

To compute $P(x \mid C)$, we make the *naive Bayes assumption* that attributes are statistically independent. Given that $x$ is a vector of $n$ attribute values [i.e., $x = (x_1, x_2, \ldots, x_n)$], this assumption leads to:

$$P(x \mid C) = P(x_1, x_2, \ldots, x_n \mid C) = \prod_{i=1}^{n} P(x_i \mid C)$$

Each $P(x_i \mid C)$ is calculated as the proportion of documents from class $C$ that include attribute value $x_i$. $P(C)$ is the probability of sampling for class $C$, which is calculated as the proportion of the training documents that fall in class $C$. $P(x)$ is a common denominator, which is not needed in the calculations if only the class label is to be determined.

Now to find the class of the Theatre document, we compute the conditional probability of class A and class B given that this document has already occurred. For

**TABLE 5.6 Boolean Document Vectors with Class Labels**

|  | *history* | *science* | *research* | *offers* | *students* | *hall* | Class |
|---|---|---|---|---|---|---|---|
| Anthropology | 0 | 1 | 1 | 0 | 1 | 1 | A |
| Art | 0 | 0 | 0 | 1 | 1 | 1 | B |
| Biology | 0 | 1 | 1 | 0 | 1 | 1 | A |
| Chemistry | 0 | 1 | 0 | 0 | 1 | 1 | A |
| Communication | 0 | 0 | 0 | 1 | 1 | 0 | B |
| Computer Science | 0 | 1 | 0 | 0 | 1 | 1 | A |
| Criminal Justice | 0 | 0 | 0 | 0 | 1 | 0 | B |
| Economics | 0 | 0 | 1 | 0 | 0 | 0 | A |
| English | 0 | 0 | 0 | 1 | 0 | 1 | B |
| Geography | 0 | 1 | 0 | 0 | 1 | 0 | A |
| History | 1 | 0 | 0 | 1 | 0 | 0 | B |
| Mathematics | 0 | 1 | 1 | 1 | 1 | 1 | A |
| Modern Languages | 0 | 0 | 0 | 1 | 0 | 1 | B |
| Music | 1 | 0 | 0 | 0 | 1 | 1 | B |
| Philosophy | 1 | 0 | 0 | 1 | 0 | 1 | B |
| Physics | 0 | 0 | 1 | 0 | 1 | 1 | A |
| Political Science | 0 | 1 | 1 | 0 | 1 | 1 | A |
| Psychology | 0 | 0 | 1 | 1 | 1 | 1 | A |
| Sociology | 0 | 0 | 1 | 1 | 1 | 1 | A |
| Theatre | 0 | 0 | 0 | 0 | 1 | 1 | ? (B) |

class A we have

$$P(A \mid \text{Theatre}) = \frac{P(\text{Theatre} \mid A)\, P(A)}{P(\text{Theatre})}$$

$$P(\text{Theatre} \mid A) = P(\text{history} = 0 \mid A) \times P(\text{science} = 0 \mid A) \times P(\text{research} = 0 \mid A)$$
$$\times\, P(\text{offers} = 0 \mid A) \times P(\text{students} = 1 \mid A) \times P(\text{hall} = 1 \mid A)$$

To calculate each of the probabilities above, we take the proportion of the corresponding attribute value in class A. For example, in the *science* column we have 0's in four documents out of 11 from class A. Thus, $P(\text{science} = 0 \mid A) = 4/11$. Similarly, we calculate the rest of the terms in the product and obtain

$$P(\text{Theatre} \mid A) = \tfrac{11}{11} \times \tfrac{4}{11} \times \tfrac{3}{11} \times \tfrac{8}{11} \times \tfrac{10}{11} \times \tfrac{9}{11} = 0.0536476$$

For class B we obtain

$$P(\text{Theatre} \mid B) = \tfrac{5}{8} \times \tfrac{8}{8} \times \tfrac{8}{8} \times \tfrac{2}{8} \times \tfrac{4}{8} \times \tfrac{5}{8} = 0.0488281$$

The probabilities of classes A and B are estimated with the proportion of documents in each: $P(A) = 11/19 = 0.578947$ and $P(A) = 8/19 = 0.421053$. Plugging all this in the Bayes formula and then dropping the common denominator $P(\text{Theatre})$ results in the following probability estimates (*likelihoods*):

$$P(A \mid \text{Theatre}) = \frac{(0.0536476)(0.578947)}{P(\text{Theatre})} \approx 0.0310591$$

$$P(B \mid \text{Theatre}) = \frac{(0.0488281)(0.421053)}{P(\text{Theatre})} \approx 0.0205592$$

At this point we can make the decision that Theatre belongs to class A, because its likelihood is higher. Or we can normalize the likelihoods to get the correct probabilities:

$$P(A \mid \text{Theatre}) = \frac{0.0310591}{0.0310591 + 0.0205592} = 0.601707$$

$$P(B \mid \text{Theatre}) = \frac{0.0205592}{0.0310591 + 0.0205592} = 0.398293$$

Compared to the original class label of the document (B), this prediction is incorrect. Interestingly, the same prediction was made by the 19-NN algorithm with weighting, which uses the entire training set (as Bayes does), while the 1-NN prediction was B. Although the prediction made by 1-NN is correct, it is based on a single document. Assuming that we don't have the original label (or are not sure that it has been assigned correctly), these observations raise a question of which classification is more feasible. The intuition suggests that the classification that uses more information must be more feasible. Although the Boolean naive Bayes algorithm uses all training documents (and thus may be assumed as more feasible than 1-NN), it ignores the term counts. So our next step is to investigate how a Bayesian model based on term counts will classify our test document.

Assume that there are $m$ terms $t_1, t_2, \ldots, t_m$ (corresponding to the attributes in the document description) and $n$ documents $d_1, d_2, \ldots, d_n$ from class C. Let us denote the number of times that term $t_i$ occurs in document $d_j$ as $n_{ij}$, and the probability with which term $t_i$ occurs in all documents from class C as $P(t_i|C)$. The latter can be estimated with the number of times that $t_i$ occurs in all documents from class C over the total number of terms in the documents from class C.

$$P(t_i|C) = \frac{\sum_{j=1}^{n} n_{ij}}{\sum_{i=1}^{m} \sum_{j=1}^{n} n_{ij}}$$

The *multinominal distribution* defines the probability of document $d_j$ given class $C$ as

$$P(d_j|C) = \left( \sum_{i=1}^{m} n_{ij} \right)! \prod_{i=1}^{m} \frac{P(t_i|C)^{n_{ij}}}{n_{ij}!}$$

This formula looks similar to the naive Bayes assumption. The basic differences are the factorials. They are added to account for all possible orderings of each word ($n_{ij}!$) and all words in the document $\left[ \left( \sum_{i=1}^{m} n_{ij} \right)! \right]$. The reason for this is that according to the bag-of-words model, the ordering of words is ignored.

Let us now see how the multinominal model will classify our test document Theatre. Table 5.7 includes the original data for our six-attribute department collection, where each cell includes the number of occurrences of the corresponding term in the document. This is, in fact, the row data that we have used so far to represent documents

**TABLE 5.7 Term-Count Representation of the Department Collection**

|  | *history* | *science* | *research* | *offers* | *students* | *hall* | Class |
|---|---|---|---|---|---|---|---|
| Anthropology | 0 | 1 | 1 | 0 | 4 | 1 | A |
| Art | 0 | 0 | 0 | 2 | 1 | 1 | B |
| Biology | 0 | 1 | 3 | 0 | 1 | 1 | A |
| Chemistry | 0 | 2 | 0 | 0 | 1 | 1 | A |
| Communication | 0 | 0 | 0 | 1 | 2 | 0 | B |
| Computer Science | 0 | 5 | 0 | 0 | 2 | 1 | A |
| Criminal Justice | 0 | 0 | 0 | 0 | 1 | 0 | B |
| Economics | 0 | 0 | 1 | 0 | 0 | 0 | A |
| English | 0 | 0 | 0 | 2 | 0 | 1 | B |
| Geography | 0 | 1 | 0 | 0 | 2 | 0 | A |
| History | 7 | 0 | 0 | 2 | 0 | 0 | B |
| Mathematics | 0 | 1 | 1 | 1 | 1 | 1 | A |
| Modern Languages | 0 | 0 | 0 | 1 | 0 | 1 | B |
| Music | 1 | 0 | 0 | 0 | 1 | 1 | B |
| Philosophy | 1 | 0 | 0 | 2 | 0 | 1 | B |
| Physics | 0 | 0 | 1 | 0 | 1 | 1 | A |
| Political Science | 0 | 5 | 2 | 0 | 1 | 1 | A |
| Psychology | 0 | 0 | 2 | 1 | 2 | 1 | A |
| Sociology | 0 | 0 | 1 | 1 | 2 | 1 | A |
| Theatre | 0 | 0 | 0 | 0 | 4 | 1 | ? (B) |

in various ways (TF, TFIDF, and Boolean). Now we use this information directly as a representation of our documents. First we calculate the probabilities $P(t_i \mid C)$. Within each class (rows with the corresponding label) we take the sum of the counts in the corresponding column and divide it by the total count for all columns. There are situations, however, where the sum for a particular column is zero. This results in zero probability $P(t_i \mid C)$, which when raised to a nonzero power may turn the entire product into zero no matter what the values of the other terms in the product are. For example, this happens with the term *history* and class A; that is, $P(history \mid A) = 0$. Consequently, the documents, which have a nonzero count for *history* will have zero probability in class A. That is $P(\text{History} \mid A) = 0$, $P(\text{Music} \mid A) = 0$, and $P(\text{Philosophy} \mid A) = 0$. A common approach to avoid this problem is to use the *Laplace estimator*. The idea is to add 1 to the frequency count in the numerator and 2 (or the number of classes, if more than two) to the denominator. The Laplace estimator helps to deal with a zero probability situation, which may also happen with the discrete probabilities in the Boolean representation that we discussed earlier.

Now we compute the probabilities of each term given each class using the Laplace estimator. For example, $P(history \mid A) = (0 + 1)/(57 + 2) = 0.017$ and $P(history \mid B) = (9 + 1)/(29 + 2) = 0.323$. Plugging all these probabilities in the formula results in

$$P(\text{Theatre} \mid A) = 5! \times \frac{0.017^0}{0!} \times \frac{0.288^0}{0!} \times \frac{0.22^0}{0!} \times \frac{0.068^0}{0!} \times \frac{0.305^4}{4!} \times \frac{0.017^1}{1!}$$

$$P(\text{Theatre} \mid B) = 5! \times \frac{0.323^0}{0!} \times \frac{0.0323^0}{0!} \times \frac{0.0323^0}{0!} \times \frac{0.355^0}{0!} \times \frac{0.194^4}{4!} \times \frac{0.194^1}{1!}$$

Similar to the Boolean case, we compute $P(\text{A} \mid \text{Theatre})$ and $P(\text{B} \mid \text{Theatre})$ by using only the numerator of the Bayes rule and then normalize the likelihoods. The calculations can be simplified further by omitting the factorial in front of the product because it occurs in both classes and will disappear in the normalization process. Thus, we obtain $P(\text{A} \mid \text{Theatre}) \approx 0.0000354208$ and $P(\text{B} \mid \text{Theatre}) \approx 0.00000476511$, and after normalization, $P(\text{A} \mid \text{Theatre}) = 0.88$ and $P(\text{B} \mid \text{Theatre}) = 0.12$. The winner is class A, with even more significant advantage over the boolean case (0.60 to 0.40).

Interestingly, when classifying Theatre using all documents for training (including Theatre itself) we get the same prediction. This may be an indication that the class label is not assigned properly. Further evidence for this is that the same kind of misclassification happens with the Criminal Justice document, which appeared to be most similar to Theatre in the NN experiment. In fact, these are the only two misclassifications in the LOO-CV evaluation, which thus produces 90% accuracy.

Finally, we compare the performance of the three versions of the naive Bayes algorithm that we have discussed so far: with TFIDF attributes (normal distribution), with Boolean attributes (discrete distribution), and with term counts (multinominal distribution). The data representation used by each of these algorithms is illustrated by the six-attribute samples shown in Tables 5.1, 5.6 and 5.7, respectively. We use an experimental setting similar to that used earlier for nearest-neighbor evaluation. For each representation the attributes are ranked by the *information gain method*, and samples with an increasing number of attributes (decreasing rank) are used for LOO-CV evaluation of the corresponding version of naive Bayes. The results of the experiments are shown in Figure 5.3.

The clear winner in this experiment is the multinominal Bayes. For all samples with 3 to 100 attributes it achieves 100% accuracy and after that stays well above the others and achieves the highest accuracy (85%) with all attributes. Next best is the Boolean naive Bayes. It also achieves relatively high accuracy up to 100 attributes, but then its accuracy curve goes down quickly and reaches 55% with all attributes. Note that 55% is the accuracy of the *majority predictor* that assigns class labels according to their probability in the training set. Thus, accuracies lower than 55% indicate poor

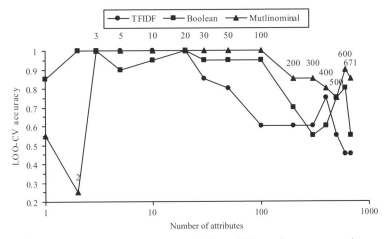

**Figure 5.3**    Naive Bayes accuracy with three different data representations.

performance, which is also the case with the TFIDF naive Bayes for 500 and more attributes.

The drop of the multivariate curve at two attributes (25% accuracy) illustrates an interesting conceptual difference between the multivariate and Boolean cases. This situation may seem counterintuitive, because the two attributes in question are *research* and *science*, the top two in the relevance ranking. The key to understanding this is the way that attribute probability $P(t_i \mid C)$ is used. In multivariate Bayes it is raised to a power equal to the term count. The terms *research* and *science* both have 0 counts in class B, which means that their probabilities are both 1. Thus the product is 1 (ignoring the factorial in front), and when multiplied by the class probability, which is greater for class A, all documents from class B are misclassified. The reasoning behind this is that if a term count is 0, the corresponding attribute is ignored from the process of classification (its probability becomes 1 and thus it does not affect the value of the product in any way). This allows the other attributes to make their contribution to document probability. However, in the present situation there are no other attributes, and thus the document probability is determined solely by the class probability. In the Boolean case, a term count of zero is treated differently. Zero is a legitimate *nominal value* whose occurrences in the document vectors are counted (just like the occurrence of 1), and thus it obtains a proper discrete probability, which is then used to compute the document probability. This may be seen as an advantage of the Boolean (nominal) naive Bayes because the absence of a term has the same importance for the overall classification as its presence does.

The experimental results from the evaluation of the three versions on naive Bayes can be explained easily if we look into the underlying document modeling framework: the *bag-of-words approach*, where the only information used is the number of occurrences of words in documents. Multinominal Bayes shows the best performance because it incorporates this information directly into the classification mechanism. The next-best algorithm, Boolean naive Bayes, uses only a part of this information—whether or not a word occurs in the document—whereas the TFIDF framework transforms the representation and changes the types of the attributes (counts into continuous values). Then it assumes that the resulting data have a normal distribution, which may not be true. So the poor performance of TFIDF Bayes in our experiments comes as no surprise. In fact, the objective of the TFIDF transformation is to represent documents as points (or vectors) in a *metric vector space*, with the underlying assumption that similar documents are represented by close points in the vector space. Therefore, the TFIDF representation is suitable for similarity- and metric-based approaches to classification. If we look at the performance evaluation of the nearest-neighbor algorithm (Figure 5.2), we see that its accuracy is comparable to the accuracy of multinominal Bayes. In the next section we discuss a metric-based approach to classification, linear regression, that also uses the TFIDF representation.

To summarize, the multinominal naive Bayes algorithm is suitable for domains with large vocabularies, such as the Web. It may work relatively well without the need for selecting a small subset of relevant attributes. Although it is based on the independence assumption, which is almost never present in real data, the naive Bayes algorithm works surprisingly well in practice. A possible explanation is that classification doesn't require accurate probability estimates as long as maximum probability is assigned to the correct class. Another advantage of naive Bayes is that it is more efficient than nearest neighbor, because the probabilities may be precomputed at learning time and used in the actual classification, which will then be straightforward. Also, there is no need to store all training documents.

## NUMERICAL APPROACHES

In the TFIDF vector space framework, we have used *cosine similarity* primarily as a measure of document similarity. However, the same vector representation allows documents to be considered as *points in a metric space*, where the similarity is defined by the *Euclidean distance*. In these terms the classification problem can be expressed as a separation problem. That is, given a set of points, the objective is to find a surface that divides the space in two parts, so that the points that fall in each part belong to a single class. *Linear regression*, the most popular approach based on this idea, uses a *hyperplane* as a separating surface.

Linear regression is a standard technique for numerical prediction. It works naturally with numerical attributes (including the class). The class value $C$ predicted is computed as a *linear combination* of the attribute values $x_i$ as follows:

$$C = w_0 + w_1 x_1 + \cdots + w_m x_m$$

The objective is to find the coefficients $w_i$ given a number of training instances $x_i$ with their class values $C$.

There are several approaches to the use of linear regression for classification (predicting class labels). One simple approach to binary classification is to substitute class labels with the values $-1$ and $1$. Then the predicted class is determined by the sign of the linear combination. For example, consider our six-attribute document vectors (Table 5.1). Let us use $-1$ for class A and $1$ for class B. Then the task is to find seven coefficients $w_0, w_1, \ldots, w_6$ which satisfy a system of 19 linear equations (we leave the Theatre vector for testing):

$$-1 = w_0 + w_1 \times 0 + w_2 \times 0.537 + w_3 \times 0.477 + w_4 \times 0 + w_5 \times 0.673 + w_6 \times 0.177$$
$$1 = w_0 + w_1 \times 0 + w_2 \times 0 + w_3 \times 0 + w_4 \times 0.961 + w_5 \times 0.195 + w_6 \times 0.196$$
$$\vdots$$
$$-1 = w_0 + w_1 \times 0 + w_2 \times 0 + w_3 \times 0.639 + w_4 \times 0.570 + w_5 \times 0.459 + w_6 \times 0.237$$

The solution for the vector of coefficients $(w_0, w_1, \ldots, w_6)$ is

$$(1.1397, -0.0549, -1.8396, -1.9736, -0.0175, -0.3912, -0.623)$$

Let us now compute the class value of Theatre:

$$1.1397 + 0 + 0 + 0 + 0 + -0.3912 \times 0.967 + -0.623 \times 0.254 = 0.603168$$

The result is positive, and thus the class predicted for Theatre is B. This prediction is correct and also agrees with the prediction of 1-NN, the vector-space classification approach that we discussed earlier.

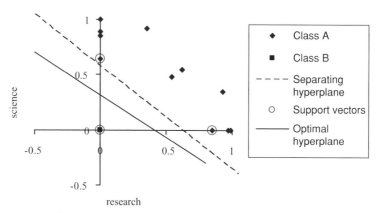

**Figure 5.4** Classification by linear regression and SVM.

We are not going into the details of how the coefficients are derived. We only mention that there exist standard numerical analysis techniques for this purpose. The idea is to *minimize the squared error*, which is the sum of the squared difference between the predicted and actual class values through all training instances. Generally, a solution exists if there are *more instances than attributes*. Of course, in some cases the squared error may be too large, so that no correct predictions can be made even on the training set. This happens when classes are not *linearly separable*, that is, cannot be separated by a hyperlane (or line in two dimensions). The simplest example of this is the XOR problem, defined with two attributes, $x$ and $y$, and a class value equal to the Boolean function $x \oplus y$ ($0 \oplus 0 = 0$, $0 \oplus 1 = 1$, $1 \oplus 0 = 1$, $1 \oplus 1 = 0$).

Figure 5.4 shows a two-dimensional projection of the six-dimensional vector space that we used in the example. The documents are plotted as points and their classes are indicated by different markers. All points from class B collapse into one point: (0,0). The *separating hyperplane* found by the linear regression algorithm is shown as a dashed line. Its equation includes the coefficients $w_i$ from the linear combination that we found earlier:

$$1.1397 - 0.0549x_1 - 1.8396x_2 - 1.9736x_3 - 0.0175x_4 - 0.3912x_5 - 0.623x_6 = 0$$

There are various extensions of the linear regression approach to classification. We discuss two that are particularly important: the maximum margin hyperplane and support vector machines (SVM).

A *maximum margin hyperplane* is a special kind of separating hyperplane with the maximum distance from the nearest points. The idea of such a hyperplane is illustrated in Figure 5.4. The nearest points to it, called *support vectors* (marked with circles in the figure), are at the same distance from the hyperplane. There is always at least one support vector from each class. The use of a maximum margin hyperplane makes the learning algorithm more stable and less sensitive to irrelevant instances because only the support vectors determine the position and orientation of the hyperplane; other instances are ignored. For the same reason, this approach helps avoiding overfitting.

The *support vector machine* (SVM) *approach* addresses the biggest disadvantage of linear regression: its inability to represent nonlinear boundaries between classes. The basic idea is to use a nonlinear mapping (called a *kernel*), which transforms the original vector space with nonlinear class boundaries into a new (usually higher-dimensional) space where the class boundaries are linear. SVMs are also combined with the maximum margin hyperplane approach, which makes them the most accurate classifier, especially suitable for nonlinear cases. It is also considered as the most accurate text classifier. Its basic disadvantage is that training algorithms for SVMs are computationally expensive.

## RELATIONAL LEARNING

All classification methods that we have discussed so far are based solely on the document content and more specifically on the bag-of-words model. Thus, many additional document features, such as the internal HTML structure, language structure, and interdocument link structure, are ignored. All this may, however, be a valuable source of information for the classification task. The basic problem with incorporating this information into the classification algorithm is the need for uniform representation. For example, content-based classification works well with vector-space representation, while hyperlink-based classification can be implemented by using graph models (e.g., subgraph isomorphism). In this section we discuss briefly an approach that allows various types of information to be represented in a uniform way and used for web document classification. The idea is known as *relational learning* or *first-order learning*. Another, narrower term also used in this context is *inductive logic programming* (ILP), which uses the language of logic programming (or Prolog) as a representation language for learning.

Let us start by extending our content-based approach to a relational representation. In our domain we have documents $d$ and terms $t$ connected with the basic relation *contains*. That is, if term $t$ occurs in document $d$, the relation contains($d$, $t$) is true. To represent the document class, we may use the unary relations class_A($d$) and class_B($d$). For example, the Boolean document representation with six attributes (from Table 5.6) is expressed in relational form by the set of relations (facts) shown partially in Figure 5.5 (some of the "contains" facts are omitted for brevity).

This set is called *background knowledge* and is used by the relational learning system to generate *clauses* (also called *rules*) for the *target relations*. The target relations for our task are *class_A* and *class_B*. Thus, the system generates the following clauses:

class_A(D) :- contains(D, *research*).

class_A(D) :- contains(D, *science*).

class_B(D) :- not contains(D, *science*), not contains(D, *research*).

| | | |
|---|---|---|
| class_A('Anthropology'). | class_B('Art'). | contains('Anthropology', *science*). |
| class_A('Biology'). | class_B('Communication'). | contains('Anthropology', *research*). |
| class_A('Chemistry'). | class_B('Criminal Justice'). | contains('Anthropology', *students*). |
| class_A('Computer Science'). | class_B('English'). | contains('Anthropology', *hall*). |
| class_A('Economics'). | class_B('History'). | contains('Art', *offers*). |
| class_A('Geography'). | class_B('Modern Languages'). | contains('Art', *students*). |
| class_A('Mathematics'). | class_B('Music'). | contains('Art', *hall*). |
| class_A('Physics'). | class_B('Philosophy'). | contains('Biology', *science*). |
| class_A('Political Science'). | class_B('Theatre'). | : |
| class_A('Psychology'). | | contains('Theatre', *students*). |
| class_A('Sociology'). | | contains('Theatre', *hall*). |

**Figure 5.5**  Background knowledge for relational learning.

The notation used here is based on Prolog syntax, where ":-" indicates implication ($\leftarrow$), "," indicates logical conjunction, and "not" indicates logical negation. Strings beginning with an uppercase letter are variables and those beginning with a lowercase letter or in single quotes are constants. Thus, these clauses read: "If a document contains *science*, its class is A. If a document contains *research*, its class is A. If a document does not contain *science* and does not contain *research*, its class is B." Note that this is exactly the meaning of the hypothesis $H_1$ that we discussed in Chapter 4 in the context of model-based clustering. Note also that the relational description is more concise and easily readable. In $H_1$ we had to list all possible combinations of values of the attributes *science* and *research*, whereas here we only specify explicitly what is true and all other possibilities are assumed to be false. This useful technique is based on the *closed world assumption* (CWA) and plays an important role in the definition of logical negation in Prolog. It is used in the third clause, where "not contains(D, *science*)" means that "contains(D, *science*)", where D has the value of a particular document, is not present in (or more precisely, does not logically follow from) the background knowledge.

There are various algorithms for first-order learning. Hereafter we describe briefly the algorithm FOIL [7], which is simple and efficient and uses an entropy-based technique to guide the search for clauses similar to the one we have discussed earlier for attribute evaluation.

Let us look into the process of generation of the clauses for the "class_A" relation. The instances of this relation (shown in the first column in Figure 5.5) are called *positive examples*. Given the positive examples, the algorithm automatically generates a set of *negative examples* by using the CWA approach (there is also an option that allows specifying them explicitly). The negative examples are instances of the same relation, where its argument takes all values from the contrasting class B (Art, Communication, Criminal Justice, etc.). The objective of the learning system is to find clauses that *cover*[1] all positives and do not cover any negatives (the latter condition may be relaxed in the presence of noise, i.e., some percentage of negative examples may be covered, too).

---

[1] A clause covers an example if there are substitutions for its variables such that when applied the clause head coincides with the example and each of its body literals occurs in (or follows from) the background knowledge.

TABLE 5.8    Literals and Examples Covered

| Candidate Literal | Number of Positives Covered | Number of Negatives Covered |
|---|---|---|
| contains(D, *history*). | 0 | 3 |
| contains(D, *science*). | 7 | 0 |
| contains(D, *research*). | 8 | 0 |
| contains(D, *offers*). | 3 | 6 |
| contains(D, *students*). | 10 | 5 |
| contains(D, *hall*). | 9 | 6 |

The algorithm works in general to specific fashion starting from the most general hypothesis, "class_A(D)." It covers all positives, however all negatives too. Therefore, it should be specialized by adding body literals. The candidates are generated using relations and arguments from the background knowledge. Also, they have to include the variable D, because otherwise the coverage does not change. For example, a clause such as "class_A(D) :- contains(X, *history*)" is equivalent to "class_A(D)." The potential candidate literals along with the number of positive and negative examples covered by the clause after adding the literal are shown in Table 5.8.

After generating all candidates, the algorithm computes an *information gain evaluation function*, which selects the best literal. We are not going into the details, but the idea is to maximally reduce the total number of bits needed to encode the classification of all positive examples covered by the clause. In the particular case, "contains(D, *research*)" and "contains(D, *science*)" are the clear winners (no negatives covered), which comes at no surprise because the attributes *research* and *science* are also on top of the entropy ranking that we discussed earlier in the chapter. Thus, the algorithm picks "contains(D, *research*)" and creates the clause

class_A(D) :- contains(D, *research*).

This clause does not cover negative examples, so it needs no further specialization and the algorithm stops looking for more literals to add. Otherwise, the clause would have to be extended with more literals until it covers no negative examples. This terminates the inner loop of the algorithm, which at each run creates a single clause.

If the clause found by the inner loop covered all positive examples, the algorithm would stop. However, it covers only eight. Therefore, more clauses are needed to cover the rest of the positive examples. The eight examples already covered are excluded from the original set of positives and the algorithm enters the inner loop again with the remaining ones: {class_A('Chemistry'), class_A('Computer Science'), class_A('Geography')}. Now it finds the clause "class_A(D) :- contains(D, *science*)," which happens to cover all remaining examples.

To simplify the discussion, we omitted the fact that negated literals such as "not contains(D, *science*)" are also considered as candidates and evaluated in the same way as the nonnegated literals. This is how the clause for relation "class_B" has been found.

After being generated, the clauses for the target relation can be used to classify new documents. For this purpose the new document is first represented as a set of

directory_page('Departments').    contains('Theatre', *johnson*).    link_to('Departments', 'Anthropology').
directory_page('Dept. Directory'). contains('Theatre', students).    link_to('Departments', 'Biology').
department_page('Theatre').    contains('Theatre', *hall*).
:    :    link_to('Departments', 'Theatre').
:    :
faculty(*johnson*).    contains('Dept. Directory', *johnson*). :
:    contains('Dept. Directory', *perrotta*). link_to('Departments', 'Dept. Directory').
:    :
staff(*perrotta*).    :
:
chairperson(*johnson*, 'Theatre').

**Figure 5.6**    Background knowledge for the department domain.

relations "contains" with the terms that it includes. Then a deductive system (e.g., Prolog) checks which of the relations "class_A" and "class_B" with the document specified as an argument is covered. Because the clauses are easy to read and understand, the definition of the target relation also provides an *explanation* of the class of documents in terms of the relations from the background knowledge. This is essentially the *knowledge discovery* step (turning data into knowledge) in the process of web mining.

There are various ways in which the relational language can be used to represent web data and knowledge. The approach that we have used defines objects as one-argument relations such as "class_A('History')" and relations among objects as two-argument predicates such as "contains('Art', *students*)". This approach also allows us to represent the web hyperlink structure as well as types (or categories) of web pages, terms, and other objects involved in the representation. We illustrate this idea by representing the domain of our department example.

Consider the web graph that includes the neighborhood of the department page ('Departments') shown in Figure 1.3. This page has links to our 20 well-known department pages and also a link to a school directory page that lists the department chairs and contact information ('Dept. Directory'). Figure 5.6 shows some of the relations from the background knowledge that describe this domain. The web pages are classified into two categories: directory page and department page. Categories (faculty, staff) are also associated with terms that represent personal names.

Assume that we want to generate a definition for the relation "chairperson" using the other relations available. First we have to specify a number of positive examples, that is, instances of the target relation, such as "chairperson (*johnson*, 'Theatre')." The negative examples will be instances of the target relation, which are logically false (should not follow from the background knowledge): for example, "chairperson(*perrotta*, 'Theatre')" and "chairperson(*johnson*, 'Biology')." Given all this information, a relational learning system such as FOIL will generate a rule like the following:

chairperson(X, D) :- department_page(D), contains(D, X), link_to(D1, D),

        link_to(D1, D2), directory_page(D2), contains(D1, X).

The literals "department_page(D)," "contains(D, X)," and "contains(D1, X)" ensure that the chairperson's name is mentioned in the department description page D (see the text of such a page in Figure 1.4) as well as in the department directory page

D1. The "link_to" literals check if the department directory page D2 belongs to that particular school (with departments listed in page D1) where department D belongs. If another person's name (e.g., the department secretary, whose name also occurs in the department directory) is included in some department description, an additional body literal may be needed, such as "faculty(X)".

This clause can now replace the positive examples, instances of "chairperson(X, D)." Most important, adding the clause to the background knowledge will allow a deductive reasoning system (such as Prolog) to answer questions about the truth value of other instances of "chairperson" not defined explicitly as positive or negative examples. The system may also infer the objects for which the relation is true. For example (the Prolog answer is given in italics):

?- chairperson(X, 'Computer Science').

*X = calvert*

?- chairperson(*craine*, D).

*D =* 'Mathematics'

This simple example illustrates the process of *learning knowledge bases from the Web*, which is one of the important objectives of web mining. A major project in this area is Carnegie Mellon University's Web->KB project [8]. The ultimate goal of this and similar projects is to create knowledge bases *automatically* that will make the information on the Web available in formalized, computer-understandable form so that it can be used for advanced information retrieval and problem solving.

# REFERENCES

1. D. J. Newman, S. Hettich, C. L. Blake, and C. J. Merz. *UCI Repository of Machine Learning Databases*, Department of Information and Computer Science, University of California, Irvine, CA; 1998, http://www.ics.uci.edu/~mlearn/MLRepository.html.
2. S. Hettich and S. D. Bay. *The UCI KDD Archive*, Department of Information and Computer Science, University of California, Irvine, CA; 1999, http://kdd.ics.uci.edu.
3. David W. Aha, Dennis F. Kibler, and Marc K. Albert, Instance-based learning algorithms, *Mach. Learn.*, 6:37–66, 1991.
4. I. Kononenko, Estimating attributes: analysis and extensions of RELIEF, in *Proceedings of the European Conference on Machine Learning*, 1994.
5. J. Ross Quinlan, Induction of decision trees, *Mach. Learn.*, 1(1):81–106, 1986.
6. U. M. Fayyad and K. B. Irani, Multi-interval discretisation of continuous-valued attributes for classification learning, in *Proceedings of the 13th International Joint Conference on Artificial Intelligence*, Morgan Kaufmann, San Francisco, CA, 1993.
7. J. Ross Quinlan, Learning logical definitions from relations, *Mach. Learn.*, 5:239–266, 1990.
8. Mark Craven, Dan DiPasquo, Dayne Freitag, Andrew McCallum, Tom M. Mitchell, Kamal Nigam, and Seán Slattery, Learning to construct knowledge bases from the World Wide Web, *Artif. Intell.*, 118(1–2): 69–113, 2000, http://www.cs.cmu.edu/~webkb/.
9. Ian H. Witten and Eibe Frank, *Data Mining: Practical Machine Learning Tools and Techniques*, 2nd ed., Morgan Kaufmann, San Francisco, CA, 2005.

# EXERCISES

1. Use the *k*-nearest neighbor algorithm (Weka's IBk) with the binary, term-count, and TFIDF data sets (the files "Top-100-websites-binary.arff," "Top-100-websites-counts.arff," and "Top-100-websites-TFIDF.arff," available from the book series Web site, www.dataminingconsultant.com). Vary the parameter *k*, the weighting scheme, and the normalization. Examine how each of these parameters affects the classification accuracy measured with 10-fold cross-validation (create graphs whenever possible). Find the setting that produces maximal accuracy. Comment on it.

2. Use the data set that produced maximal accuracy in Exercise 1 and apply information gain (Weka's InfoGainAttributeEval) and similarity (Weka's ReliefFAttributeEval) attribute evaluation. This can be done through Weka's attribute selection panel (to examine the attribute ranking) or in preprocess mode through filters (to actually rank and select attributes).

   **a.** Use IBk with the parameter setting that produced maximal accuracy in Exercise 1. Apply each of the filters and then run the algorithm with an increasing number of attributes chosen from the beginning of the ranked list. Use a proper logarithmic scale for the number of attributes and plot the accuracies in a graph similar to Figure 5.2. Which attribute selection method works better? Comment on this. Determine the optimal number of attributes for classification.

   **b.** Use IBk with *k*-NN=1. Apply each of the filters and then run the algorithm with the increasing number of attributes chosen from the beginning of the ranked list. Use a logarithmic scale for the number of attributes and plot the accuracies in a graph similar to that of Figure 5.2. Which attribute selection method works better? Comment on this. Determine the optimal number of attributes for classification.

   **c.** Compare the results in the experiments in parts a and b. Explain the differences.

3. Use the naive Bayes algorithm (Weka's NaiveBayes) with the binary, term-count, and TFIDF data sets (the files "Top-100-websites-binary.arff," "Top-100-websites-counts.arff," and "Top-100-websites-TFIDF.arff," available from the book series Web site www.dataminingconsultant.com). Compare the accuracies (produced with 10-fold cross-validation) and comment on the results.

4. Use the multinominal naive Bayes algorithm (Weka's NaiveBayesMultinomial) with the binary, term-count, and TFIDF data sets (the files "Top-100-websites-binary.arff," "Top-100-websites-counts.arff," and "Top-100-websites-TFIDF.arff," available from the book series Web site, www.dataminingconsultant.com). Compare the accuracies (produced with 10-fold cross-validation) and comment on the results.

5. Using the results from the experiments in Exercises 3 and 4, compare the performance of the two versions of naive Bayes (normal distribution and multinominal distribution) on each of the data sets. Comment on the results.

6. Run the SVM algorithm (Weka's SMO) on the TFIDF data set "Top-100-websites-TFIDF.arff" (available from the book series Web site, www.dataminingconsultant.com). Try the full set of attributes as well as subsets selected by InfoGain. Compare the 10-fold cross validation accuracies. Comment on the results.

7. Review the results achieved by *k*-NN, naive Bayes, and SVM on the binary, term-count, and TFIDF data sets (Exercises 1 to 6) and find the best algorithm and the best

representation in terms of classification accuracy. Also examine the run times, the time taken to build the model (reported by Weka in the classifier output window) and the total run time, including the testing step (available from the Log). Comment on this.

8. Experiment with Weka's "Supplied test set" test option. Remove a number of instances from a data set (say, "Top-100-websites-binary.arff") and store them in a new data file (test file) with the same header as that of the original file. Then load the new file through the "Set" option in the Weka classify panel. Run a classifier and examine the classifier errors through the "Visualize classifier errors" option (right-click on the result line). In this option, Weka shows the actual and predicted class labels for each instance (click on an instance to see them; the squares indicate errors) or allows saving this information on a file. This is how new instances with unknown labels can be classified. Use any label (or just a guess) in the test data set and Weka will provide the classification of the test instances by showing the labels predicted.

9. (Advanced project: web page classification)   Develop an approach to using the model created by Weka on the training data to classify new web pages by topic.

   a. Create a data set using a collection of web pages labeled manually by topic. Follow the approach suggested in Exercise 1 of Chapter 3 or use the file "Top-100-websites-binary.arff."

   b. Using experiments with feature selection, identify a subset of terms that will be used both for creating the model and classification of new web pages.

   c. Find a proper application or write a program (e.g., using the open source of Weka) which given a web document and the set of terms generates a binary vector representation of the documents in ARFF format. This will be the Weka test file.

   d. Use the Weka test set option (described in Exercise 8) to classify the new web documents.

10. (Advanced project: intelligent web browser)   Follow the steps of Exercise 9 but with the web pages labeled according to user preferences. In the collection phase, the web user while browsing the web pages labels them as like/dislike or uses a numerical scale depending on whether he or she finds their text content interesting. Then after the training (model creation) phase, new web pages will automatically be classified and presented to the web user with the label predicted. All this can be built in an "intelligent" web browser that will learn its user preferences automatically and then give recommendations about the interestingness of pages that the user is about to visit. Another application of this approach is user profiling: i.e. learning user models and identifying web users by their preferences.

PART

# WEB USAGE MINING

**I**n earlier chapters, we learned about web structure mining and web content mining. Next, we begin to learn about *web usage mining*, defined by Srivastava et al. [3] as follows: "Web usage mining is the application of data mining techniques to discover usage patterns from Web data, in order to understand and better serve the needs of Web-based applications." Note that web usage mining differs from web structure mining and web content mining, in that web usage mining reflects the behavior of humans as they interact with the Internet. Because of this, web usage mining is of intense interest for e-marketing and e-commerce professionals. Analysis of user behavior can provide insights leading to customization and personalization of a user's web experience.

# INTRODUCTION TO WEB USAGE MINING

## DEFINITION OF WEB USAGE MINING

Using standard data mining techniques such as clustering and association rules [2], a particular user may be associated with other users exhibiting similar behavior patterns and preferences. Then this user may be offered specialized links and sales opportunities tailored to his or her own preferences, based on information provided by the clustering or association rule algorithms. For example, the e-vendor may provide a choice of items to the user based on items the user has already browsed. "Customers who bought this book also bought . . . " (from `Amazon.com`, arguably the world leader in applied web usage mining). Recommendation making is one of the most common applications of knowledge gained through web usage mining.

Further, web usage mining offers a "reality check" to the developers of a Web site, sometimes indicating that the actual user behavior differs from the behavior expected as reflected in the design of the Web site. For example, web usage analysis may indicate that many customers are clicking from horror movies to a navigational page to science fiction movies. The web developers could use this information to add

*Data Mining the Web: Uncovering Patterns in Web Content, Structure, and Usage*
By Zdravko Markov and Daniel T. Larose   Copyright © 2007 John Wiley & Sons, Inc.

a direct link to science fiction movies from the horror movies page so that the user is not required to click through the navigation page.

Web usage mining can take place at several different levels. For example, as indicated above, developers may be interested in the sequence of clicks by a single user, in order to provide that user with a specialized experience. On the other hand, developers may be interested in the aggregate behavior of a large number of users, say, all users within a one-week period, in order to assess issues such as ease of navigation.

## CROSS-INDUSTRY STANDARD PROCESS FOR DATA MINING

Like data mining, web usage mining may be viewed in the context of the Cross-Industry Standard Process for Data Mining (CRISP–DM). According to CRISP–DM, a given data mining project has a life cycle consisting of six phases, as illustrated in Figure 6.1. Note that the phase sequence is *adaptive*. That is, the next phase in the sequence often depends on the outcomes associated with the previous phase. The most significant dependencies between phases are indicated by the arrows. For example, suppose that we are in the modeling phase. Depending on the behavior and

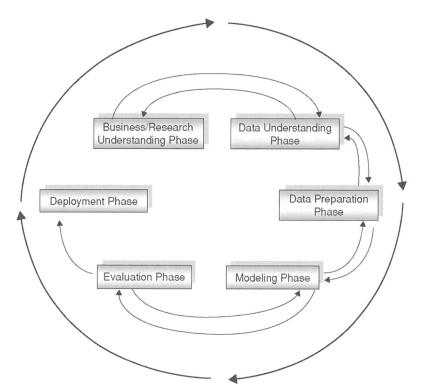

**Figure 6.1** CRISP–DM is an iterative, adaptive process.

characteristics of the model, we may have to return to the data preparation phase for further refinement before moving forward to the model evaluation phase. The six phases are as follows.

1. *Business understanding phase.* The first phase in the CRISP–DM standard process may also be termed the *research understanding phase.*

   a. Clearly enunciate the project objectives and requirements in terms of the business or research unit as a whole.

   b. Translate these goals and restrictions into the formulation of a data mining problem definition.

   c. Prepare a preliminary strategy for achieving these objectives.

2. *Data understanding phase*

   a. Collect the data.

   b. Use exploratory data analysis to familiarize yourself with the data, and discover initial insights.

   c. Evaluate the quality of the data.

   d. If desired, select interesting subsets that may contain actionable patterns.

3. *Data preparation phase*

   a. This labor-intensive phase covers all aspects of preparing the final data set, used for all subsequent phases, from the initial raw data.

   b. Select the cases and variables that you want to analyze and that are appropriate for your analysis.

   c. Perform transformations on certain variables, if needed.

   d. Clean the raw data so that they are ready for the modeling tools.

4. *Modeling phase*

   a. Select and apply appropriate modeling techniques.

   b. Calibrate model settings to optimize results.

   c. Often, different techniques may be used for the same data mining problem.

   d. Looping back to the data preparation phase may be required to bring the form of the data into line with the specific requirements of a particular data mining technique.

5. *Evaluation phase*

   a. The modeling phase has delivered one or more models. These models must be evaluated for quality and effectiveness before we deploy them for use in the field.

   b. Determine whether the model in fact achieves the objectives set for it in phase 1.

   c. Establish whether some important facet of the business or research problem has not been accounted for sufficiently.

   d. Finally, come to a decision regarding use of the data mining results.

**6.** *Deployment phase*

   **a.** Model creation does not signify completion of the project. We need to make use of models created according to business objectives.

   **b.** Provide an example of simple deployment: Generate a report.

   **c.** Provide an example of more complex deployment: Implement a parallel data mining process in another department.

   **d.** For businesses, the customer often carries out the deployment based on the model.

For more on CRISP–DM, see Chapman et al. [1], Larose [2], or `www.crisp-dm.org`. In this section we demonstrate web usage mining through the CRISP–DM context. In this chapter we examine the types of web log data that web usage miners usually work with; this is part of the data understanding phase in CRISP–DM. In Chapter 7, we discuss data preparation for web usage mining, which is clearly part of the data preparation phase. In Chapter 8, we examine exploratory data analysis for web usage mining, which is also part of the data understanding phase. In Chapter 9, we look at several different modeling methods and briefly discuss evaluative methods; these are part of the modeling and evaluation phases.

Another framework for web usage mining is that proposed by Srivastava et al. [3]. This process consists of four phases: the input stage, the preprocessing stage, the pattern discovery stage, and the pattern analysis stage.

1. *Input stage.* At the input stage, three types of raw web log files are retrieved—access logs, referrer logs, and agent logs—as well as registration information (if any) and information concerning the site topology. In this chapter we discuss these data sources and become familiar with the type of web log data used in web usage mining.

2. *Preprocessing stage.* The raw web logs do not arrive in a format conducive to fruitful data mining. Therefore, substantial data preprocessing must be applied. The most common preprocessing tasks are (1) data cleaning and filtering, (2) de-spidering, (3) user identification, (4) session identification, and (5) path completion. In Chapter 7, we look more closely at each of these tasks.

3. *Pattern discovery stage.* Once these tasks have been accomplished, the web data are ready for the application of statistical and data mining methods for the purpose of discovering patterns. These methods include (1) standard statistical analysis, (2) clustering algorithms, (3) association rules, (4) classification algorithms, and (5) sequential patterns. We examine methods and models for pattern discovery in Chapters 8 and 9.

4. *Pattern analysis stage.* Not all of the patterns uncovered in the pattern discovery stage would be considered interesting or useful. For example, an association rule for an online movie database that found "If Page = Sound_of_Music then Section = Musicals" would not be useful, even with 100% confidence, since this wonderful movie is, of course, a musical. Hence, in the pattern analysis stage,

human analysts examine the output from the pattern discovery stage and glean the most interesting, useful, and actionable patterns. This stage is discussed in Chapter 9.

## CLICKSTREAM ANALYSIS

Web usage mining is sometimes referred to as *clickstream analysis*. A *clickstream* is the aggregate sequence of page visits executed by a particular user navigating through a Web site. In addition to page views, clickstream data consist of logs, cookies, metatags, and other data used to transfer web pages from server to browser. When loading a particular web page, the browser also requests all the objects embedded in the page, such as .gif or .jpg graphics files. The problem is that each request is logged separately. All of these separate hits must be aggregated into *page views* at the preprocessing stage. Then a series of page views can be woven together into a *session*. Thus, clickstream data require substantial preprocessing before user behavior can be analyzed.

Nevertheless, once the clickstream data have been preprocessed, analysts can begin to tackle questions such as the following:

- Which web page is the most common point of entry for users?
  - Are visitors entering through the gateway constructed by the Web site developers, or are they somehow bypassing the gateway and landing in the middle of the Web site?
- In which order have the pages been viewed?
  - Is this page sequencing as the developers might have expected, or is there something the users are trying to tell us about how the Web site should be structured?
- Which other Web sites referred the users to your Web site?
  - Which referrer sites are providing us with the greatest number of referrals? Which unproductive referrer sites should our marketers consider reassessing?
- How many web pages have been viewed in the typical visit?
  - If we find that users tend to "cut and run" after just a couple of page views, should we perhaps consider an extensive redesign of the site to make it more user friendly?
- How long does the typical visitor stay on our Web site?
  - Similar to the previous question, if we find that the total clock time spent by users on our site is less than expected, perhaps we should ask ourselves why.
- Which web page is the most common departure point for users?
  - Should the developers examine why customers are leaving at this point? Is this page a natural point of departure, or is there some other reason why the page is detracting from the user's experience?

## WEB SERVER LOG FILES

Before we can begin clickstream analysis, we must familiarize ourselves with the types of data forms available for the analysis of clickstream behavior. Web usage information takes the form of *web server log files*, or *web logs*. For each request from a user's browser to a web server, a response is generated automatically, called a *web log file*, *log file*, or *web log* (not to be confused with *blogs*, of course, which are essentially web journals, sometimes called web logs). This response takes the form of a simple single-line transaction record that is appended to an ASCII text file on the web server. This text file may be comma-delimited, space-delimited, or tab-delimited.

A sample web log is the excerpt, shown in Figure 6.2, from the venerable EPA web log data available from the Internet Traffic Archive at `http://ita.ee.lbl.gov/html/traces.html`. Each line in this file represents a particular action requested by a user's browser, received by the EPA web server in Research Triangle Park, North Carolina. Each line (record) contains the fields described below.

---

141.243.1.172 [29:23:53:25] "GET /Software.html HTTP/1.0" 200 1497
query2.lycos.cs.cmu.edu [29:23:53:36] "GET /Consumer.html HTTP/1.0" 200 1325
tanuki.twics.com [29:23:53:53] "GET /News.html HTTP/1.0" 200 1014
wpbfl2-45.gate.net [29:23:54:15] "GET /default.htm HTTP/1.0" 200 4889
wpbfl2-45.gate.net [29:23:54:16] "GET /icons/circle_logo_small.gif HTTP/1.0"
    200 2624
wpbfl2-45.gate.net [29:23:54:18] "GET /logos/small_gopher.gif HTTP/1.0" 200 935
140.112.68.165 [29:23:54:19] "GET /logos/us-flag.gif HTTP/1.0" 200 2788
wpbfl2-45.gate.net [29:23:54:19] "GET /logos/small_ftp.gif HTTP/1.0" 200 124
wpbfl2-45.gate.net [29:23:54:19] "GET /icons/book.gif HTTP/1.0" 200 156
wpbfl2-45.gate.net [29:23:54:19] "GET /logos/us-flag.gif HTTP/1.0" 200 2788
tanuki.twics.com [29:23:54:19] "GET /docs/OSWRCRA/general/hotline HTTP/1.0"
    302 -
wpbfl2-45.gate.net [29:23:54:20] "GET /icons/ok2-0.gif HTTP/1.0" 200 231
tanuki.twics.com [29:23:54:25] "GET /OSWRCRA/general/hotline/ HTTP/1.0"
    200 991
tanuki.twics.com [29:23:54:37] "GET /docs/OSWRCRA/general/hotline/95report
    HTTP/1.0" 302 -
wpbfl2-45.gate.net [29:23:54:37] "GET /docs/browner/adminbio.html HTTP/1.0"
    200 4217
tanuki.twics.com [29:23:54:40] "GET /OSWRCRA/general/hotline/95report/
    HTTP/1.0" 200 1250
wpbfl2-45.gate.net [29:23:55:01] "GET /docs/browner/cbpress.gif HTTP/1.0"
    200 51661
dd15-032.compuserve.com [29:23:55:21] "GET /Access/chapter1/s2-4.html
    HTTP/1.0" 200 4602

---

**Figure 6.2**   Sample web log from the EPA Web site.

## Remote Host Field

This field consists of the Internet IP address of the remote host making the request, such as "141.243.1.172". If the remote host name is available through a DNS lookup, this name is provided, such as "wpbfl2-45.gate.net."

To obtain the domain name of the remote host rather than the IP address, the server must submit a request, using the Internet domain name system (DNS) to resolve (i.e., translate) the IP address into a host name. Since humans prefer to work with domain names and computers are most efficient with IP addresses, the DNS system provides an important interface between humans and computers. For more information about DNS, see the Internet Systems Consortium, `www.isc.org`.

## Date/Time Field

The EPA web log uses the following specialized date/time field format: "[DD:HH:MM:SS]," where DD represents the day of the month and HH:MM:SS represents the 24-hour time, given in EDT. In this particular data set, the DD portion represents the day in August, 1995 that the web log entry was made. However, it is more common for the date/time field to follow the following format: "DD/Mon/YYYY:HH:MM:SS offset," where the offset is a positive or negative constant indicating in hours how far ahead of or behind the local server is from Greenwich Mean Tim (GMT). For example, a date/time field of "09/Jun/1988:03:27:00 -0500" indicates that a request was made to a server at 3:27 a.m. on June 9, 1988, and the server is 5 hours behind GMT.

## HTTP Request Field

The HTTP request field consists of the information that the client's browser has requested from the web server. The entire HTTP request field is contained within quotation marks. Essentially, this field may be partitioned into four areas: (1) the request method, (2) the uniform resource identifier (URI), (3) the header, and (4) the protocol. The most common request method is GET, which represents a request to retrieve data that are identified by the URI. For example, the request field in the first record in Figure 6.2 is "GET /Software.html HTTP/1.0," representing a request from the client browser for the web server to provide the web page Software.html. Besides GET, other requests include HEAD, PUT, and POST. For more information on the latter request methods, refer to the W3C World Wide Web Consortium at `www.w3.org`.

The uniform resource identifier contains the page or document name and the directory path requested by the client browser. The URI can be used by web usage miners to analyze the frequency of visitor requests for pages and files. The header section contains optional information concerning the browser's request. This information can be used by the web usage miner to determine, for example, which keywords are being used by visitors in search engines that point to your site. The HTTP request field also includes the protocol section, which indicates which version of the HyperText Transfer Protocol (HTTP) is being used by the client's browser. Then, based on the relative frequency of newer protocol versions (e.g., HTTP/1.1), the web developer may decide to take advantage of the greater functionality of the newer versions and provide more online features.

## Status Code Field

Not all browser requests succeed. The status code field provides a three-digit response from the web server to the client's browser, indicating the status of the request, whether or not the request was a success, or if there was an error, which type of error occurred. Codes of the form "2xx" indicate a success, and codes of the form "4xx" indicate an error. Most of the status codes for the records in Figure 6.2 are "200," indicating that the request was fulfilled successfully. A sample of the possible status codes that a web server could send follows.

- Successful transmission (200 series)
  - Indicates that the request from the client was received, understood, and completed.
    - 200: success
    - 201: created
    - 202: accepted
    - 204: no content
- Redirection (300 series)
  - Indicates that further action is required to complete the client's request.
    - 301: moved permanently
    - 302: moved temporarily
    - 303: not modified
    - 304: use cached document
- Client error (400 series)
  - Indicates that the client's request cannot be fulfilled, due to incorrect syntax or a missing file.
    - 400: bad request
    - 401: unauthorized
    - 403: forbidden
    - 404: not found
- Server error (500 series)
  - Indicates that the web server failed to fulfill what was apparently a valid request.
    - 500: internal server error
    - 501: not implemented
    - 502: bad gateway
    - 503: service unavailable

## Transfer Volume (Bytes) Field

The transfer volume field indicates the size of the file (web page, graphics file, etc.), in bytes, sent by the web server to the client's browser. Only GET requests that have been completed successfully (Status = 200) will have a positive value in the transfer volume field. Otherwise, the field will consist of a hyphen or a value of zero. This field is useful for helping to monitor the network traffic, the load carried by the network throughout the 24-hour cycle.

# COMMON LOG FORMAT

Web logs come in various formats, which vary depending on the configuration of the web server. The *common log format* (CLF or "clog") is supported by a variety of web server applications and includes the following seven fields:

- Remote host field
- Identification field
- Authuser field
- Date/time field
- HTTP request
- Status code field
- Transfer volume field

## Identification Field

This field is used to store identity information provided by the client only if the web server is performing an identity check . However, this field is seldom used because the identification information is provided in plain text rather than in a securely encrypted form. Therefore, this field usually contains a hyphen, indicating a null value.

## Authuser Field

This field is used to store the authenticated client user name, if it is required. The authuser field was designed to contain the authenticated user name information that a client needs to provide to gain access to directories that are password protected. If no such information is provided, the field defaults to a hyphen.

# EXTENDED COMMON LOG FORMAT

The extended common log format (ECLF) is a variation of the common log format, formed by appending two additional fields onto the end of the record, the referrer field, and the user agent field. Both the common log format and the extended common log format were created by the National Center for Supercomputing Applications (http://www.ncsa.uiuc.edu/).

## Referrer Field

The referrer field lists the URL of the previous site visited by the client, which linked to the current page. For images, the referrer is the web page on which the image is to be displayed. The referrer field contains important information for marketing purposes, since it can track how people found your site. Again, if the information is missing, a hyphen is used.

## User Agent Field

The user agent field provides information about the client's browser, the browser version, and the client's operating system. Importantly, this field can also contain information regarding bots, such as web crawlers. Web developers can use this information to block certain sections of the Web site from these web crawlers, in the interests of preserving bandwidth. Further, this field allows the web usage miner to determine whether a human or a bot has accessed the site, and thereby to omit the bot's visit from analysis, on the assumption that the developers are interested in the behavior of human visitors. This is known as *de-spidering* and is discussed further in Chapter 7.

## Example of a Web Log Record

Consider the following example of an extended common log format (ECLF). For privacy purposes, the URL has been partly masked.

```
149.1xx.120.116 -- smithj [28/OCT/2004:20:27:32
-5000] ``GET /Default.htm HTTP/1.1'' 200
1270 ``http:/www.dataminingconsultant.com/''
``Mozilla/4.0+(compatible;+MSIE+6.0;+Windows+NT+5.0)''
```

- Remote host: 149.1xx.120.116
- Identification: –
- Authuser: smithj
- Date/time: [28/OCT/2004:20:27:32 -5000]
- Request: "GET /Default.htm HTTP/1.1"
- Status code: 200
- Transfer volume: 1270
- Referrer: "http:/www.dataminingconsultant.com/"
- User agent: "Mozilla/4.0+(compatible;+MSIE+6.0;+Windows+NT+5.0)"

Consider Figure 6.3, which contains a subset of the records from Figure 6.2 for the user at wpbfl2-45.gate.net. Note that the first record is a request for the server to provide *default.htm* (the label often used for the home page of a Web site). However,

```
wpbfl2-45.gate.net [29:23:54:15] "GET /default.htm HTTP/1.0" 200 4889
wpbfl2-45.gate.net [29:23:54:16] "GET /icons/circle_logo_small.gif HTTP/1.0"
   200 2624
wpbfl2-45.gate.net [29:23:54:18] "GET /logos/small_gopher.gif HTTP/1.0" 200 935
wpbfl2-45.gate.net [29:23:54:19] "GET /logos/small_ftp.gif HTTP/1.0" 200 124
wpbfl2-45.gate.net [29:23:54:19] "GET /icons/book.gif HTTP/1.0" 200 156
wpbfl2-45.gate.net [29:23:54:19] "GET /logos/us-flag.gif HTTP/1.0" 200 2788
wpbfl2-45.gate.net [29:23:54:20] "GET /icons/ok2-0.gif HTTP/1.0" 200 231
```

**Figure 6.3**    Single click turns into multiple hits.

note that over the next 5 seconds, a further series of requests are made, all of which are for .gif image files. These six image files are stored on the server and must be provided to the client browser, which aligns them in their proper places on the default.htm web page.

Thus, we see that a web page is actually a collection of objects, each of which must be requested from the Web server. On sophisticated Web sites, the web server may forward requests to other servers, such as ad servers, shopping cart servers, and so on. Thus, when a user makes a single click on a link to request a single web page, this request results in multiple hits on the web server, one line in the log file for each document or object requested. The collection of hits in Figure 6.3 represents a single *page view*, which is discussed in Chapter 7. It is clear from Figure 6.3 that these log file records belong together, resulting from the actions of a single user. However, Figure 6.2 shows that the web server may be receiving many hits from other clients at nearly the same time. Thus, the hits associated with one particular client or even one particular page view are not recorded in sequence. Thus, the web usage miner must first preprocess the data to uncover the page views within the data, as we discuss in Chapter 7.

## MICROSOFT IIS LOG FORMAT

There are other log file formats besides the common and extended common log file formats. The Microsoft IIS log format includes the following fields:

- Client IP address
- User name
- Date
- Time
- Service and instance
- Server name
- Server IP
- Elapsed time

- Client bytes sent
- Server bytes sent
- Service status code
- Windows status code
- Request type
- Target of operation
- Parameters

The IIS format records more fields than the other formats, so that more information can be uncovered. For example, the elapsed processing time is included, along with the bytes sent by the client to the server; also, the time recorded is local time. Note that web server administrators need not choose any of these formats; they are free to specify which fields they believe are most appropriate for their purposes. Now that we have been introduced to the type of data used for web usage mining, in Chapter 7, we must learn how to preprocess this raw web log data to make it ready for the exploratory methods in Chapter 8 and the modeling algorithms and methods in Chapter 9.

## AUXILIARY INFORMATION

Besides web logs, further auxiliary information may be available in the form of user registration information, user demographic information, and so on. These data usually reside on separate servers from the web log data and will need to be merged with the web logs before preprocessing can be done. Finally, to perform the preprocessing task known as *path completion*, the analyst will need to have knowledge of the *topology* or structure of the Web site, the network of hierarchies and relationships among the web pages, and so on. We discuss path completion in Chapter 7.

## REFERENCES

1. Peter Chapman, Julian Clinton, Randy Kerber, Thomas Khabaza, Thomas Reinart, Colin Shearer, and Rudiger Wirth, *CRISP–DM Step-by-Step Data Mining Guide*, 2000, http://www.crisp-dm.org/.
2. Daniel Larose, *Discovering Knowledge in Data: An Introduction to Data Mining*, Wiley, Hoboken, NJ, 2005.
3. Jaideep Srivastava, Robert Cooley, Mukund Deshpande, and Pang-Ning Tan, Web usage mining: discovery and applications of usage patterns from web data, *SIGKDD Explor.*, 1(12), Jan. 2000.

## EXERCISES

1. Each of these fields belongs to the common log format except:

   **a.** Host

   **b.** Agent

   **c.** Transfer volume

   **d.** Authuser

2. The most common method for the HTTP request field is:

   **a.** Get

   **b.** Post

   **c.** Head

   **d.** Put

**3.** A search engine hit, including the keywords they used to locate your site, would be located in which field?

   **a.** Authuser

   **b.** Request

   **c.** Agent

   **d.** None of the above

**4.** The following web log entry is in which format? `207.86.139.145 - jwb [09/Sep/1997:10:47:43 -0800]` `` ``GET /www.ping/index.htm HTTP/1.0"  200 954 ``

   **a.** CLF

   **b.** ECLF

   **c.** MIIS

   **d.** None of the above

**5.** The directory path and object name being requested by the client browser is contained in which of the following?

   **a.** HTTP request field

   **b.** URI

   **c.** CLF

   **d.** All of the above

# PREPROCESSING FOR WEB USAGE MINING

NEED FOR PREPROCESSING THE DATA

DATA CLEANING AND FILTERING

DE-SPIDERING THE WEB LOG FILE

USER IDENTIFICATION

SESSION IDENTIFICATION

PATH COMPLETION

DIRECTORIES AND THE BASKET TRANSFORMATION

FURTHER DATA PREPROCESSING STEPS

## NEED FOR PREPROCESSING THE DATA

As we mentioned in Chapter 6, raw web log data must first be preprocessed before modeling may be applied fruitfully. Consider that, to apply data mining models, the input data format would ideally contain, among other things, information regarding:

- The page views
- The identification of each user
- The user session, specifically:
  - Which pages were viewed?
  - In which order?
  - For how long?

Unfortunately, the raw web log files cannot be used directly for modeling purposes without preprocessing. Why do we need to preprocess the data? Preprocessing is needed in order to:

*Data Mining the Web: Uncovering Patterns in Web Content, Structure, and Usage*
By Zdravko Markov and Daniel T. Larose    Copyright © 2007 John Wiley & Sons, Inc.

- *Clean up the data.* That is, filter out from the data set the automatic requests (e.g., for graphics files) generated by the web page, which were not specifically requested by the user.

- *Rid the web log file of nonhuman access behavior.* Spiders, crawlers, and other automatic web bots are constantly crawling around the World Wide Web, performing exhaustive searches of Web sites. The behavior of the bots differs qualitatively from human behavior and is not considered interesting from a web usage mining standpoint.

- *Identify each distinct user.* The free-form structure of the Internet means that most user accesses to most Web sites are done anonymously. The web usage miner combines IP address information with available cookie and registration information in order to identify each user.

- *Identify the user session.* That is, for each visit, determine which pages were requested, the order of the requests, and the duration of each page view. Also, try to estimate when the user left the Web site.

- *Perform path completion.* Many people use the "Back" button on their browsers to return to a page viewed previously. When this happens, the browser returns to a page that has previously been cached locally rather than accessing the web server again. This leads to "holes" in the web server's record of the user's path through the Web site. Knowledge of site topology must be applied to complete these paths.

In this chapter we examine each of these preprocessing tasks in turn. We use two data sets to demonstrate some of these tasks: the EPA web log file and the CCSU web log file. The EPA data are the same EPA web log data that we met in Chapter 6. So that the reader may learn web usage mining by doing web usage mining, we have made this data set available on the book series Web site. The EPA web log file contains only five fields, which helps to soften our learning curve. Even though this file is somewhat old (1995), the methods that we demonstrate for this simple data set can be extrapolated to larger, more complex web log formats later.

The second data set we shall work with is the CCSU web log file, the web log file for the Central Connecticut State University Web site, www.ccsu.edu, for the date October 28, 2004. For privacy purposes, the client IP address and the client user name have been altered and the query search strings have been omitted. The CCSU server IP address and server port fields have been omitted because they contain only one (or nearly only one) value. Unfortunately, for privacy purposes, this data set will not be made available for download. The CCSU web log file contains the following 11 fields:

- Date
- Time
- Client IP address (altered for privacy)
- Client user name (altered for privacy)
- CCSU server IP address (omitted due to singular value)

- CCSU server port (omitted due to nearly singular value)
- Request method
- Request URI stem (i.e., page requested)
- Request query search string (omitted for privacy)
- Status code
- Client user agent

## DATA CLEANING AND FILTERING

Recall that the EPA web log file contains the following fields:

- Remote host field (IP Address)
- Date/time field
- HTTP request
- Status code field
- Transfer volume field

Figure 7.1 shows the first 20 records (of a total of 47,747 records) in the web log, in raw form, before any preprocessing has been applied. The first web log entry represents a request from a user at IP address 141.243.1.172, at 11:53:25 p.m. on August 29, 1995 (remember that the specialized date format of this data set provides only the date DD in August 1995 when the web log entry was made). The user's browser requested the web server to GET the page "/Software.html" using protocol version HTTP 1.0. The status code "200" represents a success, with a resulting transfer volume of 1497 bytes. The next hit on the web server occurred 11 seconds later, from a different user, and the next hit after that occurred another 17 seconds later from still another user.

| | IP Address | Date / Time | HTTP Request | Status Code | Transfer Volume |
|---|---|---|---|---|---|
| 1 | 141.243.1.172 | [29:23:53:25] | GET /Software.html HTTP/1.0 | 200 | 1497 |
| 2 | query2.lycos.cs.cmu.edu | [29:23:53:36] | GET /Consumer.html HTTP/1.0 | 200 | 1325 |
| 3 | tanuki.twics.com | [29:23:53:53] | GET /News.html HTTP/1.0 | 200 | 1014 |
| 4 | wpbfl2-45.gate.net | [29:23:54:15] | GET / HTTP/1.0 | 200 | 4889 |
| 5 | wpbfl2-45.gate.net | [29:23:54:16] | GET /icons/circle_logo_small.gif HTTP/1.0 | 200 | 2624 |
| 6 | wpbfl2-45.gate.net | [29:23:54:18] | GET /logos/small_gopher.gif HTTP/1.0 | 200 | 935 |
| 7 | 140.112.68.165 | [29:23:54:19] | GET /logos/us-flag.gif HTTP/1.0 | 200 | 2788 |
| 8 | wpbfl2-45.gate.net | [29:23:54:19] | GET /logos/small_ftp.gif HTTP/1.0 | 200 | 124 |
| 9 | wpbfl2-45.gate.net | [29:23:54:19] | GET /icons/book.gif HTTP/1.0 | 200 | 156 |
| 10 | wpbfl2-45.gate.net | [29:23:54:19] | GET /logos/us-flag.gif HTTP/1.0 | 200 | 2788 |
| 11 | tanuki.twics.com | [29:23:54:19] | GET /docs/OSWRCRA/general/hotline HT... | 302 | - |
| 12 | wpbfl2-45.gate.net | [29:23:54:20] | GET /icons/ok2-0.gif HTTP/1.0 | 200 | 231 |
| 13 | tanuki.twics.com | [29:23:54:25] | GET /OSWRCRA/general/hotline/ HTTP/1.0 | 200 | 991 |
| 14 | tanuki.twics.com | [29:23:54:37] | GET /docs/OSWRCRA/general/hotline/95... | 302 | - |
| 15 | wpbfl2-45.gate.net | [29:23:54:37] | GET /docs/browner/adminbio.html HTTP/... | 200 | 4217 |
| 16 | tanuki.twics.com | [29:23:54:40] | GET /OSWRCRA/general/hotline/95report... | 200 | 1250 |
| 17 | wpbfl2-45.gate.net | [29:23:55:01] | GET /docs/browner/cbpress.gif HTTP/1.0 | 200 | 51661 |
| 18 | dd15-032.compuserve.... | [29:23:55:21] | GET /Access/chapter1/s2-4.html HTTP/1.0 | 200 | 4602 |
| 19 | tanuki.twics.com | [29:23:55:23] | GET /docs/OSWRCRA/general/hotline/95... | 200 | 56431 |
| 20 | wpbfl2-45.gate.net | [29:23:55:29] | GET /docs/Access HTTP/1.0 | 302 | - |

**Figure 7.1** EPA web log file, first 20 records of raw, unpreprocessed data.

Now note that these fields are all formatted as text, since the raw web logs are text files. Also, note that some fields contain more than a single piece of information. For example, the date/time field naturally contains two variables, the date and the time. The HTTP request field contains the request method, the uniform resource identifier (i.e., page or document requested), the protocol version, and optionally, some search information. Before we can perform any analysis, we must extract these masked variables.

Thus, the first step in web log preprocessing is the variable extraction step:

### Data Cleaning/Filtering Step 1: Variable Extraction

1. From the date/time field, extract the date variable.

2. From the date/time field, extract the time variable.

3. From the HTTP request field, extract the request method.

4. From the HTTP request field, extract the page (URI).

5. From the HTTP request field, extract the protocol version.

These extractions may be accomplished using the string manipulation functions of your software. Next, it is useful to create a date/time stamp using both the date and time variables so that the software recognizes that 12:01 a.m. (00:01) on August 30 occurs later than 11:59 p.m. (23:59) on August 29. Of course, different software packages encode date information differently. One way to create the time/stamp is as follows.

### Data Cleaning/Filtering Step 2: Creating a Time Stamp

1. First find out how many days there are between the web log entry date and the software's baseline date.

2. Multiply this number of days by 86,400, which represents the number of seconds in a 24-hour day.

3. Find the time in seconds since midnight that is represented by the time in the web log entry.

4. Add (2) and (3).

The result of (1) through (4) is to create a time stamp, an integer-typed variable that represents the number of seconds elapsed since midnight of the baseline date. The time stamp is useful for estimating the duration of the user's visit to the Web site and for maintaining the sequence of web requests across days. Figure 7.2 shows the results from our variable extraction and time stamp creation. Note that the time stamp for the second entry is 11 greater than that of the first entry, representing the 11 seconds elapsed between the two entries. (The baseline date for this example is January 1, 1995.)

Turning to the CCSU web log data, Figure 7.3 shows the first 20 records (of a total of 193,704 records) in the web log, containing the eight remaining fields in raw form, before preprocessing. The first web log entry represents a request from a user at IP address 549.152.17.23, at 12:00:02 a.m. on October 28, 2004. The user's browser requested the web server to GET the default web page at "/athletictraining/Services/." The status code "302" represents a dynamic redirection message; that is, the user's

| | IP Address | Date | Time | Method | Page | HTTP_version | TimeStamp |
|---|---|---|---|---|---|---|---|
| 1 | 141.243.1.172 | 29 | 23:53:25 | GET | /Software.html | HTTP/1.0 | 20822005 |
| 2 | query2.lycos.cs.cmu.edu | 29 | 23:53:36 | GET | /Consumer.html | HTTP/1.0 | 20822016 |
| 3 | tanuki.twics.com | 29 | 23:53:53 | GET | /News.html | HTTP/1.0 | 20822033 |
| 4 | wpbfl2-45.gate.net | 29 | 23:54:15 | GET | / | HTTP/1.0 | 20822055 |
| 5 | wpbfl2-45.gate.net | 29 | 23:54:16 | GET | /icons/circle_logo_small.gif | HTTP/1.0 | 20822056 |
| 6 | wpbfl2-45.gate.net | 29 | 23:54:18 | GET | /logos/small_gopher.gif | HTTP/1.0 | 20822058 |
| 7 | 140.112.68.165 | 29 | 23:54:19 | GET | /logos/us-flag.gif | HTTP/1.0 | 20822059 |
| 8 | wpbfl2-45.gate.net | 29 | 23:54:19 | GET | /logos/small_ftp.gif | HTTP/1.0 | 20822059 |
| 9 | wpbfl2-45.gate.net | 29 | 23:54:19 | GET | /icons/book.gif | HTTP/1.0 | 20822059 |
| 10 | wpbfl2-45.gate.net | 29 | 23:54:19 | GET | /logos/us-flag.gif | HTTP/1.0 | 20822059 |
| 11 | tanuki.twics.com | 29 | 23:54:19 | GET | /docs/OSWRCRA/general/... | HTTP/1.0 | 20822059 |
| 12 | wpbfl2-45.gate.net | 29 | 23:54:20 | GET | /icons/ok2-0.gif | HTTP/1.0 | 20822060 |
| 13 | tanuki.twics.com | 29 | 23:54:25 | GET | /OSWRCRA/general/hotline/ | HTTP/1.0 | 20822065 |
| 14 | tanuki.twics.com | 29 | 23:54:37 | GET | /docs/OSWRCRA/general/... | HTTP/1.0 | 20822077 |
| 15 | wpbfl2-45.gate.net | 29 | 23:54:37 | GET | /docs/browner/adminbio.ht... | HTTP/1.0 | 20822077 |
| 16 | tanuki.twics.com | 29 | 23:54:40 | GET | /OSWRCRA/general/hotlin... | HTTP/1.0 | 20822080 |
| 17 | wpbfl2-45.gate.net | 29 | 23:55:01 | GET | /docs/browner/cbpress.gif | HTTP/1.0 | 20822101 |
| 18 | dd15-032.compuserve.... | 29 | 23:55:21 | GET | /Access/chapter1/s2-4.html | HTTP/1.0 | 20822121 |
| 19 | tanuki.twics.com | 29 | 23:55:23 | GET | /docs/OSWRCRA/general/... | HTTP/1.0 | 20822123 |
| 20 | wpbfl2-45.gate.net | 29 | 23:55:29 | GET | /docs/Access | HTTP/1.0 | 20822129 |

**Figure 7.2**   EPA data: extracted variables and time stamp for the first 20 entries.

browser will be redirected to another address. This client's browser is Microsoft Internet Explorer 6.0, and the client's browser is Windows NT (5.1). The next hit on the web server occurred 4 seconds later, from a different user. The status of 304 for this second client represents a "conditional GET," indicates that the server is checking if the document in cache is the current version, and asks the browser to open the cached version.

Note that entries 2 to 7 of Figure 7.3 are all from the same IP address, 50.2.32.186. The original request for the /Default.htm page prompted requests for all the other objects that reside on that page, such as the header and the navigation bar, lines 4 and 6, respectively. To simplify the web usage mining process, these ancillary requests should be filtered out, since they are performed automatically by the browser; the user is only aware that he or she requested the single web page /Default.htm. Also, note that the CCSU web log data need not undergo the date/time variable extraction step, since it already includes separate fields for date, time, request

| date | Time | IP Address | cs-... | cs-... | Page | sc-... | cs(User-Agent) |
|---|---|---|---|---|---|---|---|
| 2004-10-28 | 00:00:02 | 549.152.17.23 | - | GET | /athletictraining/Services/ | 302 | Mozilla/4.0+(compatible;+MSIE+6.0;+Windows+NT+ |
| 2004-10-28 | 00:00:06 | 50.2.32.186 | - | GET | /Default.htm | 304 | Mozilla/4.0+(compatible;+MSIE+6.0;+Windows+NT+ |
| 2004-10-28 | 00:00:06 | 50.2.32.186 | - | GET | /Images/Bac.jpg | 304 | Mozilla/4.0+(compatible;+MSIE+6.0;+Windows+NT+ |
| 2004-10-28 | 00:00:06 | 50.2.32.186 | - | GET | /Images/Headers/Header.gif | 304 | Mozilla/4.0+(compatible;+MSIE+6.0;+Windows+NT+ |
| 2004-10-28 | 00:00:06 | 50.2.32.186 | - | GET | /Images/Slides/imgload.js | 304 | Mozilla/4.0+(compatible;+MSIE+6.0;+Windows+NT+ |
| 2004-10-28 | 00:00:06 | 50.2.32.186 | - | GET | /images/LeftNavigation/Nav.gif | 304 | Mozilla/4.0+(compatible;+MSIE+6.0;+Windows+NT+ |
| 2004-10-28 | 00:00:06 | 50.2.32.186 | - | GET | /images/slides/revolverB.gif | 304 | Mozilla/4.0+(compatible;+MSIE+6.0;+Windows+NT+ |
| 2004-10-28 | 00:00:08 | 8.247.1.176 | - | GET | /images/slides/revolverA.gif | 200 | Mozilla/4.0+(compatible;+MSIE+6.0;+Windows+NT+ |
| 2004-10-28 | 00:00:10 | 34.213.236.89 | - | GET | /caribstudy/pr-photos.html | 200 | Mozilla/4.0+(compatible;+MSIE+6.0;+Windows+NT+ |
| 2004-10-28 | 00:00:12 | 34.252.0.236 | - | GET | /Default.htm | 304 | Mozilla/4.0+(compatible;+MSIE+6.0;+Windows+98) |
| 2004-10-28 | 00:00:12 | 34.252.0.236 | - | GET | /Images/Bac.jpg | 304 | Mozilla/4.0+(compatible;+MSIE+6.0;+Windows+98) |
| 2004-10-28 | 00:00:12 | 34.252.0.236 | - | GET | /Images/Headers/Header.gif | 304 | Mozilla/4.0+(compatible;+MSIE+6.0;+Windows+98) |
| 2004-10-28 | 00:00:12 | 34.252.0.236 | - | GET | /images/LeftNavigation/Nav.gif | 304 | Mozilla/4.0+(compatible;+MSIE+6.0;+Windows+98) |
| 2004-10-28 | 00:00:13 | 34.252.0.236 | - | GET | /Images/Slides/imgload.js | 304 | Mozilla/4.0+(compatible;+MSIE+6.0;+Windows+98) |
| 2004-10-28 | 00:00:13 | 607.194.17.97 | - | GET | /images/slides/revolverG.gif | 200 | Mozilla/4.0+(compatible;+MSIE+6.0;+Windows+NT+ |
| 2004-10-28 | 00:00:13 | 34.213.236.89 | - | GET | /caribstudy/Other_Images/he... | 200 | Mozilla/4.0+(compatible;+MSIE+6.0;+Windows+NT+ |
| 2004-10-28 | 00:00:13 | 34.252.0.236 | - | GET | /images/slides/revolverA.gif | 304 | Mozilla/4.0+(compatible;+MSIE+6.0;+Windows+98) |
| 2004-10-28 | 00:00:13 | 34.213.236.89 | - | GET | /caribstudy/images/pr-header... | 200 | Mozilla/4.0+(compatible;+MSIE+6.0;+Windows+NT+ |
| 2004-10-28 | 00:00:15 | 64.2.203.196 | - | GET | /Career/Default.htm | 304 | Mozilla/4.0+(compatible;+MSIE+6.0;+Windows+NT+ |

**Figure 7.3**   CCSU data: first 20 records of raw, unpreprocessed data.

TABLE 7.1    Most Popular Page Extensions in the
EPA Web Log

| Page Extension | Count of Web Log Entries |
|---|---|
| .gif | 22,094 |
| None | 13,546 |
| .html | 8,609 |
| .xbm | 850 |
| .htm | 341 |
| .pdf | 107 |
| .exe | 82 |
| .zip | 69 |
| .txt | 68 |
| .wp | 52 |
| .jpg | 25 |

method, and page. It still needs the time stamp step, however, and it was applied here (not shown) using a baseline date of January 1, 2000.

## Page Extension Exploration and Filtering

Although we have extracted and derived new variables for the EPA data, the web log is still rather raw and difficult to interpret directly. For example, the web log entries are not sorted by IP address, making it difficult to examine the behavior of individual users. Also, it is not clear whether all 47,747 records indicate actual user clicks, or whether there are large numbers of requests generated automatically by the browser's call to a web page.

We therefore explore the page extensions in the EPA web log file to determine whether any extensions should be removed. Restricting ourselves to the GET method, the 11 most popular page extensions are shown in Table 7.1. The web usage miner should peruse these page extensions and determine which extensions may be considered irrelevant from a user-behavior point of view. Typically, graphics file extensions (e.g., .gif, .xbm, .jpg) may safely be removed, unless either (1) the Web site considers graphics to be content and wishes to track downloads of the graphics files, or (2) the analyst is interested in tracking bandwidth consumption. The pages with no extensions represent the requests for the default page for a particular directory, such as "GET /" for the default page in the root directory or "GET/Access/" for the default page in the "/Access/" directory.

Since we assume that the EPA Web site does not consider graphics to be content, and since we are not (at the moment) interested in tracking bandwidth usage, we proceed to eliminate the entries in the web log that contain these graphics extensions: .gif, .xbm, and .jpg. This reduces the size of our database by about half, thereby simplifying our analysis tasks. This process is known as *filtering*, since we are filtering out from the web log file those entries that are not relevant to the analytical problems of interest. We retain only the following page extensions: .doc, .exe, .gz, .htm, .html, .pdf, .ps, .tar, .txt, .wp, .wpd, .zip, and the empty page extension indicating a directory (e.g., record 4 in Table 7.2).

TABLE 7.2   Most Popular Page Extensions in the
CCSU Web Log

| Page Extension | Count of Web Log Entries |
|---|---|
| .gif | 64,443 |
| .jpg | 55,615 |
| .htm | 35,400 |
| .js | 15,900 |
| None | 4096 |
| .JPG | 3737 |
| .pdf | 1381 |
| .css | 1346 |
| .ico | 1105 |
| .asp | 906 |
| .exe | 838 |

Figure 7.4 contains the first 20 entries in the EPA web log file after page extension filtering has been applied. Note in the shaded column that no graphics files remain. To recapitulate, the data cleaning and filtering portion of the preprocessing phase consists of the following three steps: (1) variable extraction, (2) time stamp derivation, and (3) page extension exploration and filtering. For web logs with a richer collection of fields, of course, further cleaning, derivation, and filtering is both possible and appropriate.

For the CCSU web log data, Table 7.2 contains a list of the 10 (out of 41) most popular page extensions. We shall filter the CCSU data, retaining only the following page extensions: .htm, .pdf, .asp, .exe, .txt, .doc, .ppt, .xls, and .xml. In this way, 143,185 web log entries are filtered out, leaving 48,385 entries remaining for downstream analysis. Note that here we are including the results from the GET requests only.

| | IP Address | Stat.. | Transf.. | method | Page | HTTP_ve.. | TimeStamp |
|---|---|---|---|---|---|---|---|
| 1 | 141.243.1.172 | 200 | 1497 | GET | /Software.html | HTTP/1.0 | 20822005 |
| 2 | query2.lycos.cs.cmu.edu | 200 | 1325 | GET | /Consumer.html | HTTP/1.0 | 20822016 |
| 3 | tanuki.twics.com | 200 | 1014 | GET | /News.html | HTTP/1.0 | 20822033 |
| 4 | wpbfl2-45.gate.net | 200 | 4889 | GET | / | HTTP/1.0 | 20822055 |
| 5 | tanuki.twics.com | 302 | - | GET | /docs/OSWRCRA/general/hotline | HTTP/1.0 | 20822059 |
| 6 | tanuki.twics.com | 200 | 991 | GET | /OSWRCRA/general/hotline/ | HTTP/1.0 | 20822065 |
| 7 | tanuki.twics.com | 302 | - | GET | /docs/OSWRCRA/general/hotline/95report | HTTP/1.0 | 20822077 |
| 8 | wpbfl2-45.gate.net | 200 | 4217 | GET | /docs/browner/adminbio.html | HTTP/1.0 | 20822077 |
| 9 | tanuki.twics.com | 200 | 1250 | GET | /OSWRCRA/general/hotline/95report/ | HTTP/1.0 | 20822080 |
| 10 | dd15-032.compuserve.... | 200 | 4602 | GET | /Access/chapter1/s2-4.html | HTTP/1.0 | 20822121 |
| 11 | tanuki.twics.com | 200 | 56431 | GET | /docs/OSWRCRA/general/hotline/95repor... | HTTP/1.0 | 20822123 |
| 12 | wpbfl2-45.gate.net | 302 | - | GET | /docs/Access | HTTP/1.0 | 20822129 |
| 13 | wpbfl2-45.gate.net | 200 | 617 | GET | /information.html | HTTP/1.0 | 20822146 |
| 14 | wpbfl2-45.gate.net | 302 | - | GET | /docs/Access | HTTP/1.0 | 20822163 |
| 15 | wpbfl2-45.gate.net | 200 | 2376 | GET | /Access/ | HTTP/1.0 | 20822172 |
| 16 | tanuki.twics.com | 200 | 1250 | GET | /OSWRCRA/general/hotline/95report/ | HTTP/1.0 | 20822184 |
| 17 | freenet2.carleton.ca | 200 | 4889 | GET | /emap/html/regions/four/ | HTTP/1.0 | 20822196 |
| 18 | ix-mia5-17.ix.netcom.com | 200 | 1501 | GET | /OWOW/ | HTTP/1.0 | 20822226 |
| 19 | ix-knx-tn1-22.ix.netcom.... | 200 | 4889 | GET | / | HTTP/1.0 | 20822248 |
| 20 | hmu4.cs.auckland.ac.nz | 200 | 6829 | GET | /docs/GCDOAR/EnergyStar.html | HTTP/1.0 | 20822255 |

**Figure 7.4**   After filtering, no graphics files remain in the web log file.

# DE-SPIDERING THE WEB LOG FILE

Web search engines need the most current information available from the World Wide Web to provide this information to their customers. Therefore, they dispatch spiders, crawlers, and other automatic web bots to crawl around the Web performing exhaustive searches of Web sites. The behavior of these bots differs qualitatively from human behavior; for example, the bot may request, in order, every possible link from the Web site, one after the other. This behavior is not considered interesting from a web usage mining standpoint. In fact, if this behavior is retained in the web log file, the resulting analysis will not represent an accurate appraisal of how humans use the Web site. Therefore, the web usage miner needs to try to rid the web log file of these types of nonhuman access behavior.

The most direct method of eliminating bots, spiders, and crawlers from the web log file is to identify the spider's name in the user agent field, when supplied. For contact purposes, the bots often also include a URL or an e-mail address. The webmaster may ask the operator of the crawler not to gather information from certain portions of the Web site, to avoid wasting bandwidth. An example of a crawler bot is the Google bot; to learn more, including how to ask Google not to visit certain parts of your Web site, visit the Google bot site at `http://www.google.com/bot.html`. Other crawlers include the MSN bot (`search.msn.com/msnbot.htm`), and Yahoo! Slurp (`help.yahoo.com/help/us/ysearch/slurp/`). Once sessionizing has been completed, a second level of de-spidering may be applied by identifying the types of access behavior patterns that are typical of spiders, crawlers, and bots.

Since the EPA web log data set does not contain a user agent field, we turn instead to the CCSU web log data to provide a demonstration of de-spidering. Consider Figure 7.5, which contains a lis of the most popular user agents for the CCSU web log data. Note the presence of three different crawlers and bots, including the Google bot (two different types of entries), Yahoo! Slurp, and the Scirus crawler. Scirus (`www.scirus.com`) is a web crawler "for scientific information only." Further, there appears to be an automatic "Servers Alive URL check" routine running. These web log entries, along with all the bot and crawler entries, should be filtered out before proceeding to model human behavior on the Web site. Here we did so, filtering out

| Value | Proportion | % | Count |
|---|---|---|---|
| Mozilla/4.0+(compatible;+MSIE+6.0;+Windows+NT+5.1;+.NET+CLR+1.1.4322) | | 29.08 | 14068 |
| Mozilla/4.0+(compatible;+MSIE+6.0;+Windows+NT+5.0) | | 6.52 | 3157 |
| Mozilla/4.0+(compatible;+MSIE+6.0;+Windows+NT+5.1) | | 5.87 | 2841 |
| Mozilla/4.0+(compatible;+MSIE+6.0;+Windows+NT+5.1;+SV1;+.NET+CLR+1.1.4322) | | 5.42 | 2623 |
| Mozilla/4.0+(compatible;+MSIE+6.0;+Windows+NT+5.1;+SV1) | | 4.14 | 2004 |
| Mozilla/5.0+(compatible;+Googlebot/2.1;++http://www.google.com/bot.html) | | 3.3 | 1596 |
| FAST-WebCrawler/3.8/Scirus+(scirus-crawler@fast.no;+http://www.scirus.com/srsapp/contactus/) | | 1.93 | 935 |
| Mozilla/4.0+(compatible;+MSIE+6.0;+Windows+98) | | 1.71 | 829 |
| Googlebot/2.1+(+http://www.google.com/bot.html) | | 1.5 | 724 |
| Mozilla/4.0+(compatible;+MSIE+6.0;+Windows+NT+5.1;+SV1;+.NET+CLR+1.0.3705) | | 1.39 | 671 |
| Mozilla/4.0+(compatible;+MSIE+6.0;+Windows+NT+5.0;+.NET+CLR+1.1.4322) | | 1.28 | 619 |
| Servers+Alive+URL+check | | 1.07 | 520 |
| Mozilla/4.0+(compatible;+MSIE+6.0;+Windows+NT+5.1;+.NET+CLR+1.0.3705;+.NET+CLR+1.1.43... | | 1.05 | 508 |
| Mozilla/4.0+(compatible;+MSIE+6.0;+Windows+NT+5.1;+.NET+CLR+1.0.3705) | | 1.0 | 484 |
| Mozilla/4.0+(compatible;+MSIE+6.0;+Windows+NT+5.0;+T312461) | | 0.97 | 469 |
| Mozilla/5.0+(compatible;+Yahoo!+Slurp;+http://help.yahoo.com/help/us/ysearch/slurp) | | 0.84 | 408 |

**Figure 7.5**   Most popular user agents for the CCSU web log file.

| Value ▲ | Proportion | % | Count |
|---|---|---|---|
| bot | ▇ | 10.75 | 5201 |
| not bot | ▇▇▇▇▇▇▇▇▇▇▇▇ | 89.25 | 43184 |

**Figure 7.6**   Over 10% of the CCSU web log entries are from bots, crawlers, and spiders.

5201 entries from recognized bots, spiders, and crawlers, leaving us with 43,184 entries. A bar chart of the "bot" vs. "not bot" entries is provided in Figure 7.6.

## USER IDENTIFICATION

Here, the goal is to identify each distinct user. Ideally, this would be accomplished easily if the user provided his or her registration information, such as user name and password, each time the Web site was accessed. Unfortunately, the free-form structure of the Internet means that most user accesses to most Web sites are done anonymously, so that registration information is not available. Another way of describing this situation is to say that the Internet is essentially *stateless*, meaning that each request for a web page gets treated as an isolated event, unrelated to all other requests for the site's web pages. User identification is one way of introducing a state into this stateless system.

Another means of identifying users is the use of *cookies*. A cookie is an arbitrary text string, usually set by a web server, containing whatever information the server wishes to place. In this way, cookies can be used to connect current web page accesses to previous accesses. In addition to tracking user access, the most common uses for cookies are:

- To avoid requiring returning registered users from signing in again each time they access the site
- To personalize the user's experience: for example, with individualized recommendations
- To maintain the user's shopping cart for e-commerce sites

However, many users are concerned that the abuse of cookie information can lead to violations of privacy. Further, cookies can be blocked or cleared by the user. Therefore, the web usage miner needs recourse to other strategies for identifying users.

The remote host field, or IP address field, may in principle be used to identify users. However, the widespread use of proxy servers, corporate firewalls, and local caches renders problematic the use of the IP address as a substitute for user identification. For example, several users may be accessing the same site, using a proxy server, which will provide the web server with the same IP address for each user. To provide an example of how sparse the user name field is for a typical Web site, we show a table of the most common values for this field in the CCSU web log data, given in Table 7.3. The server name has been changed, as have the user names provided here. Note that over 99.5% of the user names are blank, taking the "-" value in the web

TABLE 7.3 Most Common Values for the User Name Field, CCSU Data

| Value | Proportion | Count |
| --- | --- | --- |
| — | 0.9955034 | 192,833 |
| CCSU_Server\smith | 0.001115 | 216 |
| CCSU_Server\jones | 0.000780 | 151 |
| CCSU_Server\akhbar | 0.000614 | 119 |
| CCSU_Server\ivanov | 0.000361 | 70 |
| CCSU_Server\chang | 0.000217 | 42 |
| CCSU_Server\feliciano | 0.000186 | 36 |
| CCSU_Server\chagnon | 0.000181 | 35 |
| CCSU_Server\johnson | 0.000176 | 34 |
| CCSU_Server\washington | 0.000134 | 26 |
| CCSU_Server\rivera | 0.000129 | 25 |

log entry. Since users by and large do not provide their own identification, we should seek alternative methods to identify them.

Next, consider Table 7.4, containing an excerpt from the fictional web log for an imaginary Web site. Note that all the IP addresses are the same, which would at first glance seem to indicate that all the entries are from the same user. However, such a conclusion would be mistaken. We shall use the following *heuristic*, which seems to be a reasonable assumption: If the agent field differs for two web log entries, the requests are from two different users. Although this assumption ignores users who access the same Web site with two different browsers on the same machine, this sort of behavior is relatively rare.

Consider the sample web log file for an imaginary Web site in Table 7.4. Applying this heuristic to the entries in the table, we can discern that there are at least two users represented here, one using Windows NT and MS Internet Explorer, the other using Linux and Firefox. Based on this, we can postulate the following paths through the Web site taken by each user:

- *User 1:* A → B → E → K → I → O → E → L
- *User 2:* A → C → G → M → H → N

However, do you see a problem with these reconstructions? If we apply the information available from the referrer field, along with the Web site topology, we can uncover the highly likely result that "user 1" here is actually two different users. Why is this? Follow the referrer field along user 1's path through the Web site. We see that access to B.html has been referred from A.html, access to E.html referred from B.html, and access to K.html referred from E.html.

However, unexpectedly, there is no referrer shown for the page I.html request. Also, consider the Web site topology shown in Figure 7.7. The arrows indicate link directionality. There is no direct link between K.html and I.html. Thus, it appears highly unlikely that the user who was traversing A → B → E → K then proceeded to **I**. It is more likely that this request for page I.html came from a third user, who accessed the page directly, probably by entering the URL directly into the browser using the

**TABLE 7.4 Sample Web Log File for an Imaginary Web Site**

| IP Address | Time | Method | Referrer | Agent |
|---|---|---|---|---|
| 987.654.32.1 | 00:00:02 | "GET A.html HTTP/1.1" | — | Mozilla/4.0 (Windows NT 5.1, MSIE6.0) |
| 987.654.32.1 | 00:00:05 | "GET B.html HTTP/1.1" | A.html | Mozilla/4.0 (Windows NT 5.1, MSIE6.0) |
| 987.654.32.1 | 00:00:06 | "GET A.html HTTP/1.1" | — | Mozilla/5.0 (Linux 1.0, Firefox/0.9.3) |
| 987.654.32.1 | 00:00:10 | "GET E.html HTTP/1.1" | B.html | Mozilla/4.0 (Windows NT 5.1, MSIE6.0) |
| 987.654.32.1 | 00:00:17 | "GET K.html HTTP/1.1" | E.html | Mozilla/4.0 (Windows NT 5.1, MSIE6.0) |
| 987.654.32.1 | 00:00:20 | "GET C.html HTTP/1.1" | A.html | Mozilla/5.0 (Linux 1.0, Firefox/0.9.3) |
| 987.654.32.1 | 00:00:27 | "GET I.html HTTP/1.1" | — | Mozilla/4.0 (Windows NT 5.1, MSIE6.0) |
| 987.654.32.1 | 00:00:36 | "GET G.html HTTP/1.1" | C.html | Mozilla/5.0 (Linux 1.0, Firefox/0.9.3) |
| 987.654.32.1 | 00:00:49 | "GET 0.html HTTP/1.1" | I.html | Mozilla/4.0 (Windows NT 5.1, MSIE6.0) |
| 987.654.32.1 | 00:00:57 | "GET M.html HTTP/1.1" | G.html | Mozilla/5.0 (Linux 1.0, Firefox/0.9.3) |
| 987.654.32.1 | 00:03:15 | "GET H.html HTTP/1.1" | — | Mozilla/5.0 (Linux 1.0, Firefox/0.9.3) |
| 987.654.32.1 | 00:03:20 | "GET N.html HTTP/1.1" | H.html | Mozilla/5.0 (Linux 1.0, Firefox/0.9.3) |
| 987.654.32.1 | 00:31:27 | "GET E.html HTTP/1.1" | K.html | Mozilla/4.0 (Windows NT 5.1, MSIE6.0) |
| 987.654.32.1 | 00:31:34 | "GET L.html HTTP/1.1" | E.html | Mozilla/4.0 (Windows NT 5.1, MSIE6.0) |

*Source:* Adapted from ref. 1.

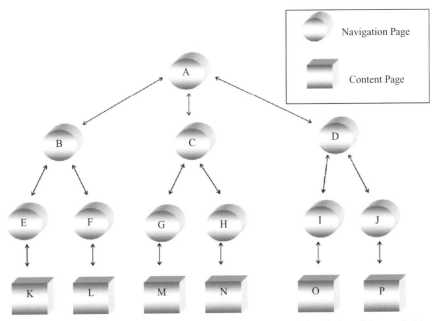

**Figure 7.7**   Topology of the imaginary Web site, showing links. (Adapted from ref. 1.)

same browser version and operating system. Further, note that the only way to access page O.html is from I.html. The referrer information supports the inference that this third user clicked from I.html to O.html. Thus, it appears that we have evidence in this web log file for the presence of three distinct users:

- *User 1:* A → B → E → K → E → L
- *User 2:* A → C → G → M → H → N
- *User 3:* I → O

## User Identification Procedure

In general, the following procedure could be used to identify users:

1. Sort the web log file by ID address and then by time stamp.
2. For each distinct ID address, identify each agent as belonging to a different user.
3. For each user identified in step 2, apply path information garnered from the referrer field and the site topology to determine whether this behavior is more likely the result of two or more users.
4. To identify each user, combine the user identification information from steps 1 to 3 with available cookie and registration information.

## SESSION IDENTIFICATION

Next we turn to the important concept of a *user session*, which may be defined roughly as the set of web pages viewed by a particular user for a particular purpose. Baglioni et al. [2] recommend the *reference length* approach, where it is assumed that the length of time that a user spends on a web page is proportional to the interest of the user in the page's content. The reference length approach allows us to distinguish between *navigational pages*, which contain only links and no content, and *content pages*, which contain the information desired by the user.

Define the time delay $d_{A \to B}$ to be the time difference between the request for page A and the request for page B. Then, in the absence of other information, for a given time threshold $t$, we may provisionally classify page A to be a content page if $d_{A \to B} > t$, and a navigational page otherwise. Baglioni et al. then define a user session to be "a sequence of navigational URLs followed by one content URL." However, this definition is too restrictive for our purposes, since conceivably the user could move from content page to navigation page to content page in the same session.

The concept of user session is important because it corresponds to what is often considered to be a "visit" to a site. As the web usage miner should not be expected to divine the purpose of a user visiting the site, standardized heuristics are available. For example, suppose that a particular user makes two visits to a particular Web site twice within a 24-hour period. Suppose that the visits are 6 hours apart. If the user identification methods examined earlier are applied to the web log for this 24-hour period, the two visits will be sorted together and identified with this user. But clearly, a distinction should be made between the two visits. This is where *sessionizing*, or *session identification*, comes in. Sessionizing is a process by which the aggregate page requests made by a particular user over a long period of time are partitioned into individual sessions.

Perhaps the most straightforward sessionizing method is simply to apply a time-out after a certain length of time has passed since the user's last request. For example, using empirical data, Catledge and Pitkow [3] determined a timeout threshold of 25.5 minutes. Many web usage analysts and commercial applications set the timeout threshold at 30 minutes. A session identification algorithm can then apply this timeout threshold to the web log data and define a new session to be started whenever the difference between two requests exceeds the threshold.

For example, consider again Table 7.4, which contains the sample web log for our imaginary Web site. Note that for user 1, there is more than a 30-minute delay between the request for page K.html (at time 00:00:17) and the second request for page E.html (at time 00:31:27). The sessionizing algorithm would therefore presumably identify the second request for page E.html as the start of a new session, giving us the following four sessions from this web log:

- *Session 1 (user 1):* A $\to$ B $\to$ E $\to$ K
- *Session 2 (user 2):* A $\to$ C $\to$ G $\to$ M $\to$ H $\to$ N
- *Session 3 (user 3):* I $\to$ O
- *Session 4 (user 1):* E $\to$ L

### Session Identification Procedure

The session identification procedure may be summarized as follows:

1. For each distinct user identified in the preceding section, assign a unique session ID.
2. Define the timeout threshold $t$.
3. For each user, perform the following:
   a. Find the time difference between every two consecutive web log entries.
   b. If this difference exceeds the threshold $t$, assign a new session ID to the later entry.
4. Sort the entries by session ID.

Returning to the EPA web log data, we apply this session identification procedure to the cleaned and filtered EPA web log data. First, we assign a unique session ID to each user identified. (Since this data set contains neither the referrer nor the agent fields, we default to assigning users by IP address only.) Then we define a timeout threshold of 30 minutes (1800 seconds) for defining the start of a new session. Finally, for each user, we determine whether any requests are delayed by more than 30 minutes; if so, a new session ID is issued. Finally, the entries are sorted by session ID. A portion of the results are provided in Figure 7.8 All entries in the figure are from the same user. However, note the difference in time stamp between the shaded entries: $20878108 - 20872908 = 5200$ seconds $= 86.67$ minutes, exceeding the timeout threshold of 30 minutes. Therefore, the algorithm assigned a new session ID, "Session 21," starting at this entry.

| | IP Address | method | TimeStamp | Page | Session ID |
|---|---|---|---|---|---|
| 173 | 128.165.180.61 | GET | 20872485 | / | Session_20 |
| 174 | 128.165.180.61 | GET | 20872511 | /docs/WhatsNew.html | Session_20 |
| 175 | 128.165.180.61 | GET | 20872554 | /Offices.html | Session_20 |
| 176 | 128.165.180.61 | GET | 20872737 | /cgi-bin/imagemap/eparegio... | Session_20 |
| 177 | 128.165.180.61 | GET | 20872738 | /docs/eparegions/region4.ht... | Session_20 |
| 178 | 128.165.180.61 | GET | 20872777 | /Standards.html | Session_20 |
| 179 | 128.165.180.61 | GET | 20872787 | /docs/OPPTS_Harmonized | Session_20 |
| 180 | 128.165.180.61 | GET | 20872789 | /OPPTS_Harmonized/ | Session_20 |
| 181 | 128.165.180.61 | GET | 20872840 | /Consumer.html | Session_20 |
| 182 | 128.165.180.61 | GET | 20872866 | /cgi-bin/imagemap/eparegio... | Session_20 |
| 183 | 128.165.180.61 | GET | 20872867 | /docs/eparegions/region6.ht... | Session_20 |
| 184 | 128.165.180.61 | GET | 20872908 | /docs/Environment.html | Session_20 |
| 185 | 128.165.180.61 | GET | 20878108 | / | Session_21 |
| 186 | 128.165.180.61 | GET | 20878205 | / | Session_21 |
| 187 | 128.165.180.61 | GET | 20878228 | /Info.html | Session_21 |
| 188 | 128.165.180.61 | GET | 20878236 | /docs/Procurement.html | Session_21 |
| 189 | 128.165.180.61 | GET | 20878266 | /docs/conlist | Session_21 |
| 190 | 128.165.180.61 | GET | 20878267 | /conlist/ | Session_21 |
| 191 | 128.165.180.61 | GET | 20878287 | /docs/conlist/conlist.html | Session_21 |
| 192 | 128.165.180.61 | GET | 20878792 | /docs/OPP_TECHNICAL_S... | Session_21 |

**Figure 7.8**   Session identification for EPA web log data.

The web log files record the time whenever a request from the web server is made. However, when the user leaves the site, no record of this is made on the original web server; instead, the time is recorded on whatever server hosts the next Web site the user visited. This situation makes it difficult to estimate when the session ended or how long the session lasted.

It is possible that the user left the site immediately to check the sports scores; on the other hand, the user may have remained on the last page for up to an hour. Using only the web log data, there is no way to tell for sure. If we assume that the session ended when no web entry was logged before the timeout threshold of 30 minutes, this is perhaps overestimating the session length. On the other hand, if we define the end of the session to occur when the last page was logged, this is certainly underestimating the session length. Neither solution is entirely satisfactory. Perhaps a better solution is to assign the last page a duration similar to the duration of other users who visited the same number of pages. Can you think of any other solutions to this problem? You are invited to do so in the exercises.

## PATH COMPLETION

Not all page views seen by the user are recorded in the web server log. For example, many people use the "Back" button on their browsers to return to a page viewed previously. When this happens, the browser returns to a page that was previously cached locally rather than accessing the web server again. This leads to "holes," missing pages, in the web server's record of the user's path through the Web site. Knowledge of site topology must be applied to complete these paths, in a process known as *path completion*.

Once the missing pages have been identified, they are inserted into the session file along with an estimate of the duration spent on the missing page. These duration estimates may be classified according to whether the missing page is a navigation page, with a shorter duration estimate, or a content page, with a longer duration estimate.

Consider again session 2 identified in the preceding section:

- *Session 2 (user 2):* $A \rightarrow C \rightarrow G \rightarrow M \rightarrow H \rightarrow N$

Note from the topology in Figure 7.6 that there is no direct link between page M.html and page H.html. Therefore, the user is presumed to have hit the "Back" button on the browser twice, retracing the path back through page G.html to page C.html, where a direct link to H.html can be found. Therefore, the path completion process leads us to insert "$\rightarrow G \rightarrow C$" into the session path for session 2, giving us the following "final" forms for the four sessions:

- *Session 1 (user 1):* $A \rightarrow B \rightarrow E \rightarrow K$
- *Session 2 (user 2):* $A \rightarrow C \rightarrow G \rightarrow M \rightarrow G \rightarrow C \rightarrow H \rightarrow N$
- *Session 3 (user 3):* $I \rightarrow O$
- *Session 4 (user 1):* $E \rightarrow L$

## DIRECTORIES AND THE BASKET TRANSFORMATION

The directory structure of a Web site may contain information that will prove useful when the time comes to do some modeling, such as finding which pages are associated with which other pages, and so on. It is therefore helpful to derive a new variable that contains the top directory, or first directory, of the page requested. Then, if we wish, we may aggregate the pages by directory, and analyze patterns and trends by directory.

Figure 7.9 contains a list of the most commonly requested directories for the CCSU Web site, with the root directory accounting for 48.8% of the requests. Note the "/datamining" directory, with 274 requests. This is the Web site for Data Mining @CCSU, the program offering a master of science in data mining with all classes completely online. The program director is the author. See www.ccsu.edu/datamining (of course) for more information.

At present, the data are not in a format that is easy for most data mining algorithms to work with. What we would prefer would be to transform the values in the web log entries into a collection of flag variables, each flag variable indicating, for example, whether or not a particular page or directory were requested. This collection of flag variables would represent a single session using a single record, which is much more appropriate than the web log file structure for most data mining algorithms. This

| Value | Proportion | % | Count ▽ |
|---|---|---|---|
|  |  | 48.8 | 21075 |
| /Index/ |  | 6.41 | 2769 |
| /its/ |  | 3.19 | 1377 |
| /catalogs/ |  | 3.04 | 1312 |
| /grad/ |  | 2.83 | 1222 |
| /career/ |  | 2.4 | 1038 |
| /admission/ |  | 2.4 | 1037 |
| /business/ |  | 2.27 | 982 |
| /registrar/ |  | 2.1 | 908 |
| /search/ |  | 1.91 | 826 |
| /index/ |  | 1.19 | 515 |
| /Calendar/ |  | 1.11 | 478 |
| /Admission/ |  | 1.1 | 473 |
| /virtualtour/ |  | 1.07 | 460 |
| /Personnel/ |  | 1.02 | 441 |
| /planning/ |  | 0.82 | 355 |
| /Career/ |  | 0.81 | 351 |
| /athletictraining/ |  | 0.79 | 339 |
| /Catalogs/ |  | 0.73 | 317 |
| /datamining/ |  | 0.63 | 274 |
| /cie/ |  | 0.6 | 259 |
| /ResLife/ |  | 0.55 | 238 |
| /Italian/ |  | 0.54 | 234 |
| /HowDoI/ |  | 0.53 | 227 |

**Figure 7.9**   Directories requested most from the CCSU Web site.

| Value | Proportion | % | Count ▽ |
|---|---|---|---|
| /Default.htm | ■■■ | 38.1 | 16453 |
| /academics.html | | 2.14 | 925 |
| /Index/ | | 1.85 | 797 |
| /Index/Default.htm | | 1.67 | 722 |
| /Current.htm | | 1.6 | 691 |
| /career/_vti_bin/fpcount.exe | | 1.15 | 495 |
| /Future.htm | | 1.13 | 488 |
| /Faculty.htm | | 1.02 | 442 |
| /search/ | | 0.91 | 395 |
| /search/Default.htm | | 0.89 | 384 |
| /Courses.htm | | 0.75 | 324 |
| /registrar/Forms/CentralPipeline_R... | | 0.74 | 319 |
| /admission/PDF/Application.pdf | | 0.73 | 315 |
| /Personnel/jobs.html | | 0.65 | 279 |
| /Academic_Departments.html | | 0.63 | 270 |
| /Index/C.htm | | 0.5 | 216 |

**Figure 7.10**  Web pages requested most from the CCSU Web site.

procedure is called the *basket transformation* because the collection of flag variables are considered to comprise the basket of information about a particular session, all summarized in one record.

Before applying the basket transformation, the web usage miner should try to get an idea of which variables might be important for analysis farther downstream. For example, it would make sense for the variable we just derived, the first directory, to be important for association rules, since presumably pages within a single directory would be likely to be requested together. Thus, we shall create flag variables for each of the directories found in Figure 7.9, which contains all the directories that have 0.5% or more of the page requests. We also create flag variables for each of the pages found in Figure 7.10, which contains all pages that have 0.5% or more requests.

A *flag variable* is a special case of an *indicator variable* (also known as a *dummy variable*), for use when we wish to indicate whether or not a record has a particular characteristic. A flag variable is a binary 0/1 variable which takes the value 1 if the observation belongs to a given category, and 0 otherwise. For example, to indicate whether or not a particular session included a request for the "/academics.html" web page, we define the following flag variable:

$$\text{Page\_/academics.html} = \begin{cases} T & \text{if session included /academics.html page} \\ F & \text{otherwise} \end{cases}$$

Figure 7.11 shows an intermediate stage of this basket transformation on the page variable for a few of the sessions. Note that whenever the page variable takes a particular value, the corresponding flag variable takes on a value T (true), and F (false) otherwise. For a particular page or directory, only a single flag variable may take a true value. For the first page in Session_0, /Default.htm, the flag variable Page_/Default.htm is the only one to take on a true value. Similarly, Page_/Future.htm

| Session ID | Page | Page _/Default.htm | Page _/Future.htm | Page _/admission/PDF/App.. | Page _/academics.html |
|---|---|---|---|---|---|
| Session_0 | /Default.htm | T | F | F | F |
| Session_0 | /Future.htm | F | T | F | F |
| Session_0 | /Admission/adminapp.htm | F | F | F | F |
| Session_0 | /admission/Application_W.htm | F | F | F | F |
| Session_0 | /admission/PDF/Application.pdf | F | F | T | F |
| Session_0 | /admission/PDF/Application.pdf | F | F | T | F |
| Session_0 | /admission/PDF/Application.pdf | F | F | T | F |
| Session_0 | /admission/PDF/Application.pdf | F | F | T | F |
| Session_0 | /admission/PDF/Application.pdf | F | F | T | F |
| Session_1 | /Default.htm | T | F | F | F |
| Session_10 | /Default.htm | T | F | F | F |
| Session_10 | /academics.html | F | F | F | T |

**Figure 7.11**   Creating flag variables for web pages with frequency > 0.5%.

is the only one to show a true value for the second page in the session, Future.htm. Note that there are no flag variables turned on for the third and fourth pages in this session, since these variables evidently did not make it to the 0.5% threshold for inclusion as flag variables.

The web usage miner should check a few of the flag variables to make sure that they are being transformed accurately. To do this, simply check the frequency distribution of the flag variable against the proportions found in Figure 7.9 and 7.10. For example, the frequency distribution of the flag variable "first_dir_/datamining/" is given in Figure 7.12. Note that the count and proportion of true records in Figure 7.12 are exactly the same as for the directory /datamining/ given in Figure 7.9.

Figure 7.11 is not in the final basket transformation format, since there is more than one record per session. The final step is to aggregate the flags over each session. The rule here is as follows, for each session: "For a given page A, if a true value occurs for page A anywhere in the session, the aggregate value for page A in the basket transformation format is true." Programmers would state that we are "OR-ing" the individual web log entry flags to give us the session flag. For the session flag to be false, all individual entry flags would have to be false.

An excerpt from the resulting basket-transformed CCSU web log is shown in Figure 7.13. Note that there is only one record per session; note also that more than one flag variable can take on a true value, since the session represents more than one page. Later, when we move to modeling, the data mining algorithms will greatly prefer the data in this form.

| Value | Proportion | % | Count |
|---|---|---|---|
| F | | 99.37 | 42910 |
| T | | 0.63 | 274 |

**Figure 7.12**   Frequency distribution of "first_dir_/datamining/."

| Session ID | Page _/Default.htm | Page _/Future.htm | Page _/admission/PDF/Application.pdf | first_dir _/index/ |
|---|---|---|---|---|
| Session_0 | T | T | T | F |
| Session_1 | T | F | F | F |
| Session_10 | T | F | F | F |
| Session_100 | T | F | F | F |
| Session_1000 | F | F | F | F |

**Figure 7.13**   Excerpt from the basket-transformed CCSU web log.

## FURTHER DATA PREPROCESSING STEPS

In this chapter we presented specialized preprocessing methods for handling web log data. Once these methods have been completed, the web usage miner must still apply the usual data mining preprocessing steps [4, Chapt. 2]. Space constraints prevent us from describing these steps. Suffice to list some of them:

- Data quality monitoring
- Handling missing data
- Identifying misclassifications
- Identifying outliers using both graphical and numerical methods
- Normalization and standardization

For more on data preprocessing for data mining, see Larose [4] or Pyle [5].

## REFERENCES

1. R. Cooley, B. Mobasher, and J. Srivastava, Data preparation for mining world wide web browsing patterns, *Journal of Knowledge and Information System*, 1(1): 5–32, 1999.
2. M. Baglioni, U. Ferrara, A. Romei, S. Ruggieri, and F. Turini, Preprocessing and mining web log data for web personalization, *Advances in Artificial Intelligence*, Volume 2829, Springer, Berlin, 2003.
3. L. Catledge and J. Pitkow, Characterizing browsing strategies in the world wide web, *Computer Networks and ISDN Systems*, 27: 1065–1073, 1995.
4. Daniel Larose, *Discovering Knowledge in Data: An Introduction to Data Mining*, Wiley, Hoboken, NJ, 2005.
5. Dorian Pyle, *Data Preparation for Data Mining*, Morgan Kaufmann, San Francisco, CA, 1999.

## EXERCISES

1. The series of requests for pages received by Web site servers is known as what?
   a. Clickstream
   b. Sessionization
   c. Path completion
   d. Spamming

2. Which of the following is not a part of the web log preparation process?
   a. De-spidering
   b. Sessionization
   c. Path completion
   d. Reporting

3. What is the best way of estimating when a session has ended?

  **a.** Session over if there has been no page request for 30 minutes.

  **b.** Session over when the last page is requested.

  **c.** Session over when your spouse calls demanding that you get off the Internet.

  **d.** None of the above.

4. Why are many page requests never recorded in the server log?

  **a.** The server is a Mac and it does not stoop to record PC hits.

  **b.** Caching

  **c.** Spiders

  **d.** Sessionization

5. Suggest two creative solutions to estimating the length of stay on the last page.


**Hands-on Analysis**

6. For the following web log data sets, download the data, and perform the web log pre-processing steps given below. The full data sets are available from the Internet traces web site, `http://ita.ee.lbl.gov/html/contrib/NASA-HTTP.html`. We use only a subset of the data. The data subsets are available from the book series web site, `www.dataminingconsultant.com`.

  - *The NASA-HTTP web log data*. We use only the first 131,904 records.
  - *The Calgary-HTTP web log data*. We use only the first 65,536 records.

  **a.** Extract the date and time variables, if needed.

  **b.** Extract the method, page, and protocol version variables, if needed.

  **c.** Create a **time stamp** that represents the number of seconds elapsed since a particular convenient date, such as January 1, 1995. (For Clementine users, don't forget to set the proper time format in file > stream properties.)

  **d.** Perform filtering.

    (1) Construct a table of the 10 most popular page extensions, with their counts.

    (2) Filter out all but the following extensions: .htm, .html, .pdf, .asp, .exe, .txt, .doc, .ppt, .xls, and .xml. Retain records with empty page extensions.

    (3) Explain clearly why we are doing all this.

  **e.** De-spider the data.

    (1) Construct a table of all of the bots and crawlers.

    (2) Report the relative proportions of these hits.

    (3) Eliminate all bots, spiders, and crawlers from the data.

    (4) Clearly explain why we are doing this.

  **f.** Try to perform user identification.

    (1) Discuss how much the user name field helps us.

    (2) Is there a referrer field?

    (3) Do we have the site topology?

**g.** (Extra credit)

(1) Perform some path completion using the actual entries. Document your work clearly.

(2) Construct an "empirical" topology by visiting the site yourself.

**h.** Apply session identification.

(1) Use the unique IP addresses and a timeout threshold of 30 minutes.

(2) Provide a table of some of your results, sorted by session ID and time stamp.

**i.** Apply the basket transformation to the directory structure of the web log entries.

(1) Make a table of the 20 directories with the greatest number of hits.

(2) Make a table of the web pages requested most.

(3) Derive flag variables for these 20 directories and all pages showing at least 0.5% frequency of hits.

(4) Provide documentation that your basket transformation is working, such as a table of some sessions with the pages shown along with the flag variables.

(5) Provide a table showing the final form of your basket transformation, which should contain only one entry per session.

**j.** Discuss the difficulty we face when estimating the duration of the last page of a session. Suggest a *creative* means of estimating the duration of the last page of a session.

**k.** Identify and handle missing data.

**l.** Identify outliers.

# EXPLORATORY DATA ANALYSIS FOR WEB USAGE MINING

## INTRODUCTION

Now that the heavy lifting of web log preprocessing has been completed, and before we begin modeling the web usage data, it is helpful to perform some exploratory data analysis (EDA). One can learn quite a lot about user behavior using some simple EDA techniques, as discussed in Chapter 3 of *Discovering Knowledge in Data* [1]. In general, EDA allows the analyst to probe deeper into the data set, inspect the interrelationships among the variables, and reveal interesting subsets of the records. Fruitful areas for further investigation downstream could be indicated, based on relationships uncovered in the EDA process, using simple graphs and tables. In this chapter we use exploratory methods to delve into the EPA data set.

## NUMBER OF VISIT ACTIONS

Later, when we begin profiling visitors to the Web site, one of the factors may be the visit length, in terms of how many *visit actions* (e.g., page requests) are made by users on the site, where *visit* is a synonym for *session*. Also, we would be interested in obtaining some site statistics regarding the aggregate behavior of visitors in terms of

*Data Mining the Web: Uncovering Patterns in Web Content, Structure, and Usage*
By Zdravko Markov and Daniel T. Larose    Copyright © 2007 John Wiley & Sons, Inc.

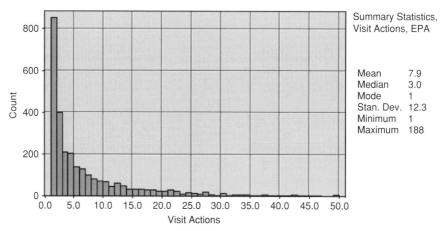

**Figure 8.1**   Distribution of visit actions, EPA.

the numbers of visit actions, such as the mean number of visit actions per session. The number of visit actions is simply the count of the web log entries for each session ID.

Figure 8.1 includes summary statistics for visitors to the EPA Web site. The mean number of user requests per session is almost eight, which seems like a fairly healthy number—good news for web developers. However, comparison with other statistics reveals evidence that the distribution of visit actions is strongly right-skewed. For example, the mean is higher than the median, the mode is the same as the minimum, and the maximum is very large.

Figure 8.1 confirms our deduction that the distribution is right-skewed. (To increase granularity, the visit actions above 50 have been omitted from the graph. Inclusion of these records would have made the graph even more right-skewed.) What this shows us is that the great majority of sessions last fewer than five actions, half last three or fewer, and a disappointingly large number of sessions consist of only a single page request. This is not such good news for web developers. Why are visitors leaving so soon? Is the site sufficiently user friendly? How can we change the site to tempt visitors to linger? Actually, the developers should not be too unhappy, since the majority of visits to most Web sites worldwide contain fewer than 10 actions.

For the CCSU web log data, the distribution of visit actions is even more strongly right-skewed (Figure 8.2, capped at 50 actions). The summary statistics for the visit actions are included in the figure. Broadly, the visit action behavior is somewhat similar to that of the EPA Web site, with the minimum, median, and mode values equal to just one visit action. The mean for the EPA site is higher, however. The reason for this may be that the EPA data were not de-spidered; search engines and spiders often systematically traverse an entire site, thereby increasing the mean visit length.

## SESSION DURATION

Apart from the number of user clicks per session, another important variable is the time duration per session that the user spent on the Web site. Unfortunately, because

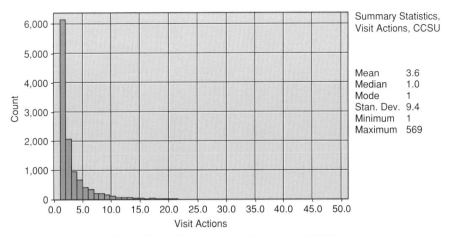

**Figure 8.2** Distribution of visit actions, CCSU.

we do not know how long the user spent on the last page of a session, the exact amount of time per session will prove to be elusive. Thus, when we calculate the session duration, we need to restrict the sessions to those that contained more than a single action; otherwise, there is no measured duration at all for a single web log entry.

### Session Duration Calculation Procedure

The process for calculating the session duration is as follows:

1. Select only those sessions that contain more than a single action.
2. For each session, do the following:
   a. Select only the first and last page requests.
   b. Find the session time by subtracting the time stamp of the first page request from the time stamp of the last page request.

It is important to note, of course, that this method of calculating session duration inevitably leads to an underestimate of the total session duration, since the time spent on the last page is not counted. Once the session duration has been calculated, we may explore further the behavior of this new statistic. For the reasons discussed above, we restrict our analysis to those users who requested more than one page. Figure 8.3 contains the summary statistics for session duration for the EPA data.

The mean session duration is 752.4 seconds, or 12.54 minutes. Again, this seems pretty encouraging, until we remember that for right-skewed data (see Figure 8.3) the median is a better summary statistic than the mean. The median session duration is 317 seconds, or about 5.28 minutes, which is a more realistic estimate of the typical session duration, among those who requested more than one page. Figure 8.3 shows the distribution of session duration (also known as *visit time*) for multipage sessions. Again, to increase granularity, the upper tail has been clipped at 4000 seconds for this graph.

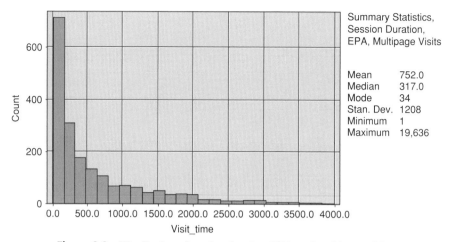

**Figure 8.3** Distribution of session duration, EPA, and multipage visits.

Does this mean that the typical session lasted about 5.28 minutes? Well, this statistic represents only those who clicked through at least two pages. It is probably a fair assumption that those users (sessions) that only visited one page typically spent less than 5.28 minutes on this single page. Therefore, this 5.28 minutes probably overestimates the median session duration for all sessions, although we cannot know for sure.

The CCSU session duration again exhibits broadly similar behavior, as shown in Figure 8.4. Note that the mean session duration for the CCSU data is higher than that of the EPA data, even though the mean visit actions for the CCSU data is less than half that of the EPA data. This may indicate further evidence for the presence of unaccounted-for web crawler activity on the EPA Web site, which would produce many hits of short duration. This also indicates evidence that the mean time per page

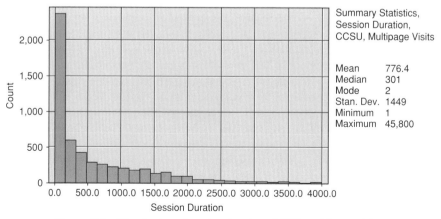

**Figure 8.4** Distribution of session duration, CCSU, multipage visits.

for visitors to the CCSU Web site is longer than for visitors to the EPA Web site. In the next section we investigate this result further.

The low mode (2) for the CCSU data may or may not be noteworthy, since the mode can be an unstable statistic in certain situations. The maximum session duration for the CCSU data represents a session of over 12 hours in length, with no break of 30 minutes or longer. This is the same session that performed the maximum 569 actions, of which, as it turned out, 430 were requests for the CCSU Web site default page. Perhaps the web analyst may wish to take another look at this user, to better understand this type of behavior.

## RELATIONSHIP BETWEEN VISIT ACTIONS AND SESSION DURATION

Next, we turn to the relationship between session duration and the number of visit actions. For example, would it make sense that on average, an increase in the number of user actions per session is associated with an increase in the session duration? The type of graph that would help here is a scatter plot of the relationship between session duration ($y$, vertical axis) and visit actions ($x$, horizontal axis), shown in Figure 8.5 (visit actions capped at 80 to enhance granularity). As expected, there appears to be evidence of a positive association, or correlation, between the number of visit actions and the duration of the session.

It would be nice if we could somehow quantify this association. That is, an additional page request is associated with how much of an increase in session duration, on average? A handy tool for ascertaining this is regression analysis [2, Chap. 2]. In simple linear regression, a straight line is used to approximate the relationship between a single numerical predictor variable and a single numerical response variable.

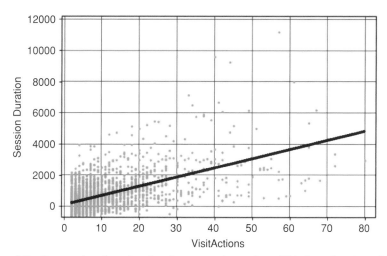

**Figure 8.5**   Scatter plot of session duration vs. session actions, EPA data, showing evidence of positive association. The estimated regression line is shown.

**TABLE 8.1 Regression Coefficients for Relationship Between Session Duration and Session Actions, EPA Data[a]**

| Model | | Unstandardized Coefficients | | Standardized Coefficients | | |
|---|---|---|---|---|---|---|
| | | B | Std. Error | β | t | Sig. |
| 1 | (Constant) | 112.073 | 25.235 | | 4.441 | 0.000 |
| | Visit Actions | 59.330 | 1.451 | 0.671 | 40.901 | 0.000 |

[a] Dependent variable: session duration.

Applying regression analysis to the relationship between session duration and visit actions gives us the results shown in Table 8.1. The estimated regression equation is therefore:

"The estimated session duration equals 112.073 seconds plus 59.33 seconds times the number of visit actions."

The line

$$\text{estimated duration} = 112.073 + 59.33\,(\text{actions})$$

is graphed in Figure 8.5.

We may use this estimated regression equation to make predictions for the session duration, given a particular number of visit actions. For example, a session consisting of 10 actions would have an estimated duration of $112.073 + (59.33)(10) = 705.373$ seconds, or about 11.76 minutes. Also, the interpretation of the value for the regression slope is useful. Here the slope estimate is 59.33 seconds, meaning that for every additional visit action (page request), the estimate increase in session duration is 59.33 seconds (always remembering that we are talking about sessions with more than one page request). Note that this is not simply an average time per page, but rather, the slope of the regression line, which has a $y$-intercept of 112 seconds. The literal meaning of the $y$-intercept is the estimated duration for a session of zero actions, but this literal meaning does not make sense in the present context.

The relationship between session duration and session actions for the CCSU data is similar to that for the EPA data. Figure 8.6 is a scatter plot of session duration against session actions, with an estimated regression line overlay. Here the estimated regression equation is

$$\text{estimated duration} = 310.496 + 73.675\,(\text{actions})$$

as shown by Table 8.2. The interpretation of the slope value 73.675 is that for each additional action (page view), the estimated increase in session duration is about 74 seconds. This is somewhat greater than the 59.33 seconds for the EPA data set, and supports the surmise in the preceding section that CCSU visitors spent more time per page than was spent by EPA visitors.

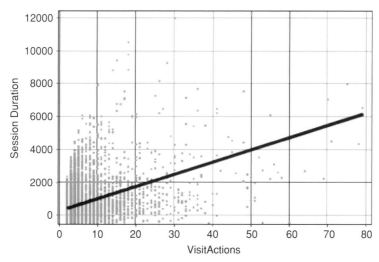

**Figure 8.6**   Scatter plot of session duration vs. visit actions, CCSU data. The estimated regression line is shown.

**TABLE 8.2    Regression Coefficients for Relationship Between Session Duration and Session Actions, CCSU Data[a]**

| Model | | Unstandardized Coefficients | | Standardized Coefficients | $t$ | Sig. |
|---|---|---|---|---|---|---|
| | | $B$ | Std. Error | $\beta$ | | |
| 1 | (Constant) | 310.496 | 15.903 | | 19.524 | 0.000 |
| | VisitActions | 73.675 | 1.102 | 0.660 | 66.869 | 0.000 |

[a] Dependent variable: session duration.

## AVERAGE TIME PER PAGE

Next, we calculate the average time per page over all sessions. This is found by deriving a new variable for each session:

$$\text{average time per page} = \frac{\text{session duration}}{\text{number of visit actions } - 1}$$

Why do we subtract 1 from the number of visit actions? Because the last page visited is not counted as part of the session duration but is counted in the number of visit actions. The summary statistics for the average time per page are provided in Figure 8.7 So here we have an overall mean of 118.6 seconds per page across all sessions. The figure shows that the distribution is again right-skewed, however, meaning that the median is perhaps a better summary of the average time per page across all sessions. (Observations over 600 have been clipped for the graph only.) This median time per page of 53.6 seconds is not far from our earlier regression slope estimate of 59.33 seconds. It seems that, typically, visitors to the EPA Web site are spending

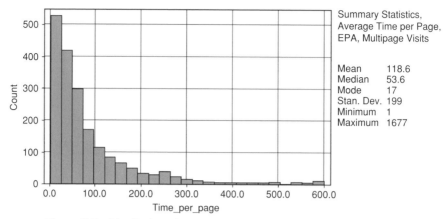

**Figure 8.7** Distribution of average time per page, EPA multipage sessions.

about 1 minute per page. This average of about 1 minute per page is aggregated over both navigation pages and content pages. Later we investigate whether there is a difference in average time per page between the various types of pages.

The distribution of average time per page for the CCSU multipage sessions shown in Figure 8.8 indicates a right-skewed distribution with both a heavier tail and a more pronounced spike at the left bound than for the EPA data set. This greater spread is reflected in the larger value for the standard deviation, 369 vs. 199, as seen from the summary statistics in the figure. The mean and median are both larger for the CCSU data than for the EPA data, reinforcing our earlier findings that the average time per page was longer for visitors to the CCSU Web site. Note that the median of about 80 seconds per page is not far from the regression slope estimate of 74 seconds for each additional page.

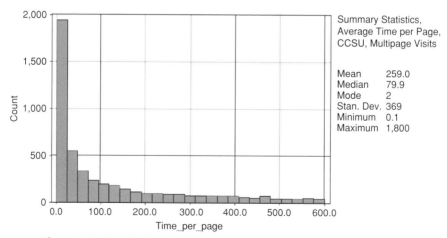

**Figure 8.8** Distribution of average time per page, CCSU multipage sessions.

| | Session ID | VisitActions | User Agent | Session Duration | Time_per_page |
|---|---|---|---|---|---|
| 1 | Session_7325 | 22 | htdig/3.1.6+(silentbob@ccsu.edu) | 2 | 0.1 |
| 2 | Session_1192 | 36 | Scooter/3.3 | 8 | 0.2 |
| 3 | Session_11995 | 14 | Mozilla/4.0+(compatible;+MSIE+6.0;+Win... | 4 | 0.3 |
| 4 | Session_4910 | 4 | Mozilla/4.0+(compatible;+MSIE+6.0;+Win... | 1 | 0.3 |
| 5 | Session_5266 | 7 | Mozilla/4.0+(compatible;+MSIE+6.0;+Win... | 2 | 0.3 |
| 6 | Session_8613 | 4 | Mozilla/4.0+(compatible;+MSIE+6.0;+Win... | 1 | 0.3 |
| 7 | Session_812 | 3 | Mozilla/4.0+(compatible;+MSIE+6.0;+Win... | 1 | 0.5 |
| 8 | Session_4933 | 3 | Mozilla/4.0+(compatible;+MSIE+6.0;+Win... | 1 | 0.5 |
| 9 | Session_9565 | 3 | Mozilla/4.0+(compatible;+MSIE+6.0;+Win... | 1 | 0.5 |
| 10 | Session_5872 | 3 | Mozilla/4.0+(compatible;+MSIE+6.0;+Win... | 1 | 0.5 |
| 11 | Session_6763 | 3 | Mozilla/4.0+(compatible;+MSIE+6.0;+Win... | 1 | 0.5 |
| 12 | Session_6761 | 3 | Mozilla/4.0+(compatible;+MSIE+6.0;+Win... | 1 | 0.5 |
| 13 | Session_7496 | 5 | Mozilla/4.0+(compatible;+MSIE+6.0;+Win... | 2 | 0.5 |
| 14 | Session_11632 | 3 | Mozilla/4.0+(compatible;+MSIE+6.0;+Win... | 1 | 0.5 |
| 15 | Session_11756 | 4 | Mozilla/4.0+(compatible;+MSIE+6.0;+Win... | 2 | 0.7 |
| 16 | Session_5754 | 2 | Mozilla/4.0+(compatible;+MSIE+6.0;+Win... | 1 | 1.0 |
| 17 | Session_9531 | 2 | Mozilla/4.0+(compatible;+MSIE+5.22;+M... | 1 | 1.0 |
| 18 | Session_4647 | 2 | Mozilla/4.0+(compatible;+MSIE+6.0;+Win... | 1 | 1.0 |
| 19 | Session_12019 | 2 | Mozilla/4.0+(compatible;+MSIE+6.0;+Win... | 1 | 1.0 |
| 20 | Session_9509 | 2 | Mozilla/4.0+(compatible;+MSIE+6.0;+Win... | 1 | 1.0 |

**Figure 8.9**   Lowest average times per page, CCSU data.

The minimum average time per page for the CCSU data is worrisome, however, with a value of only 0.1 second per page. Further investigation is called for. Figure 8.9 provides a listing of the 20 lowest average times per page across all CCSU sessions. Note that the first record in the figure, Session ID 7325, represents a session of 22 page requests in 2 seconds. That's some mighty fast clicking! Similarly, the second record represents a session (ID 1192) that requested 36 pages in 8 seconds. Presumably, these sessions were not the result of human activity, but rather the result of bots, which somehow eluded the bot-catching net we applied in the de-spidering section. The third record also stretches the bounds of credulity with its 14 actions in 4 seconds, but the user agent field does not identify it as a crawler or bot, so we choose to overlook this.

However, we must return to the preprocessing stage to eliminate the entries made by the two crawlers we uncovered here, htdig and Scooter. Note that this occurrence underscores the interactive nature of the web usage mining process. The web usage miner should be prepared to iterate between phases, such as the preprocessing phase and the exploratory phase, in order to fine tune the data and the models.

# DURATION FOR INDIVIDUAL PAGES

Visits to most Internet Web sites tend to be rather short in terms of page requests; most visits last for fewer than a dozen actions. Thus, if the web usage miner is interested in profiling the visitors, for example, for the purpose of making a sales recommendation, such profiling should perhaps be done as quickly as possible. In this section we derive attributes labeling the first three pages requested by the user in each session. Later, the analyst may wish to use labels such as these to form purchase or link recommendations.

Also in this section we explore the duration for each of the first three pages visited. To find the duration for the first $n$ pages of a session, use the following procedure.

1. Sort the web log by session ID and then by time stamp.
2. For each session, do the following:
   a. Label the first page visited, $page_1$.
   b. For page $i = 2, \ldots, n$:
      i. Label each page visited, $page_i$.
      ii. Find the duration of $page_{i-1}$ by subtracting the time stamp of $page_{i-1}$ from the time stamp of $page_i$.

We surmise that the duration of navigation pages will be less than that of content pages, overall. Unfortunately, we lack precise knowledge as to either the topology of the Web site or to which pages are navigation and which pages are content. Recall from Chapter 7 that we retained entries with the following extensions, on the assumption that these extensions indicated some sort of content: .doc, .exe, .gz, .htm, .html, .pdf, .ps, .tar, .txt, .wp, .wpd, and .zip. Entries with an empty page extension, indicating a directory default page, were assumed to be navigation pages. However, note that these are assumptions, not facts. The site may not even be divided formally into navigation and content pages. Nevertheless, a brief exploration may shed some light on the situation.

If we find that the mean duration of our content pages is greater than that of our navigation pages, this would represent evidence in support of our categorization scheme. Table 8.3 provides the mean page duration for each of the first two pages visited, across all sessions, broken down as follows: the overall mean duration for all pages, the mean duration for the navigation pages, and the mean duration for the content pages. For each page, the content pages had a longer mean duration than the navigation pages. This supports our categorization of the pages as such. Now a statistician looks at this type of data and immediately thinks: two-sample $t$-test. Certainly, we could carry out that type of statistical inference on these data, and we may indeed find significance. But we are here in the exploratory phase of the process, where inference does not belong. Also, the role of statistical inference in data mining as a whole is rather problematic. The huge sample sizes extant in most data mining problems leads inevitably to findings of significance, even for the smallest effect sizes.

**TABLE 8.3 Mean Page Duration for the First Two Pages Visited, EPA Data**

| Page 1 Duration | | | Page 2 Duration | | |
|---|---|---|---|---|---|
| Overall | Navigation | Content | Overall | Navigation | Content |
| 135.5 | 126.6 | 162.5 | 96.7 | 88.7 | 123.1 |

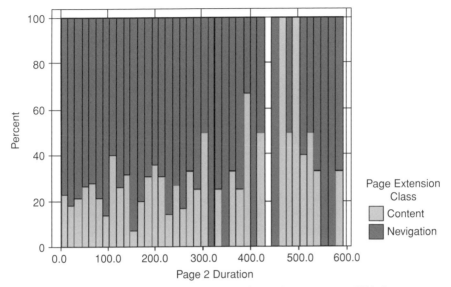

**Figure 8.10**   Page 2 durations, by navigation and content pages, EPA data.

For these reasons we approach hypothesis tests and other inferential methods with caution. Anyway, at this stage we are still exploring.

Figure 8.10 shows a graph of the page 2 durations, categorized by navigation or content page. (Note that the histogram is normalized for each category, so that each bar is the same size. This increases the contrast for the low-count areas. Also, the durations have been capped at 600 seconds to increase granularity.) Note that although navigation pages predominate overall, the proportion of lighter regions (content pages) gradually are increase as the duration increases. That is, as duration increases, page 2 is more and more likely to be a content page.

The summary statistics for the CCSU data, shown in Table 8.4, support the findings that the content pages have a higher mean duration than the navigation pages. Also, the second page has a shorter duration than the first page for both data sets. The difference in duration between the content and navigation pages is consistent but not overwhelming. This is perhaps because many web pages actually contain elements of both navigation and content.

**TABLE 8.4   Mean Page Duration for First Two Pages Visited, CCSU Data**

| | Page 1 Duration | | | Page 2 Duration | |
| --- | --- | --- | --- | --- | --- |
| Overall | Navigation | Content | Overall | Navigation | Content |
| 277.5 | 239.7 | 278.3 | 241.8 | 178.4 | 243.8 |

## REFERENCES

1. Daniel Larose, *Discovering Knowledge in Data: An Introduction to Data Mining*, Wiley, Hoboken, NJ, 2005.
2. Daniel Larose, *Data Mining Methods and Models*, Wiley, Hoboken, NJ, 2006.

## EXERCISES

**Hands-on Analysis**

For the following web log data sets, download the data and perform the web log exploratory steps given below. (*Note*: Some steps may not be applicable to a particular data set.) The full data sets are available from the Internet traces Web site, http://ita.ee.lbl.gov/html/contrib/NASA-HTTP.html. We use only a subset of the data. The data subsets are available from the book series Web site, www.dataminingconsultant.com.

- *The NASA-HTTP web log data*. We use only the first 131,904 records.

- *The Calgary-HTTP web log data*. We use only the first 65,536 records.

(*Note*: For some histograms and scatter plots, it may be helpful to omit temporarily values above a certain very high threshold, to increase the granularity of the plot. Otherwise, the plot looks almost unary. When you do so, do not delete these records, simply omit them from the plot. Also, report the threshold you used and the number and proportion of records omitted.)

1. Examine the visit actions. Before you get too far into this, examine Exercise 4.

   **a.** Provide a histogram of the number of visit actions per session.

   **b.** Provide summary statistics, including mean, standard deviation, median, mode, min, and max.

2. Examine session duration.

   **a.** Consider sessions consisting of a single action only. What empirical evidence do we have regarding the duration of such sessions? Thus, when finding session duration, we need to restrict ourselves to the sessions that contain more than one action.

   **b.** Calculate the session duration for such sessions.

   **c.** Make a histogram of session duration, reporting the same statistics as in the preceding exercise.

   **d.** Do you think these results underestimate or overestimate the true session duration across all sessions? Why?

3. Explore the relationship between visit actions and session duration.

   **a.** Use a scatter plot and a simple linear regression model. Logically, which variable should be the predictor and which should be the response?

   **b.** Find the estimated regression equation.

   **c.** In your scatter plot, overlay the estimated regression line.

   **d.** Interpret clearly, so that a nonspecialist could understand, the meaning of the $y$-intercept and slope coefficients and whether they make sense in the present context.

4. Calculate the average time per page.

   a. Show the formula you are using to derive this.

   b. Construct a histogram of the average time per page, and report the usual summary statistics. Comment.

   c. Compare the intuitive interpretation of the average time per page with that of the estimated slope in the preceding question.

5. Do the following.

   a. Provide a table of the 20 sessions with the shortest average time per page. This is a way of checking whether you have found and eliminated all the nonhuman visitors.

   b. If the average time per page for any session is less than 0.5 second, this is evidence that this user is exhibiting nonhuman behavior. Therefore, delete these sessions and redo all the work since the de-spidering step.

   c. If you seriously think that a particular session with smaller than 0.5 second average time per page is human generated, provide documentation (including all session pages), and a darn good argument.

6. For each applicable session, find the duration of the first two pages, if any.

   a. Provide a histogram of the duration for the first page.

   b. Provide the usual statistics for the durations of both pages.

   c. Compare and comment.

7. Consider how we can use the page extensions to determine whether the page is a navigation page or a content page.

   a. Go ahead and classify the empty page extension as indicating a navigation page, and all the other (remaining) extensions as indicating a content page. (If you have a better idea of how to do this, I am all ears.)

   b. Compare the mean page duration for each of the first two pages visited, broken down by navigation vs. content.

   c. Provide a normalized histogram of mean page duration for each of the first two pages, with an overlay of navigation vs. content.

   d. Discuss whether this stuff is providing evidence in support of our method of classifying navigation vs. content.

8. Construct a bar graph of the visits per hour over the course of 24 hours.

9. Construct a bar graph of the visitors per hour over the course of 24 hours.

10. Summarize the visits using the following statistics.

   a. Total number of visits

   b. Average visit length

   c. Median visit length

11. Summarize the visitors using the following statistics.

   a. Total number of unique visitors

   b. Number of visitors who visited more than once that day

   c. Average number of visits per visitor

**12.** Summarize the hits using the following statistics.

   **a.** Successful hits for the entire site

   **b.** Home page hits

**13.** Summarize the page views using the following statistics.

   **a.** Total number of page views

   **b.** Average number of page views per visit

**14.** Construct a table of the top 20 domain names as measured by visits and by hits.

**15.** Construct a table of the top seven domain types (e.g., .com) as measured by visits and by hits.

**16.** Construct a bar graph of the average visit length over the course of 24 hours.

**17.** Construct a table of the top 10 visitors, by visits (e.g., wireless.ccsu.edu_Mozilla/4.0.).

**18.** Construct a table of the number of unique visitors, by number of visits (1 through 9).

**19.** Construct a table of the top 10 pages, by visits and by page views.

**20.** Construct a table of the top 10 directories, by visits and by hits.

**21.** Construct a table of the top 10 file types (e.g., .gif), by number of times accessed.

**22.** Construct a table of the top 10 files downloaded, by number of downloads and by visits.

**23.** Construct a table of the top 10 entry pages, by visits.

**24.** Construct a table of the top 10 exit pages, by visits.

**25.** Construct a table of the top 10 single access pages, by visits.

**26.** Find all paths of length two or three pages that have been visited 24 or more times.

**27.** Construct a table of all 404 client errors (e.g., 404 not found), by hits.

**28.** Construct a table of the top 10 files that were not found and reported, by hits.

**29.** Construct a table of the frequency of internal server errors, by hits, for each of 24 hours.

**30.** Construct a table of the number of pages viewed (0 to 12), by visits.

**31.** Construct a table of the visit duration in minutes (0 to 1 minute, 1 to 2 minutes, etc.), by visits.

**32.** Construct a table of the top six browsers, by visits and by hits.

**33.** Find the top three spiders, by visits and by hits.

**34.** Construct a table of all platforms (e.g., Windows XP), by visits.

# MODELING FOR WEB USAGE MINING: CLUSTERING, ASSOCIATION, AND CLASSIFICATION

## INTRODUCTION

After data preprocessing and exploratory data analysis have been completed, we can finally begin the modeling phase. This is the favorite part for many web usage miners, since it allows them to apply the range of their data mining skills and attack the problem at hand using an array of data mining methods, algorithms, and models. In many ways, the modeling phase also represents the beginning of the "payoff" for all the analytic effort expended throughout the web mining process, for it is here that patterns and trends that can be actionable and profitable for the end user may be uncovered.

*Data Mining the Web: Uncovering Patterns in Web Content, Structure, and Usage*
By Zdravko Markov and Daniel T. Larose    Copyright © 2007 John Wiley & Sons, Inc.

In this chapter we cover three main modeling techniques: clustering, association rules, and classification. We begin by describing clustering, which should normally be the first modeling method applied by the web usage miner or by the data miner in general. We then move to association rules, which, like clustering, is an undirected or unsupervised method, meaning that the analyst need not define a target variable. The search for association rules is sometimes called *affinity analysis* or *market basket analysis*. Finally, we turn to classification methods, where the web usage miner uses a variety of models to make predictions based on the patterns uncovered in the data.

Data mining methods may be categorized as either supervised (directed) or unsupervised (undirected). In unsupervised methods, no target variable is identified as such. Instead, the data mining algorithm searches for patterns and structure among the variables. The most common unsupervised data mining method is clustering. Another data mining method, which may be supervised or unsupervised, is association rule mining. In market basket analysis, for example, one may simply be interested in "which items are purchased together," in which case no target variable would be identified. We cover association rule mining later in the chapter.

Most data mining methods are supervised methods, however, meaning that (1) there is a particular prespecified target variable, and (2) the algorithm is given many examples where the value of the target variable is provided, so that the algorithm may learn which values of the target variable are associated with which values of the predictor variables. All classification methods are supervised methods, including the methods we use in this chapter: classification and regression trees and the C4.5 algorithm.

## MODELING METHODOLOGY

Most supervised data mining methods apply the following methodology for building and evaluating a model. First, the algorithm is provided with a *training set* of data, which includes the preclassified values of the target variable in addition to the predictor variables. For example, if we are interested in classifying *income bracket*, based on *age*, *gender*, and *occupation*, our classification algorithm would need a large pool of records, containing complete (as complete as possible) information about every field, including the target field, *income bracket*. In other words, the records in the *training set* need to be *preclassified*. A provisional data mining model is then constructed using the training samples provided in the training data set.

However, the training set is necessarily incomplete; that is, it does not include the "new" or future data that the data modelers are really interested in classifying. Therefore, the algorithm needs to guard against "memorizing" the training set and blindly applying to the future data all patterns found in the training set. For example, it may happen that all customers named "David" in a training set may be in the high-income bracket. We would presumably not want our final model to be applied to new data, to include the pattern, "If the customer's first name is David, then the customer has high income." Such a pattern is a spurious artifact of the training set and needs to be verified before deployment.

Therefore, the next step in supervised data mining methodology is to examine how the provisional data mining model performs on a *test set* of data. In the test set, a holdout data set, the values of the target variable are temporarily hidden from the provisional model, which then performs classification according to the patterns and structure it learned from the training set. The efficacy of the classifications are then evaluated by comparing them against the true values of the target variable. The provisional data mining model is then adjusted to minimize the error rate on the test set.

The adjusted data mining model is then applied to a *validation* data set, another holdout data set, where again, the values of the target variable are hidden temporarily from the model. The adjusted model is itself then adjusted, to minimize the error rate on the validation set. Estimates of model performance for future, unseen data can then be computed by observing various evaluative measures applied to the validation set. Such model evaluation techniques are discussed in Larose [1, Chapter 11].

Although we have discussed the training/test/validation partition methodology in the context of supervised methods, this methodology also applies to unsupervised methods. Data miners and web usage miners should check the validity of their clustering solutions and association rules by partitioning the data set and deriving broadly similar clusters and rules across all partitions. Otherwise, the clusters and rules lack validity and are due to "noise" rather than true patterns.

## DEFINITION OF CLUSTERING

Clustering refers to the grouping of records, observations, or cases into classes of similar objects. A *cluster* is a collection of records that are similar to one another and dissimilar to records in other clusters. Clustering differs from classification in that there is no target variable for clustering. The clustering task does not try to classify, estimate, or predict the value of a target variable. Instead, clustering algorithms seek to segment the entire data set into relatively homogeneous subgroups or clusters, where the similarity of the records within the cluster is maximized, and the similarity to records outside this cluster is minimized (see Figure 9.1).

Clustering is often performed as a preliminary step in a data mining process, with the resulting clusters being used as further inputs into a different technique downstream, such as neural networks. Due to the enormous size of many present-day databases, it is often helpful to apply clustering analysis first, to reduce the search space for the downstream algorithms. In this chapter we examine the BIRCH or two-step clustering algorithm. For more information on clustering, see Chapter 3 or ref. [1].

For optimal performance, the analyst should normalize or standardize the numerical variables for clustering, association, and classification. In this way, no particular variable or subset of variables dominates the analysis. Analysts may use either the *min-max normalization*

$$X^* = \frac{X - \min(X)}{\text{range}(X)}$$

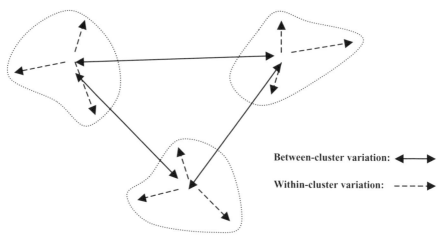

**Figure 9.1**   Clusters should have small within-cluster variation compared to between-cluster variation.

or the *Z-score standardization*:

$$X^* = \frac{X - \text{mean}(X)}{\text{SD}(X)}$$

All clustering methods have as their goal the identification of groups of records such that the similarity within the group is very high and the similarity to records in other groups is very low. In other words, as shown in Figure 9.1, clustering algorithms seek to construct clusters of records such that the *between-cluster variation* is large compared to the *within-cluster variation*. This is somewhat analogous to the concept behind analysis of variance (e.g., [2]).

## THE BIRCH CLUSTERING ALGORITHM

The BIRCH algorithm [3] requires only one pass through the data set and therefore represents a scalable solution for very large data sets. The algorithm contains two main steps and hence is termed *two-step clustering* in *Clementine*. In the first step, the algorithm preclusters records into a large number of small subclusters by constructing a cluster feature tree. In the second step, the algorithm combines these subclusters into higher-level clusters which represent the algorithm's clustering solution.

One benefit of Clementine's implementation of the algorithm is that unlike *k*-means and Kohonen clustering, the analyst need not prespecify the desired number of clusters. Thus, BIRCH clustering represents a desirable exploratory tool when just beginning to undertake the modeling phase. A detailed case study that uses the BIRCH algorithm in part is provided in Larose [4, Chapter 7]. For more information on other clustering methods, including *k*-means clustering, Kohonen networks, and hierarchical clustering methods, see Larose [1].

To provide an example of how clustering may be applied to a real-world data set, we apply the BIRCH algorithm to the CCSU web log data set. Because later we

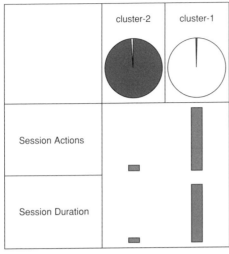

|  | Cluster-2 | Cluster-1 |
|---|---|---|
| Count | 5748 (99.2%) | 79 (0.8%) |
| Mean Session Action | 5.7 | 78.6 |
| Mean Session Action | 710 | 9106 |

**Figure 9.2**   Two clusters found by the BIRCH algorithm.

will be interested in association among pages, we restrict our analysis to sessions of two or more session actions. For explanatory purposes we restrict our input variables to two: session duration and session actions. Using only these two variables as input, the BIRCH algorithm uncovered two clusters, which are described in Figure 9.2. Cluster 2 dominates, with 99.2% of the sessions (all data are session-level), consisting of sessions that have moderate numbers of actions (mean 5.7) and are of relatively moderate duration (mean about 12 minutes). Cluster 1 is a very small cluster, containing only 0.8% of the sessions, which have a very large number of actions (mean 78.6) and a long duration (mean over 2.5 hours).

Figure 9.3 provides a view of how cluster membership varies across the scatter plot of duration vs. action values. The fewer, darker points of cluster 2 have either many

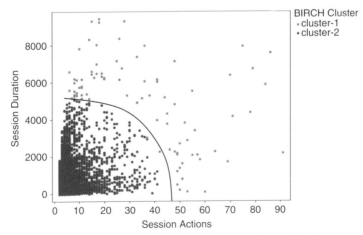

**Figure 9.3**   Scatter plot of session duration vs. session actions, with cluster membership overlay.

actions or high duration or both. The many, lighter points of cluster 1 are all huddled within the curved line superimposed on the plot. (This line is for illustration only and does not have a mathematical relationship with the algorithm results.) We illustrate clustering using only two numerical variables because it is difficult to demonstrate cluster membership graphically in higher dimensions.

Next we apply the BIRCH clustering algorithm to a large set of session-level variables from the CCSU web log data. These variables include the following:

- Session duration
- Session actions
- Average time per page
- Page 1 duration
- Page 2 duration
- All the "first directory" (top directory) flag variables
- All the "page" flag variables

The BIRCH algorithm, which is free to select the most appropriate number of clusters, again found two clusters in this large data set. An excerpt of the graphic description of the variables, by cluster, is provided in Figure 9.4.

The web usage miner should carefully review such graphs, seeking variables that take appreciably different values or proportions from cluster to cluster. These variables will then by selected for more detailed scrutiny. From Figure 9.4 we see immediately that the numerical variables time per page and session actions have notably different values between the two clusters. Session duration has a smaller change, but may be worth a look. The flag variables Page_/search/ and Page_/search/Default.htm have proportions of false and true that seem to differ by cluster. Table 9.1 present a complete list of variables that have apparent cluster differences, along with the mean value (if a numerical variable) or the proportion of true values (if a flag variable). Cluster 2 is the larger cluster, containing 4857 session records; cluster 1 contains 937 records. This enables us provisionally to identify cluster 2 as the more "typical" cluster, containing almost 84% of the records. Our cluster descriptions therefore concentrate on discriminating how cluster 1 sessions differ systematically from a typical session.

Based on the observed means and proportions in Table 9.1, we may label cluster 1 as "Index and Search Users." The index pages are requested by these users at a rate thousands of times greater than that of the typical user, and similarly for the search pages. The top directories "Index" and "Search" are requested at a much higher rate for cluster 1 users than for the typical user. Cluster 1 sessions also have more than double the session actions than the typical session (13.8 vs. 5.0), although the session duration is not that much more (983 vs. 741) because the average time per page is a fraction of that of the typical session (79 vs. 290). The typical user, on the other hand, almost never accesses either the search or the index pages. Thus, the BIRCH clustering algorithm has uncovered some interesting differences between the two session clusters. Perhaps the CCSU web masters could apply this knowledge to enhance the online experience for both types of users.

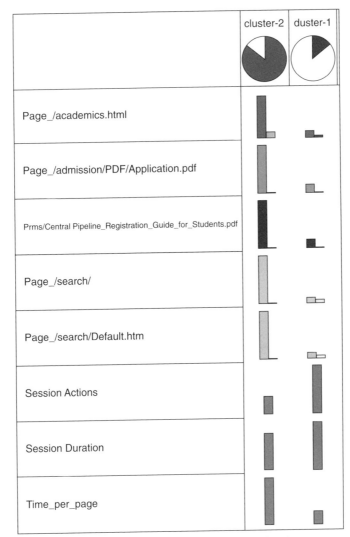

**Figure 9.4**  Graphic description of variables, by cluster.

# AFFINITY ANALYSIS AND THE A PRIORI ALGORITHM

*Affinity analysis* refers to the study of attributes or characteristics that "go together." Methods for affinity analysis, also known as *market basket analysis*, seek to uncover *associations* among these attributes; that is, it seeks to uncover rules for quantifying the relationship between two or more attributes. Association rules take the form "If *antecedent*, then *consequent*," along with a measure of the support and confidence associated with the rule. For example, a particular supermarket may find that of the 1000 customers shopping on a Thursday night, 200 bought diapers, and of those 200 who bought diapers, 50 bought beer. Thus, the association rule would be: "If buy

**TABLE 9.1    Variables that Differ Appreciably by Cluster**

| Variable | Cluster 1 | Cluster 2 |
|---|---|---|
| Page_/Index/ | 0.6949 | 0.0073 |
| Page_/Index/C.htm | 0.1908 | 0.0042 |
| Page_/Index/Default.htm | 0.6961 | 0.0022 |
| Page_/search/ | 0.3663 | 0.0006 |
| Page_/search/Default.htm | 0.3757 | 0.0006 |
| First_dir/search/ | 0.3934 | 0.0053 |
| First_dir/Index/ | 0.7256 | 0.0273 |
| Session Actions | 13.8 | 5.0 |
| Session Duration | 983 | 741 |
| Average Time per Page | 79 | 290 |
| Page 1 duration | 119 | 290 |
| Page 2 duration | 65 | 146 |

diapers, then buy beer" with a *support* of 50/1000 = 5% and a *confidence* of 50/200 = 25%.

What types of algorithms can we apply to mine association rules from a particular data set? The daunting problem that awaits any such algorithm is the curse of dimensionality: The number of possible association rules grows exponentially in the number of attributes. Specifically, if there are $k$ attributes and we limit ourselves to binary attributes and account only for the positive cases (e.g., *Buy diapers = yes*), there are on the order of $k \cdot 2^{k-1}$ possible association rules. Consider that a typical application for association rules is market basket analysis and that there may be *thousands* of binary attributes (*Buy beer? Buy popcorn? Buy milk? Buy bread?* etc.), the search problem appears at first glance to be utterly hopeless. For example, suppose that a tiny convenience store has only 100 different items and a customer could either buy or not buy any combination of those 100 items. Then there are $100 \times 2^{99} \cong 6.4 \times 10^{31}$ possible association rules that await your intrepid search algorithm.

The a priori algorithm for mining association rules, however, takes advantage of structure within the rules themselves to reduce the search problem to a more manageable size. Before we examine the a priori algorithm, which was developed by Agrawal et al. [5], however, let us consider some basic concepts and notation for association rule mining.

Let $D$ denote a set of transactions, where each transaction $T$ in $D$ represents a set of items contained in $I$, the set of all items. Suppose that we have a particular set of items $A$ (e.g., Page_/Default.htm and Page_/search/), and another set of items $B$ (e.g., Page_/index/). Then, an *association rule* takes the form *if A then B* (i.e., $A \Rightarrow B$), where the *antecedent* $A$ and the *consequent* $B$ are proper subsets of $I$, and $A$ and $B$ are mutually exclusive. This definition would exclude, for example, trivial rules such as *if Page_/Default.htm and Page_/search/, then Page_/Default.htm.*

The *support* $s$ for a particular association rule $A \Rightarrow B$ is the proportion of transactions in $D$ that contain both $A$ and $B$. That is,

$$\text{support} = P(A \cap B) = \frac{\text{number of transactions containing both } A \text{ and } B}{\text{total number of transactions}}$$

The *confidence* c of the association rule $A \Rightarrow B$ is a measure of the accuracy of the rule, as determined by the percentage of transactions in $D$ containing $A$ that also contain $B$. In other words,

$$\text{confidence} = P(B|A) = \frac{P(A \cap B)}{P(A)}$$
$$= \frac{\text{number of transactions containing both } A \text{ and } B}{\text{number of transactions containing } A}$$

Analysts may prefer rules that have either high support or high confidence, and usually both. *Strong* rules are those that meet or surpass certain minimum support and confidence criteria. For example, an analyst interested in finding which supermarket items are purchased together may set a minimum support level of 20% and a minimum confidence level of 70%. On the other hand, a fraud detection analyst or a terrorism detection analyst would need to reduce the minimum support level to 1% or less, since comparatively few transactions are either fraudulent or terror-related. For more on association rules, including the derivation of the a priori algorithm and the GRI (generalized rule induction) algorithm, see ref. 1 Chapter 10.

Note that what Clementine calls "Support" for the a priori algorithm is actually not what we defined support to be (following Han and Kamber [7]; Hand et al. [8] and other texts). Instead, what Clementine calls "Support" is the proportion of occurrences of the antecedent alone rather than the antecedent and the consequent. (Not helpfully, Clementine's GRI and a priori algorithms define "Support" one way, and its CARMA and sequence nodes define it another way.) To find the actual support for the association rule using the Clementine results for the GRI and a priori algorithms, multiply the reported "Support" times the reported confidence. In Version 9.0, Clementine began supplying the "Rule Support" measure, which is the equivalent of the usual support measure used in the literature.

Unfortunately, the a priori algorithm does not admit numerical variables, either as input variables or consequents. The GRI method does admit numerical variables as input, but since the a priori algorithm enjoys more widespread use, we shall provide an example using the a priori algorithm applied to the CCSU Web site data.

## DISCRETIZING THE NUMERICAL VARIABLES: BINNING

Since we would like to keep our numerical variables in the model, we need to transform these numerical variables into categorical variables by the discretization process known as *binning*. We shall separate each of the three numerical variables session actions, session duration, and average time per page into three bins: Low, Medium, and High. Once binned, these variables can then be used by the a priori algorithm as both input and output.

Consider Figure 9.5, a histogram of session actions with cluster overlay. (Note that cluster 2 tends to gain in proportion gradually as the number of session

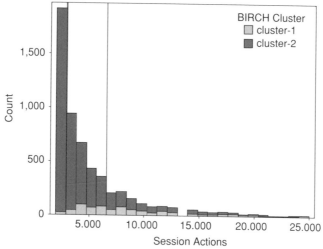

**Figure 9.5** Histogram of session actions with cluster overlay, showing bands dividing low, Medium, and High categories.

action increases.) The two vertical lines indicate where the boundaries were drawn. Clementine allows the user to place these boundaries and then uses these boundaries automatically to create a *derive* node that creates a categorical variable, in this case called "Session Actions Bin," that takes on the following values:

$$\text{Session Actions Bin} = \begin{cases} \text{Low} & \text{if Session Actions} \leq 2 \\ \text{Medium} & \text{if } 3 \leq \text{Session Actions} < 7 \\ \text{High} & \text{if Session Actions} \geq 7 \end{cases}$$

Figure 9.6 shows the distribution of this newly derived categorical variable, Session Actions Bin. This graph shows more clearly that the proportion of cluster 2 sessions grows as the number of actions moves from low to high. In the absence of a target variable, it is probably desirable for the proportions of records not be severely unequal among the bins. When binning for classification or prediction, however, one should try to arrange the boundaries for the predictor variable where its relationship with the target variable undergoes a change point [4, Chap. 4].

| Value ▲ | Proportion | % | Count |
|---|---|---|---|
| 1-Low | | 33.1 | 1918 |
| 2-Medium | | 41.51 | 2405 |
| 3-High | | 25.39 | 1471 |

BIRCH Cluster

☐ cluster-1          ■ cluster-2

**Figure 9.6** Distribution of session actions bin, with cluster overlay.

Using similar methodology, we also discretized session duration and average time per page, creating new categorical variables as follows:

$$\text{Session Duration Bin} = \begin{cases} \text{Low} & \text{if Session Duration} < 150 \\ \text{Medium} & \text{if } 150 \leq \text{Session Duration} \leq 900 \\ \text{High} & \text{if Session Duration} > 900 \end{cases}$$

$$\text{Time per Page Bin} = \begin{cases} \text{Low} & \text{if Time per Page} < 68 \\ \text{Medium} & \text{if } 68 \leq \text{Time per Page} < 504 \\ \text{High} & \text{if Time per Page} \geq 504 \end{cases}$$

## APPLYING THE A PRIORI ALGORITHM TO THE CCSU WEB LOG DATA

We are now ready to apply the a priori algorithm to the CCSU web log data, seeking to uncover some actionable association rules. Figure 9.7 provides a list of the association rules uncovered by the a priori algorithm, sorted by "rule support" (support). Consider the second rule in the list. The antecedent is Page_/Default.htm and the consequent is cluster 2. The form of the rule is therefore

$$\text{Page}_-/\text{Default.htm} \Rightarrow \text{cluster 2}$$

The support of the rule is 69.468%, meaning that the rule applies to almost 70% of the sessions in the data; this is an extremely high level of support. What does a confidence of 82.564% mean? There are a total of 5794 sessions (not shown). Of these 5794 sessions, 4875 fulfilled the antecedent condition; that is, they requested the Default.htm page at some point. Of these 4875 sessions, 82.564% of them, or 4025 sessions, belong to cluster 2.

In general, this 82.564% represents fairly solid confidence. Does that mean that this association rule is useful? No. In fact, this particular rule is worse than useless. Remember that 83.8% of sessions belong to cluster 2. Therefore, with no information at all, we could, completely blindly, select a session (that contains Page_/Default.htm) at random and be almost 83.8% confident that the session would belong to cluster 2. The problem is that we need to restrict the rules generated by the a priori algorithm to those that might in fact be useful. We therefore choose the option that selects rules

| Consequent | Antecedent | Confidence % | Rule Support % |
|---|---|---|---|
| Page _/Default.htm | BIRCH Cluster = cluster-2 | 82.870 | 69.468 |
| BIRCH Cluster = cluster-2 | Page _/Default.htm | 82.564 | 69.468 |
| Page _/Default.htm | Time Per Page Bin = 1-Low | 80.573 | 38.367 |
| Time Per Page Bin = 1-Low | Session Duration Bin = 1-Low | 91.541 | 36.607 |
| BIRCH Cluster = cluster-2 | Session Actions Bin = 2-Medium | 87.277 | 36.227 |
| Page _/Default.htm | Session Actions Bin = 2-Medium | 84.449 | 35.054 |
| BIRCH Cluster = cluster-2 | Session Duration Bin = 1-Low | 84.074 | 33.621 |
| BIRCH Cluster = cluster-2 | Session Actions Bin = 1-Low | 98.592 | 32.637 |
| BIRCH Cluster = cluster-2 | Session Actions Bin = 2-Medium Page _/Default.htm | 86.411 | 30.290 |

**Figure 9.7**  Association rules for the CCSU web log data, sorted by support.

| Consequent | Antecedent | Confidence % | Rule Support % |
|---|---|---|---|
| Time Per Page Bin = 1-Low | Session Duration Bin = 1-Low | 91.541 | 36.607 |
| BIRCH Cluster = cluster-2 | Session Actions Bin = 1-Low | 98.592 | 32.637 |
| Time Per Page Bin = 1-Low | Session Duration Bin = 1-Low<br>BIRCH Cluster = cluster-2 | 89.990 | 30.255 |
| Session Duration Bin = 1-Low | Time Per Page Bin = 1-Low<br>BIRCH Cluster = cluster-2 | 82.146 | 30.255 |
| Time Per Page Bin = 1-Low | Session Duration Bin = 1-Low<br>Page _/Default.htm | 91.548 | 28.788 |
| BIRCH Cluster = cluster-2 | Session Actions Bin = 1-Low<br>Page _/Default.htm | 100.000 | 26.355 |
| Time Per Page Bin = 1-Low | Session Duration Bin = 1-Low<br>BIRCH Cluster = cluster-2<br>Page _/Default.htm | 89.637 | 22.989 |
| Session Duration Bin = 1-Low | Time Per Page Bin = 1-Low<br>BIRCH Cluster = cluster-2<br>Page _/Default.htm | 80.825 | 22.989 |
| BIRCH Cluster = cluster-2 | Time Per Page Bin = 3-High | 97.814 | 18.536 |
| Time Per Page Bin = 1-Low | Session Actions Bin = 2-Medium<br>Session Duration Bin = 1-Low | 98.946 | 17.829 |
| Session Duration Bin = 1-Low | Session Actions Bin = 2-Medium<br>Time Per Page Bin = 1-Low | 90.694 | 17.829 |
| BIRCH Cluster = cluster-2 | Session Actions Bin = 1-Low<br>Session Duration Bin = 1-Low | 98.878 | 16.724 |
| BIRCH Cluster = cluster-2 | Time Per Page Bin = 3-High<br>Page _/Default.htm | 98.973 | 16.638 |
| BIRCH Cluster = cluster-2 | Time Per Page Bin = 3-High<br>Session Duration Bin = 3-High | 97.909 | 14.550 |

**Figure 9.8**   Association rules chosen using the confidence difference criterion.

based on the confidence difference between the prior probability of randomly selecting the consequent (the *prior*) and the posterior probability of selecting the consequent given the antecedent (the *posterior*). Those rules that provide the greatest increase in the quantity (posterior – prior) are preferred. Figure 9.8 presents a selection of such association rules, again sorted by support. Note that the rule mentioned above does not appear in this updated listing because its posterior confidence (82.564%) is less than its prior confidence (83.8%).

Consider the first rule in the list. The antecedent is Session Duration = Low and the consequent is Time per Page = Low. The form of the rule is therefore

$$\text{Session Duration} = \text{Low} \Rightarrow \text{Time per Page} = \text{Low}$$

The support is 36.607%, which is far less than the earlier rule we looked at but still not too bad. If we can design an intervention that will affect 36% of our visitors, we should by all means consider it. The (posterior) confidence is 91.541%, which is very nice. Now, is this rule useful? We check the prior proportion of the consequent and find that 47.62% (prior confidence, not shown) of sessions have a low time per page. Thus, our ability to predict a session with a low average time per page has been greatly enhanced by this simple association rule, with confidence increasing from 47.62% to 91.541%. This association rule is quite useful from a mathematical point of view. But the final arbiter of usefulness is the degree to which a rule can help solve a business or research problem. From this point of view, the usefulness of this rule is yet to be determined.

**TABLE 9.2   Some Association Rules for Identifying Sessions with Low Duration**

| Rule | Confidence | Support |
|---|---|---|
| Time per Page = Low and Cluster 2 $\Rightarrow$ Session Duration = Low | 82.146% | 30.255% |
| Time per Page = Low and Cluster 2 and Page_/Default.htm $\Rightarrow$ Session Duration = Low | 80.825% | 22.989% |
| Time per Page = Low and Session Actions = Medium $\Rightarrow$ Session Duration = Low | 90.694% | 17.829% |

Now suppose that the CCSU marketing administrators were interested in identifying users who do not spend a long time on the CCSU Web site, in order to consider strategies and interventions that would help to prolong their stay. How could we use the association rules to identify such users? Since the task is to identify sessions with short duration, we should select association rules where the consequent is Session Duration = Low. Such rules, chosen from Figure 9.8 are provided in Table 9.2. The common thread among these three rules is the presence of Time per Page = Low. Membership in cluster 2 is also predictive of a short session, especially in conjunction with short Time per Page. If marketers could design interventions that would increase the average time per page, this might increase the duration of these short sessions.

Before we leave association rules, we need to consider the difference between models and patterns. A *model* is a global description or explanation of a data set, taking a high-level perspective. Models may be descriptive or inferential. Descriptive models seek to summarize the entire data set in a succinct manner. Inferential models aim to provide a mechanism that enables the analyst to generalize from samples to populations. Either way, the perspective is global, encompassing the entire data set. On the other hand, *patterns* are essentially local features of the data. Recognizable patterns may in fact hold true for only a few variables or a fraction of the records in the data.

Classification methods, which we are about to examine, deal with global model building. Association rules, on the other hand, are particularly well suited to uncovering local patterns in the data. As soon as one applies the *if* clause in an association rule, one is partitioning the data so that, usually, most of the records do not apply. Applying the *if* clause "drills down" deeper into the data set, with the aim of uncovering a hidden local pattern, which may or may not be relevant to the bulk of the data.

For example, consider the following association rule from Table 9.2:

$$\text{Time per Page = Low and Cluster 2} \Rightarrow \text{Session Duration = Low}$$

with confidence 82.146% and support 30.255%. We see that this association rule applies to only 30.255% of the records and ignores the remaining 69.745% of the data set. Even among these records, the association rule ignores most of the variables, concentrating on only two antecedent variables and one consequent variable. Therefore, this association rule cannot claim to be global, and cannot be considered a model in the strict sense. It represents a pattern that is local to these records and these variables.

Then again, finding interesting local patterns is one of the most important goals of data mining. Sometimes, uncovering a pattern within data can lead to the deployment of new and profitable initiatives. The discovery of useful local patterns could lead to profitable policy changes. Short of this, identifying local patterns could help the analyst consider which variables are most important for the classification or predictive modeling phase. As such, the use of association rules takes on a more exploratory role. In this case we might expect the time per page variable to take a leading role in our classification models for predicting sessions of short duration. We shall see if this expectation is borne out.

# CLASSIFICATION AND REGRESSION TREES

Perhaps the most common data mining task is that of *classification*. In classification, there is a target categorical variable (e.g., *session duration bin*), which is partitioned into predetermined classes or categories, such as high, medium, and low duration. The data mining model examines a large set of records, typically called the *training data set*, where each record contains information on the target variable as well as a set of input or predictor variables. The model then looks at new data, where the value of the target variable is unknown, and assigns a classification based on the patterns observed in the training set. For more on classification, see Chapter 5 or ref. 1.

One attractive classification method involves construction of a *decision tree*. A decision tree is a collection of *decision nodes*, connected by *branches*, extending downward from the *root node* until terminating in *leaf nodes*. Beginning at the root node, which by convention is placed at the top of the decision tree diagram, attributes are tested at the decision nodes, with each possible outcome resulting in a branch. Each branch then leads either to another decision node or to a terminating leaf node. To apply a decision tree, the target variable should be categorical. Thus, decision trees represent a framework for classification. Figure 9.9 represents a simple decision tree for a good risk/bad risk credit classification. The root decision node is based on savings. Records with low savings flow to another decision node, which examines assets. Records with high savings flow to another decision node, which examine income. For this data set, records with medium savings flow directly to the leaf node, classifying them as good credit risks.

Decision trees seek to create a set of leaf nodes that are as "pure" as possible, that is, where each of the records in a particular leaf node has the same classification. In this way the decision tree may provide classification assignments with the highest measure of confidence available. However, how does one measure "uniformity," or conversely, how does one measure "heterogeneity"? Different methods for measuring leaf node purity lead to different decision tree algorithms, such as *CART* or the C4.5 algorithm.

*Classification and regression trees* (CARTs) were first suggested by Breiman et al. [9] in 1984. The decision trees produced by CARTs are strictly binary, containing exactly two branches for each decision node. CARTs recursively partition the records in a training data set into subsets of records with similar values for the target

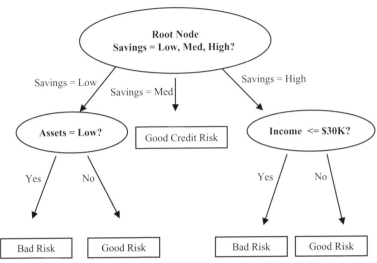

**Figure 9.9**  A Simple decision tree.

attribute. The CART algorithm grows the tree, for each decision node, by conducting an exhaustive search of all available variables and all possible splitting values, selecting the optimal split according to the following criteria of Kennedy et al. [10].

Let $\Phi(s|t)$ represent the Gini index, a measure of the "goodness" of a candidate split $s$ at node $t$, where

$$\Phi(s|t) = 2P_L P_R \sum_{j=1}^{\text{no. classes}} |P(j|t_L) - P(j|t_R)|$$

and where

$$t_L = \text{left child node of node } t$$
$$t_R = \text{right child node of node } t$$
$$P_L = \frac{\text{number of records at } t_L}{\text{number of records in training set}}$$
$$P_R = \frac{\text{number of records at } t_R}{\text{number of records in training set}}$$
$$P(j|t_L) = \frac{\text{number of class } j \text{ records at } t_L}{\text{number of records at } t}$$
$$P(j|t_R) = \frac{\text{number of class } j \text{ records at } t_R}{\text{number of records at } t}$$

Then the optimal split is whichever split maximizes the Gini index over all possible splits at node $t$. More information about decision trees and the CART algorithm may be found in ref. 1. If the CCSU marketing administrators are interested in identifying sessions with short duration, we apply CARTs to the CCSU web log data set, with session duration bin as the target variable.

Earlier, the a priori algorithm uncovered a strong association between the average time per page and the session duration. This is not surprising, since session duration is used to calculate the average time per page. To avoid this dependence, we shall not include the average time per page as a predictor variable in our decision tree for classifying session duration. Similarly, we shall not use the clusters we uncovered above as inputs to the decision tree, since the target variable, session duration, was included as an input to the clustering algorithm.

An excerpt from the resulting decision tree is shown in Figure 9.10. The root node, labeled $R-Session Duration Bin, shows the original proportions of the session duration bin classes, such as Low with 39.99% of the records, or 2317 sessions. Just under the root node is the *root node split*. In any decision tree, the root node split is the most important split in the decision tree. In general, the higher up the decision tree a split is, the more important it is, in terms of its ability to predict the outcomes of the target variable. Here, the root node split is made on the variable *time_gap1*, which measures the duration that the user spent on the first page accessed during that session. The split is

$$Time\_gap1 \leq 147.50 \text{ seconds} \qquad \text{vs.} \qquad Time\_gap1 > 147.50 \text{ seconds}$$

In a decision tree, all of the records flow down from the root node and are tested at each decision node, flowing down to the branches for which the particular field takes the value indicated. Here, all records that have *time_gap1* of not more than 147.50 seconds flow to the left branch (node 1), while all records that have time per page of more than 147.50 seconds flow to the right branch (node 14).

Note how the purity of node 14 is increased from the root node, since almost all records with low duration have been filtered out from the right branch already (only three low-duration records are left, 0.15%). Node 1's purity has also been increased, but less significantly. However, taken together, these nodes represent the optimal increase in purity over all possible splits found by the Gini index. For records in the left branch (*time_gap1* at most 147.50 seconds), the second split is made on the variable session actions:

$$Session\,Actions \leq 7.50 \qquad \text{vs.} \qquad Session\,Actions > 7.50$$

On the other hand, for records in the right branch (*time_gap1* greater than 147.50 seconds), the second split is again made on the variable *time_gap1*.

One of the most attractive aspects of decision trees lies in their interpretability, especially with respect to the construction of *decision rules*. Decision rules can be constructed from a decision tree simply by traversing any given path from the root node to any leaf. A complete set of decision rules generated by a decision tree is equivalent (for classification purposes) to the decision tree itself. Decision rules come in the form: *if antecedent, then consequent*. For decision rules, the antecedent consists of the attribute values from the branches taken by the particular path through the tree. The consequent consists of the classification value for the target variable given by the particular leaf node. The *support* of the decision rule refers to the proportion of records in the data set that rest in that particular terminal leaf node. The *confidence* of the rule refers to the proportion of records in the leaf node for which the decision rule is true.

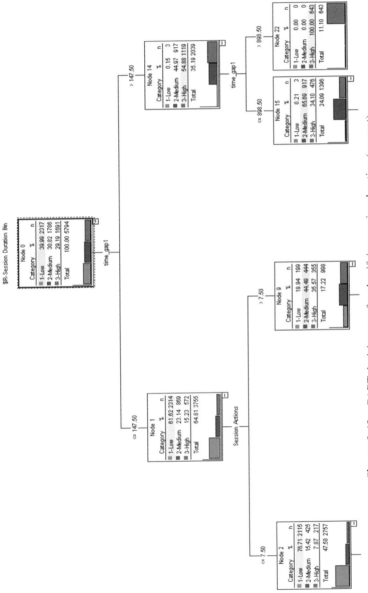

**Figure 9.10** CART decision tree for classifying session duration (excerpt).

In Figure 9.8, only one node, node 22, is a terminal leaf node; all other nodes are decision nodes (the tree continues off the page, not shown). Thus, we may use node 22 to produce the following decision rule:

| Leaf Node | Decision Rule | Confidence | Support |
|---|---|---|---|
| 22 | $\begin{aligned} & Time\_gap1 > 147.50 \\ & \text{and } Time\_gap1 > 898.50 \end{aligned} \Big\} \Rightarrow \text{Session Duration} = \text{High}$ | 100% | 11.1% = 643/5794 |

(Yes, this rule does simplify to $Time\_gap1 > 898.50 \Rightarrow$ Session Duration = High, which is perhaps not surprising, since we earlier defined high session to be of more than 900 seconds.) Note the similarity in format of decision rules to the association rules we mined earlier.

## THE C4.5 ALGORITHM

The *C4.5 algorithm* is J. Ross Quinlan's [11] extension of his own ID3 algorithm for generating decision trees. Just as with CART, the C4.5 algorithm visits each decision node recursively, selecting the optimal split, until no further splits are possible. However, there are interesting differences between CART and C4.5. Unlike CART, the C4.5 algorithm is not restricted to binary splits. Whereas CART always produces a binary tree, C4.5 produces a tree of more variable shape. For categorical attributes, C4.5 by default produces a separate branch for each value of the categorical attribute. This may result in more "bushiness" than desired, since some values may have low frequency or may naturally be associated with other values. The C4.5 method for measuring node homogeneity, which is quite different from CART's, is examined in detail below.

The C4.5 algorithm uses the concept of *information gain* or *entropy reduction* to select the optimal split. Suppose that we have a variable $X$ whose $k$ possible values have probabilities $p_1, p_2, \ldots, p_k$. What is the smallest number of bits, on average per symbol, needed to transmit a stream of symbols representing the values of $X$ observed? The answer, called the *entropy of X*, is defined as

$$H(X) = -\sum_j p_j \log_2(p_j)$$

C4.5 uses this concept of entropy as follows. Suppose that we have a candidate split $S$, which partitions the training data set $T$ into several subsets $T_1, T_2, \ldots, T_k$. The mean information requirement can then be calculated as the weighted sum of the entropies for the individual subsets:

$$H_S(T) = -\sum_{i=1}^{k} P_i \, H_S(T_i)$$

where $P_i$ represents the proportion of records in subset $i$. We may then define our *information gain* to be $\text{Gain}(S) = H(T) - H_S(T)$, that is, the increase in information produced by partitioning the training data $T$ according to this candidate split $S$. At each

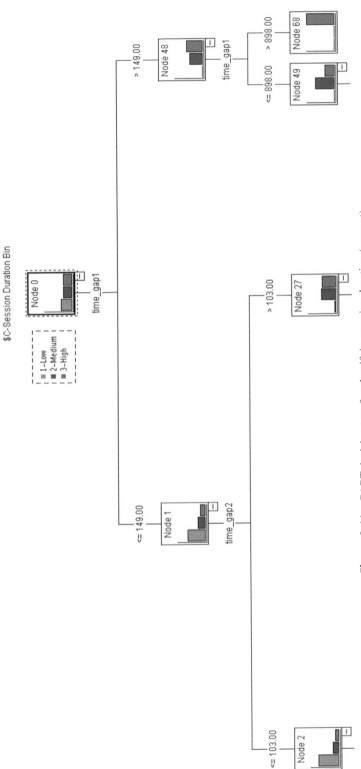

**Figure 9.11** CART decision tree for classifying session duration (excerpt).

decision node, C4.5 chooses the optimal split to be the split which has the greatest information gain, Gain($S$). For more information on the C4.5 algorithm, see ref. 1.

Applying the C4.5 algorithm (actually, Clementine uses C5.0, an update) to the CCSU data set, with session duration bin as the target variable, we generate the decision tree shown in Figure 9.11. First, it is quite similar in general structure to the CART tree above, with *Time_gap1* producing the root node split. But *Time_gap2* takes the place of session actions for the second-level split for sessions with shorter *Time_gap1*. Such similarity may be considered remarkable, considering that these two algorithms use completely different methods for determining node purity and thus where the splits should go. Yet the two algorithms have produced convergent models. We call this happy situation a *convergence of models* or a *confluence of evidence*. Such convergence reinforces our trust in the models. Other classification methods are available, including neural networks [1, Chap. 7] and logistic regression models [1, Chap. 4].

These classification models should be evaluated and verified using the training/test/validation methodology mentioned earlier. Further, model comparisons should be made, using lift charts, gains charts, error rates, false positives, and false negatives. A cost–benefit table should be constructed based on the realistic costs involved in each instance. The best model will optimize the cost–benefit table, producing the greatest gain for the least cost. For more on model evaluation techniques, see ref. 1, Chap. 11 and ref. 4, Chap. 7.

Space constraints prevent our exploration of more complex web log files such as those used in e-commerce for online purchases. In the case of e-commerce, we would be interested in predicting which users are likely to make a purchase online, in which case the attribute "Made a Purchase" would become the target variable. The methods and techniques discussed here could easily be extended to the e-commerce scenario, or to many other web usage mining situations.

## REFERENCES

1. Daniel Larose, *Discovering Knowledge in Data: An Introduction to Data Mining*, Wiley, Hoboken, NJ, 2005.
2. Robert Johnson and Patricia Kuby, *Elementary Statistics*, Brooks-Cole, Toronto, Ontario, Canada, 2004.
3. Tian Zhang, Raghu Ramakrishnan, and Miron Livny, BIRCH: an efficient data clustering method for very large databases, presented at SIGMOD'96, Montreal, Quebec, Canada, 1996.
4. Daniel Larose, *Data Mining Methods and Models*, Wiley, Hoboken, NJ, 2006.
5. Rakesh Agrawal, Tomasz Imielinski, and Arun N. Swami, Mining association rules between sets of items in large databases, in *Proceedings of the 1993 ACM SIGMOD International Conference on Management of Data*.
6. J. MacQueen, Some methods for classification and analysis of multivariate observations, in *Proceedings of the 5th Berkeley Symposium on Mathematical Statistics and Probability*, Vol. 1, pp 281–297, University of California Press, Berkeley, CA, 1967.
7. Jiawei Han and Micheline Kamber, *Data Mining Concepts and Techniques*, Morgan Kaufmann, San Francisco, CA, 2001.
8. David Hand, Heikki Mannila, and Padhraic Smith, *Principles of Data Mining*, MIT Press, Cambridge, MA, 2001.

9. Leo Breiman, Jerome Friedman, Richard Olshen, and Charles Stone, *Classification and Regression Trees*, Chapman & Hall/CRC Press, Boca Raton, FL, 1984.

10. Ruby L. Kennedy, Yuchun Lee, Benjamin Van Roy, Christopher D. Reed, and Richard P. Lippman, *Solving Data Mining Problems Through Pattern Recognition*, Pearson Education, Upper Saddle River, NJ, 1995.

11. J. Ross Quinlan, *C4.5: Programs for Machine Learning*, Morgan Kaufmann, San Francisco, CA, 1992.

# EXERCISES

1. Compare the first two rules in Table 9.2. Note that the antecedent of the second rule is a refinement (more specific specification) of the antecedent of the first rule. In general, describe the relationship between the support values for such rules.

### Hands-on Analysis

2. For the following web log data sets, download the data and perform the web log preprocessing steps given below. (*Note*: Some steps may not be applicable to a particular data set.) The full data sets are available from the Internet traces Web site, http://ita.ee.lbl.gov/html/contrib/NASA-HTTP.html. We use only a subset of the data. The data subsets are available from the book series Web site, www.dataminingconsultant.com.

   - *The NASA-HTTP web log data*. We use only the first 131,904 records.

   - *The Calgary-HTTP web log data*. We use only the first 65,536 records.

   *Important*: For your work in the following exercises, provide evidence that the solutions are consistent across both the training and the test data set.

   **a.** Clustering

      (1) Apply BIRCH (two-step) clustering to the web log data. Allow the algorithm to select its own optimal number of clusters. If the BIRCH algorithm is not available, use $k$-means or some other method.

      (2) Provide graphical and statistical summaries of the clusters in terms of the following variables: session duration, session actions, average time per page, page 1 duration, page 2 duration, all the top directory flag variables, and all the page flag variables.

      (3) Provide solid profiles of each cluster, including a label for each.

      (4) Provide scatter plots examining two-way relationships within the data, with cluster overlay.

      (5) Discuss two or three of the interesting findings that you uncover.

   **b.** Binning

      (1) In preparation for the application of affinity analysis (association rules) and classification, discretize the numerical variables (bin them), into *low*, *medium*, and *high* values, making sure that the counts per bin are not severely unequal.

      (2) For each binning, show your boundaries, such as the following example:

$$\text{Time per Page Bin} = \begin{cases} \text{Low} & \text{if Time per Page } < 68 \\ \text{Medium} & \text{if } 68 \leq \text{Time per Page } < 504 \\ \text{High} & \text{if Time per Page } \geq 504 \end{cases}$$

(3) Provide a normalized distribution of the bins with a cluster overlay. Comment on each.

**c.** A Priori Algorithm

(1) Apply the a priori algorithm to uncover association rules. Report your minimum confidence and support levels.

(2) Provide a table of the top 10 rules, sorted by rule support.

(3) Choose two of these rules and demonstrate how they are rather uninteresting.

(4) Identify the three rules with the highest rule support for identifying sessions with low duration. Discuss.

(5) Report the two rules you consider to be most interesting and/or actionable from the point of view of the Web site's developers or marketers. Discuss.

**d.** CART

(1) Suppose that marketing administrators are interested in identifying sessions with short duration. Apply CART to the CCSU web log data set, with session duration bin as the target variable.

(2) Provide a graphical excerpt from the resulting decision tree, showing the first three or four levels.

(3) Report on the most important splits, discussing these results.

(4) Provide three useful decision rules from this tree.

# INDEX

*Data Mining the Web: Uncovering Patterns in Web Content, Structure, and Usage*
By Zdravko Markov and Daniel T. Larose    Copyright © 2007 John Wiley & Sons, Inc.